A PLUME BOOK
THANK HEAVEN

LESLIE CARON has been nominated for two Academy Awards, for *Lili* and *The L-Shaped Room*, won an Emmy Award in 2007 for her role on *Law & Order: Special Victims Unit*, and continues to act today, starring most recently in *Chocolat* and *Le Divorce*. She lives in Paris, France.

"Candid, lyrically written." —*Los Angeles Times*

"In her new memoir, *Thank Heaven*, Caron reveals a darker side to the glitz and glamour that just might surprise you. Unlike many celebrity memoirists, Caron is an accomplished writer, and *Thank Heaven* truly benefits from her storytelling skills. *Thank Heaven* is an honest, no-holds-barred account of a life in Hollywood and Paris that you don't want to miss—a great gift for the actors, dancers, and film buffs in your family." —*Los Angeles Examiner*

"On screen, Leslie Caron dazzled as Lise, Lili, Gaby, Gigi, and Fanny—and that was just her first decade in film. *Thank Heaven*, her candid and canny memoir, chronicles that first decade and her subsequent five. Caron has many stories to tell, and tells them with verve." —*The Philadelphia Inquirer*

"Caron recounts her life and career as Hollywood's 'little French girl' in chatty, charming style, revealing an often troubled woman behind the glamorous image of an international movie star. . . . The little French girl spins an engrossing yarn." —*Kirkus Reviews*

"Caron provides countless dishy details about her exploits, which are sure to entertain film buffs, Caron fans, and aspiring actors." —*Booklist*

ALSO BY LESLIE CARON

Vengeance

LESLIE CARON

Thank Heaven

A Memoir

A PLUME BOOK

PLUME
Published by the Penguin Group
Penguin Group (USA) Inc., 375 Hudson Street, New York, New York 10014, U.S.A. •
Penguin Group (Canada), 90 Eglinton Avenue East, Suite 700, Toronto, Ontario, Canada
M4P 2Y3 (a division of Pearson Penguin Canada Inc.). • Penguin Books Ltd., 80 Strand,
London WC2R 0RL, England. • Penguin Ireland, 25 St. Stephen's Green, Dublin 2, Ireland
(a division of Penguin Books Ltd.). • Penguin Group (Australia), 250 Camberwell Road,
Camberwell, Victoria 3124, Australia (a division of Pearson Australia Group Pty. Ltd.). •
Penguin Books India Pvt. Ltd., 11 Community Centre, Panchsheel Park, New Delhi – 110
017, India. • Penguin Group (NZ), 67 Apollo Drive, Rosedale, North Shore 0632, New
Zealand (a division of Pearson New Zealand Ltd.). • Penguin Books (South Africa) (Pty.)
Ltd., 24 Sturdee Avenue, Rosebank, Johannesburg 2196, South Africa

Penguin Books Ltd., Registered Offices: 80 Strand, London WC2R 0RL, England

Published by Plume, a member of Penguin Group (USA) Inc. Previously published in a
Viking edition.

First Plume Printing, December 2010

10 9 8 7 6 5 4 3 2 1

All photographs from the author's collection except those below:
Corbis: insert pages 3 (bottom left), 11 (bottom left); Rex Features: 4 (top), 6 (bottom), 11
(bottom right); Lord Snowdon: 7 (top left); Courtesy of the Cecil Beaton Studio Archive at
Sotheby's: 7 (bottom left), 8 (bottom two).

Ⓟ REGISTERED TRADEMARK—MARCA REGISTRADA

The Library of Congress has catalogued the Viking edition as follows:
Caron, Leslie.
Thank heaven: a memoir / Leslie Caron.
p. cm.
ISBN 978-0-670-02134-5 (hc.)
ISBN 978-0-452-29662-6 (pbk.)
1. Caron, Leslie. 2. Actors—France—Biography. 3. Dancers—France—Biography. I. Title.
PN2638.C2525A3 2009
791.4302'8092   2009030177
[B]

Printed in the United States of America
Set in Simoncini Garamond

*Penguin is committed to publishing works of quality and integrity.
In that spirit, we are proud to offer this book to our readers;
however, the story, the experiences, and the words
are the author's alone.*

To Christopher and Jennifer

CONTENTS

ACKNOWLEDGMENTS

My thanks first go to Bruce Benderson, who, after giving me the initial push, was patient enough to teach me a few basic rules (give us details, give us dialogue, don't be shy of emotion) and a lot of encouragement. Next my thanks go to Cathy Nolan, who helped me put early events into perspective and taught me some necessary discipline—and to Judy Fayard, always there with a bagful of rich American expressions. My thanks should most particularly go to my friend Steven Englund, who recommended me to his literary agent, Georges Borchardt, who in turn believed I was capable of carrying this work through to its conclusion. Distinguished and supportive, he provided the encouragement that was my walking stick throughout. My brother, Dr. Aimery Caron, the family historian, gave me a precious résumé of our family tree. Thanks go to my writer friends Jacques Fieschi and Bernard Minoret, who insisted from the start, "Yes, you can." To my friend the architect Alberto Ponis, who said, "You must!" To my daughter, Jennifer Wilhide, who brought me the angle of her childhood recollections. To my very good friend Jack Larson, who remembers in detail the eccentricities and follies of Hollywood in the fifties. To Lorna Birch, who restrained me from certain excesses. To my friend the writer Priscilla English, for her support, as well as to my newer friend, the producer Neal Baer, for his generous backing; to my good friend Nancy Lindermeyer, for her expert advice; and to my son, my friends, and my ex-lovers and ex-husbands, who brought little pieces of mosaic to the whole panorama.

Finally my gratitude goes to my American editor, Rick Kot, who knew how to say kindly, "Nearly totally perfect. Here are five pages of corrections." And to my British editor, Jeremy Robson, who has an uncanny mind for forgotten details. They were both right (nearly) every time, and I'm forever grateful for their solicitude and enthusiasm.

AUTHOR'S NOTE

Writing one's autobiography is a huge undertaking, one that took me decades to dare contemplate. First of all, during youth one's life is so full of surprises, fireworks sparking off in so many directions, that one waits with bated breath for a clear sense of what's going on. For a minute, life appears with perfect clarity, but the line is a little short—*Let us wait for more to happen,* one thinks. Much more happens, of course, until with the mature years, life starts to gather momentum, like a bicycle without brakes gone wild—the famous fleeing forward. I was past seventy when I suddenly realized, "What am I waiting for, now's the time—or never!"

Why should I write at all, I ask myself. Yes, of course, there is nothing forcing me to reveal what is, after all, only a personal experience, considering that I'm a very secretive person who shuns self-revelation. Here was the real conflict: Should I hide like a crab under a stone and go out without a ripple, or testify and bear witness? Perhaps it is my old habit of storing everything, recycling things if I can, passing on the treasures I have accumulated, that compelled me finally to leave a trace of the remarkable people I have known and events I have experienced.

It took a friend of mine, Bruce Benderson, who asked for permission to write a book about my life, to get me going. I was more than willing to let someone else do the dirty work. Bruce requested that I keep two weeks free in May 2007, during which he would question me at length, I would reveal all my secrets into a Dictaphone, and he would then interpret my recollections and write his version of my life. Fine. But when the time came, because of his own busy schedule at the release of his latest book, whole days shrank into shorter and shorter hours. What to do with the remaining free time? I started to write on my own. After a week I had blackened ten pages—a week later fifteen. Not all good, of course, but I was on my way even if it made me dizzy at times.

The experience was fascinating but, at first, far from satisfactory. I found that the early drafts were either frivolous—one does try to please one's imagined reader—or overdramatic, to create an effect. The temptation to settle old scores also demanded several rewrites. I came to the conclusion that with enough humor you can say just about anything. I was tempted to skip embarrassing moments until my editors observed, "There is a link missing here. Tell us why this or that happened." Let's face it, there is no more useless exercise than to falsify one's biography. It is difficult enough to have a clear recollection of people and events, memory being selective, partial, and biased, but why hide the odd embarrassing moments?

My perception of an event was often recalled through small, insignificant details, but that's how it works with me, and these may be interesting years later. To my great surprise, though I thought that I had very poor memory regarding certain events, things did come back without the help of any notes or journals, things that were important, to me at least. It seems that all of one's life is filed away in the many folds of the brain, ready for a replay. Of course I consulted newspaper clippings to confirm the dates, some details were recalled by good friends or members of my family, and occasionally Google and Wikipedia helped to freshen my recall, for souvenirs are filed away in a disordered jumble. The remote often seemed near, and the close-by seemed to fade in the distance. Not surprisingly, the dark years were just as painful to recollect as when they actually bogged me down, and the good times filled me with the same joy as they originally had.

Writing *Thank Heaven* took a good deal of courage, for it's not easy to look at what you've made of this immense gift that life is. If I ultimately wrote this book for my children, I'll be glad if it interests, amuses, and even inspires my readers. But I'm the first who'd like to know who I am, and insight is not at all clear until the last page is written.

Paris, May 2009

Childhood

In my early childhood, in the 1930s, before the Second World War, my father, mother, my brother Aimery, and I lived on the top floor of the private mansion that my French paternal grandparents built in Neuilly, an elegant suburb of Paris facing the river Seine. The architecture was of the best art deco style. My grandparents were, it seems to me, extremely rich and eager to be part of everything that was modern. Perhaps all bourgeois in France lived on such a scale then. I have no point of reference.

My French grandmother's grandfather, Pierre Armand Désiré Savalle, born in 1791, was a civil engineer who had invented and patented the distiller called "la Colonne Savalle" (often referred to as "the fractional distillation column"), used ever since for producing alcohol as well as gasoline and other liquid products. He made a sizable fortune, as can be imagined.

My French great-grandfather, Ernest Adolphe Caron, after having been an eminent lawyer in the civil appellate court, turned to politics and was named president of the municipal council in Paris, which amounted to being the mayor—a title that did not exist in those days. Accumulating prestigious functions, he also became the president of the general council of the Seine Department. The list of his decorations, French and foreign, could cover half a page. Among his perks were free boxes at all the Paris theaters, the opera house, nightclubs, and about six racetracks. He was, of course, prominent in high society—a film shot in 1900 displays a portly gentleman with Edward VII mustachios, presenting the beauty queen of that year during a grand ball at the town hall. Newspaper clippings of the day also show his wife climbing Mont Blanc, one of the first women to do so. During the Second World War, we found and opened a trunk belonging to her, full of opera gloves—dozens of pairs, practically new, white, cream, or pale pink, soft as baby's skin—a useless but luxurious treasure in those lean years. They were distributed among all her descendants. I tried to make a pair of sandals out of one pair by nailing the fine suede to an ill-fitted piece of cork. It didn't work.

My grandfather, Marcel Caron, whom we called Papy (pronounced "Pah-PAY"), was also a very successful corporate lawyer, admitted to the appellate civil court. He was on the board of directors of a fair number of important firms: the Félix Potin grocery-store chain, the Mazda electric company, the Vernol paint company (Papy had obtained the large contract to paint gray the entire cement structure of the Maginot Line, the French fortifications built along their border with Germany after World War I), the luxury department store La Grande Maison de Blanc, the Rosengart auto-manufacturing company, among others. French to the point of chauvinism, he prided himself on never having left France, except for his honeymoon in Venice. He did his military service in the Alpine Corps, where he developed a love for hiking. He never owned a gun and enlisted as an ambulance driver during the First World War—a pacifist who hated strife, and a very kind man with a highly developed sense of honor, he loved pretty women and good food. Papy could not abide violence against animals as well as against humans. He was incredibly intelligent and well educated, as men in his social circles were in those days. He could answer all my questions, including any queries pertaining to history or geography. He was the first person to satisfy my appetite for learning. Courtesy was on his list of priorities. He chided me once for not specifying whether a lady whom I was introducing was to be called madame or mademoiselle. The difference was that a gentleman does not kiss the hand of an unmarried lady. (As it is, the mouth should never quite reach the hand anyway.) Considering that this particular female was an old maid, Mademoiselle Pommier, I didn't think it was important, but it was for my grandfather.

My grandmother, Mamy (pronounced "Mah-MAY"), was in every way a grand lady. She had been one of the three ravishing and rich Savalle girls, who were fond of putting on plays for the entertainment of their social circle. She loved to manage her properties with a large retinue of servants, and to host lavish parties and theme balls. A thwarted architect, she had a passion for building. It was said in the family that in exchange for shutting her eyes to my grandfather's peccadilloes she would obtain yet another pool, another landscaped garden. . . . She was an enthusiastic Anglophile—her four children had English nannies, and the "fifth o'clock tea" (her mispronunciation of "five o'clock tea") was practiced wherever she was in residence. I had the conviction that I was Mamy's most beloved grandchild, but it may have been wishful thinking. In any case I was indeed the youngest of all her grandchildren and as a result received more trinkets, jewels, and favors of every kind than the others. She used to enjoy ordering smocked dresses for me in La Grande Maison de Blanc.

In the mornings, on our way to school or to the playground, we would stop at my grandparents' bedroom to kiss Papy and Mamy good morning. We were taught to use the respectful pronoun *vous*—only my parents were modern enough to allow us to use the familiar *tu* when addressing them.

Wearing his striped pajamas, Papy prickled our cheeks with his mustache and rough, unshaven cheeks. He would grumble an inaudible "Morning, children" while scratching his arms to get the circulation going. Mamy, who was very religious, would first bless me by drawing the sign of the cross on my forehead. She usually adjusted the corkscrewed stockings on my brother, already untidy. My thoughts during this morning ceremony invariably turned to a stuffed red squirrel, imprisoned in a glass box hanging on the wall above Mamy's headboard. He looked so alive with his full tail in the air and his glass eyes full of mischief.

We often came in time to see the chef, in his pristine white uniform, notepad in hand, standing next to my grandmother's bed to take orders for the day—with menus for the dining room and separate ones for the staff, who usually ate the leftovers from previous meals. Desserts were for the dining room only. Such was the custom then.

If for different reasons my father and mother played little or no part in the events of my days, one man did: Alban—Mamy's butler. I was especially fond of him. He was from rural Gascony, a proud province with its own language. Dark in complexion, he had wavy black hair that was combed down with lacquer, as was my father's and most men's in that Valentino era. His Gascon accent enriched the words with extra syllables, and what he said went. His immense attraction was that he played the accordion in his off hours. The lower ground floor of the house, where the kitchen and staff rooms were, was forbidden territory to me and to my brother, Aimery, but we used to sneak down there and sit at the kitchen table, just to hear Alban play the popular tunes of the day. I was enraptured by the plaintive sounds of the instrument and their jaunty rhythms. Alban taught me to ride a bicycle on the sidewalk in front of the house—an immensely enjoyable accomplishment. I remember his impatience when I rang the front doorbell for the tenth time to be let into the house, probably in the hopes that he would come play with me.

Alban's wife answered to the charming name of Odilia. She was slim and sweet and also had dark, wavy hair. Apparently she came from the same village in the Pyrenees as her husband. She was my grandmother's private chambermaid, and I was full of respect for the lovely needlework that came from her hands. Among other needlework, she embroidered white scalloped edges on pink linen shelf-runners.

When time came to attend kindergarten, Aimery and I were driven in Mamy's large limousine—her Hotchkiss—by Lalo, her private chauffeur. I remember a stout man, quite red in the face and of a very kind disposition, tightly squeezed into a black uniform set off by a double row of black buttons.

At the end of my first kindergarten year, prizes were distributed to each child as encouragement, so that parents would feel that progress had been made. Most children were rewarded for group spirit, for imagination, for good behavior. A new category was invented for me: "initiative."

One early morning I found a carmine velvet rose on the carpeted floor of the car. A faint feminine perfume still floated around the luxurious accessory. In front of the whole class, I gave it to my teacher with a heart full of self-satisfaction. A few days later, at Sunday lunch, my Aunt Lucette burst into my grandparents' dining room. At this point I need to sketch a portrait of this most ungainly female: a long nose, sharp beady eyes, and a pencil line of a mouth had been inflicted on her by the hostile fairies who'd presided over her birth. Aunt Lucette never knew our names, or if she did, she didn't bother to use them. To her we were just *"petits."*

"Petits," articulated the witch, "has one of you found a red rose in the Hotchkiss? I left it in the car, and it isn't there anymore."

Mortified, I had to own up. "You'll have to ask your teacher to return it," she snapped. "I want it back!"

I had to go through the burning humiliation of asking for the rose. Mademoiselle was kind and understanding, but my hatred for my aunt never diminished. In her mellower years and after my stardom helped her remember my name, no amount of cajoling on her part ever erased the sting.

Among my grandparents' household staff, I also remember clearly a Moroccan servant called Ali, a Zouave (colonial infantry soldier) in full attire, who to the best of my knowledge was employed only to make coffee after the meals. He wore the most colorful costume—blue bouffant trousers and a matching gold-braided vest on top of his white shirt; his head was coiffed with a red fez from which dangled a black tassel. The coffee ceremony, held after the Sunday lunch—which we all took at my grandparents' table, usually attended by my Aunt Lucette, her son Teddy, and whoever else in the family was around—was a slow affair. We would leave the table and take our seats in the drawing room. Ali made "moka," as it was grandly called, not coffee. He would light up the little stove while everyone watched closely. The delicious brew slowly gurgled up into the top balloon, releasing the strong aroma in the whole room. I don't think that Ali stayed very long; gossip had it that he flirted with the females on the staff.

My father, Claude Caron, born in July 1905, was the third child after Lucette and Guy, and Mamy's favorite among her four children. He had dark hair, blue eyes, and a Grecian nose, and even in childhood his charm was evident. When asked for his name, he once answered, "Claude-Chéri-Caron-five-years-old." His sister Lili came two years after him, but an unfortunate fall over a staircase railing caused her a slow mental deterioration with fits of dementia and an early death. I think this cast a dark shadow in my father's childhood and was never mentioned in the family, as if it were a shameful secret.

The law didn't attract Claude, who was of a reflective and shy disposition, and in any case his elder brother, Guy, was already taking over their father's law firm. There were, however, great opportunities for development in the other family concerns. Claude chose to specialize in pharmacy and chemistry when he entered the university, graduating four years later.

My American mother, Margaret, was born on the seventeenth of March, 1900, in Topeka, Kansas. When she was very young, her father, Harry Petit, a gadabout of uncertain profession, deserted his wife and child. He hadn't even bothered to register the birth of his daughter; it is only because a national census was carried out three months later that records of her birth exist. Her mother, Cora, and she were provided for by one aunt or cousin after another. In later life, left vulnerable by dependence on charity, she suffered from real or imagined slights, the wounds of her childhood having never healed. Yet you could say that under her apparent fragility she was streetwise.

She and her mother ultimately landed in Seattle, where the adolescent Margaret pursued her studies while also starting to learn ballet from an Italian ballet master, Luigi Albertieri, who convinced her to try her luck on Broadway. Wearing the lovely costumes she often designed herself, she appeared in several reviews: *What's in a Name?* in 1920, *Greenwich Village Follies* in 1921, *Pin Wheel Review* in 1922, and *Sweet Little Devil* in 1923, where she danced to music by George Gershwin. The numbers she created were often inspired by the famous Diaghilev ballets: *Scheherazade, Prelude to the Afternoon of a Faun,* and so on. She achieved quite a nice renown: "Margaret Petit, a youthful danseuse with a delicate charm of her own . . ." reports *Vanity Fair* in August 1921, while the *New York City Telegraph* of April 25, 1922, mentions that "Margaret Petit, a dancer of originality and talent as well as symmetrical beauty, has been secured for vaudeville. When that interesting revue, *The Pin Wheel,* was staged on Broadway, she gave the most colorful of the offerings, a series of original and daring dances of her own conception." There were photographs of her in *Vogue* and *Harper's Bazaar,* where her graceful attitudes set her apart from the other dancers.

But dancing was hard and exhausting and certainly didn't lead to the financial security she longed for. She decided to give it up and came back to Seattle, where she married a rich high-school friend, Barrett Green, heir to the Seattle Bank. However, soon bored with the parochial local society—no match for scintillating New York—she escaped the rainy town and demanded a divorce. Barrett never recovered from her departure and loved her secretly to his dying day.

Now a single woman again, Margaret went on a trip to Paris with her ex-sister-in-law, Florence Green, ostensibly to study commercial art, for which she had an aptitude. Florence knew her way in French society, and the two girls enjoyed the social life in Paris. Margaret was fair and feminine, long-limbed, with remarkably fine hands and feet, the grace of a Botticelli, and a charming American accent that her friends must have considered very seductive (but for which we, her children, later teased her mercilessly). She couldn't say *grenouille* (frog) or *parapluie* (umbrella) without adding an extra vowel. After meeting Claude Caron among the Franco-American group with which the two girls mixed, Margaret decided to stay on a while longer, attracted to this handsome young man as much as by the whirling social life around the Caron family.

My father was in his last university year when their affair started, and there was still military service to go through. Understandably, the Caron family was less than enthusiastic about this match. Margaret was, despite her grace and beauty, a divorcée, a bleached-blond cigarette smoker, an ex–Broadway dancer, and five years his senior—a fast girl, not to say a fortune hunter, as far as they were concerned. But Claude, very much in love, was obstinate. Barely discharged from military service, he married Margaret in 1929.

For obvious reasons, any career with his father was difficult, so Claude was offered as a wedding present a well-situated pharmacy in the heart of fashionable Paris, at the corner of the rue de la Paix and place de l'Opéra. He also acquired a laboratory where he made health-care and beauty products and, eventually, perfume. He had offices proudly facing the Église de la Madeleine, the imposing church where the best people, including himself, got married.

Margaret's integration into the family was not easy. Perhaps because the newly married couple lived in the house of his parents, frictions arose between my mother and Aunt Lucette, who never lost an opportunity to make remarks that revealed the extent of her prejudice. My mother had supplanted Lucette's authority over my father, and she was in fact jealous.

Margaret suffered at the hands of this mean-spirited woman. Early on, scenes arose at the dinner table on the subject of the humiliations Lucette had inflicted upon her. My father, caught between his elder sister and his wife, would ineffectually try to arbitrate these recurring conflicts.

My parents were not rich, but comfortable enough. My mother received a sumptuous diamond-and-emerald ring as a wedding gift—which she wore every day, even though French etiquette decreed, "Never wear diamonds in daytime." My father owned a fashionable Rosengart automobile. Our domestic staff consisted of a housekeeper-cook and our all-important governess. I know that my brother, Aimery—born fourteen months before me—and I must have had a succession of nannies, but I remember only Greta, the blond Austrian girl with soft hugging arms, a feminine singsong voice, and a constant smile that lit up her cornflower blue eyes. At bathtime, Greta, ever thoughtful, would spread a bath towel on top of the radiator and sit me up there to dry me. The other governesses, tormented by Aimery, gave notice in record time and thus disappeared from my recall without leaving a trace.

A dream lingers in my memory, so pleasant that I still laugh when I think of it. I was at the head of the large staircase in the center of the house, and two floors below, on the ground floor, my mother and Greta were holding my panties open for me to fly down into them. I jumped, delighted by the flight, and landed lightly, my two feet passing gracefully through the leg holes!

Another early memory involves my mother, this unreachable beauty, going off to a party, dressed in glitter, suffused in a cloud of perfume. A good-night kiss, blown through the air; I don't remember any hugs or caresses. My mother had many admirable qualities, but she was not maternal. I'm sure she did have feelings for us, but her love was something abstract—the idea of having children was appropriate, though not their actual presence, and certainly not the care they demanded. She admitted readily that the Carons had made children a condition for her becoming part of the family. In any case, she did not like physical contact. My mother was not the kind to take my hand when crossing the street. She never accompanied me to school, seldom to ballet class, never to the theater or a museum. During the war I had to find my own way to the doctor's or the dentist's.

She believed that children must learn to fend for themselves as early as possible. I must have been about four or five when, on the nanny's day off, she started brushing my hair. After the first "ouch" from me, she slapped the brush into my hand with an impatient, "You do it. It's your hair anyway." I became what my mother wished for, a very independent woman, one who never looked to any man or any state to support her financially. I have come to be extremely grateful for the resourcefulness she forced me to develop—a determining factor in my life.

She also encouraged the tomboy in me, as I was physically fearless and creative. Her American heritage—she had an ancestor who had crossed the vast new continent from east to west in a covered wagon and married a squaw (this gave rise to the glorious image of a Red Indian in my childhood mythology, an image I used to my advantage among my school friends)—was the foundation for her theories on child raising, which were so foreign to the classical French upbringing. Even though she taught me to curtsy when meeting adult women (a difficult habit to lose), she was resolutely against the French precepts of prudence and mild behavior, which she considered "sissy." No bourgeois French family allowed children such freedom as we had. We were taught to swim almost at the same time as to walk. As a matter of fact, my first award was for swimming, at the Saint-Jean-de-Luz beach.

My mother held the philosophy that mothers mustn't praise their children, lest they become complacent. She didn't pretend that a child's first accomplishments were in any way remarkable. I heard "not too bad," underlined with a lenient smile, more often than "pretty good." I never heard "very good." A mother's evaluation stays with you for the rest of your life, I fear. She was just as direct when she admitted that children bored her. "Darling, I know I'm not doing much now, but I will be there when you're a star. You'll have plenty of friends and admirers, too," she told me when I pined for my old school friends during the long afternoons after I left school in order to concentrate on my ballet training. The path to excellence was clearly indicated, and my insecurity became chronic. From my teens onward, I lived in a perpetual state of creative exaltation, trying to reach an unattainable goal. No matter how futile, the project of the moment was of paramount importance. I felt guilty, really guilty, if enormous efforts hadn't been accomplished every day, to the point where I thought I didn't deserve my daily meals if I hadn't overreached myself.

From time to time, my mother would rise from her lethargic indifference to guide me through the next step toward a career she came to consider as essential. When I was around the age of fourteen, she signed me up with a children's theater for two afternoon performances a week and worked all night to make me a beautiful ballet dress, sewn by hand from one of her old silk costumes. One day as the church bells chimed morning Mass and I was leaving for the theater, I discovered the lovely gray silk dress spread out on the sofa in the salon. It brought tears of gratitude to my eyes.

If my father's gentleness and courtesy left an unforgettable memory with all the women who knew him, his upbringing, too, inhibited him from being very demonstrative. The only physical contact with him I can recall is during a trip in the Dolomite Mountains—I must have been around six—when he lifted me on top of his shoulders to cross a small brook. In fact, my father was a charming, polite, and shy man who showed me how to bone a fish to perfection—and I haven't forgotten how—as well as other rules of etiquette taught in his milieu. I learned from him that an envelope must always be handed over open to prove your trust in the person who will mail it. Civility also commands that you pull off your right-hand glove when shaking hands, as a sign of trust of the individual's cleanliness. In that respect, when years later I met Queen Elizabeth II, I was a little shocked when she offered her hand, keeping her glove firmly on. Obviously the rule doesn't apply to royalty, not in England in any case.

I know that my father loved us, but because he worked very hard, he was rarely present. He left the house at eight-thirty in the morning, came back for lunch from one to two-thirty, and disappeared again until eight o'clock or later. I think that I owe to my father the fact that, although I'm quite daring physically, I'm rather shy and secretive. Pushing myself to the front line was always torture for me. For years I hoped I would never win the Oscar, because the idea of getting up there to make a speech was like going to the scaffold. I did, however, prepare a speech every year for many years just in case—there's the paradox.

After a certain age, we children were allowed to sit at the table at lunchtime, where some English was spoken. The conversation was mostly about my father's business day. Absolutely no interest was ever paid to my studies, either in my early school days or later. In truth my mother, despite the fact that she never stopped reading, writing, and studying history and languages, considered education for girls a serious hindrance to the all-important prospect of marriage—this was, of course, before the war reorganized all the plans. "If you know better than a man, in any situation, don't let him see it. Men don't like smart girls." These words of wisdom were repeated during intimate conversations on her bed, and lest I didn't have the wits to make the right choice, she would add, "Let me tell you, rich boys can be just as nice as poor ones."

Of course things were different for boys. She helped my brother with his homework. She also taught him to dance the waltz and the fox trot when he was about fourteen, to ensure his success with girls at his first parties. I can still see the concentration on her face in her effort to teach social graces to this gawky adolescent.

My father's views on the education of children were never heard, although I'm sure he cared about my brother's. Now that I try to re-call those days, it seems clear that our family was a matriarchy. Perhaps because of the advantage of her age, and definitely due to the practical abilities she had learned through a harsher childhood, my mother took the lead. As she got older, she was the one who made the decisions. The outbreak of the war had a dramatic effect on her state of mind, however, as she didn't have the strength to combat the depression brought on by ever more restricted circumstances.

I realize that my father's main preoccupation, when life really be-came a struggle, was to keep my mother in a good mood and avoid scenes. He had a repertory of about three charming jokes, which I asked for repeatedly when my exasperated mother would threaten to leave us. At the slightest provocation, she would warn, "I have a good mind to go live in a hotel! That's it, I've had enough, I'm leaving you!" My father would quickly come to the rescue. "Did I tell you the one about the man who comes to the bakery to order a birthday cake? . . ."

During the war and after, when my memories are most vivid, Margaret slept late, having read *True Detective* or plays by Shakespeare until the wee hours. "Both unreal . . ." was her comment. As the morning wore on, she would hurriedly get up for the noon lunch, when we ate in the dining room. There were no cafeterias, no fast-food stores or sandwich shops in those days. Our father came home on his motor scooter, as did we on foot, from school. Before the war my mother was always eager to hear the morning's news and gave my father good business advice; he almost seemed like a schoolboy reporting his grades. She encouraged him to develop his pharmacy into the more innovative American-style drugstore. As early as the 1940s, you could, at Claude Caron's Pharmacy, bring your film to be developed, have a massage in a private room, or drink Coca-Cola at a little bar on the second floor. She designed the label for the slimming product that my father invented and the publicity to go with it: Padinox, "Slim while you sleep!" It was in fact a diuretic. Under her influence my father also launched at the end of the war the first multivitamin, Nutravita, with Claude Ricci, head of the Nina Ricci couture house, as a partner. During the marketing of this product, I heard of my father's endless battles with French bureaucracy's power of inertia.

My mother wasn't a writer, but she should have been. I remember her lying on her bed studying, the only relief she knew from her perpetual state of anxiety and perhaps also from the boredom of an idle life. She taught herself French, then French history, but only up to the Revolution of 1789. To her, the fate of the French nation after the abolition of privileges was a letdown. Yet she was totally democratic in her own behavior and had no sense of hierarchy or superiority toward servants or workers. She would talk to any stranger in the streets without the least sign of the French haughtiness that the rest of the family could affect, but when it came to history, she enjoyed pomp and grandeur with the same fascination as a tourist filing past Louis XVI's adorned bed in Versailles. At the end of the war, she started the long process of learning Russian. "You never know . . ." she said wisely.

I must have been about six or seven when my American grandmother, Cora Petit, whom I called "Bama," came to visit us. She lived in New York, where she had a hat shop. Near the end of her visit, she said that she wanted to give me a present for my birthday on the first of July. "What would you like, my darling?" she asked, smiling. "A ring? A bracelet?" She wasn't rich, but she wanted her visit to hold a particular significance. My brother took me aside to the next room and pressed me hard. "What do you want with a ring or that silly sort of thing? Ask for a water pistol, that would be fun!" I came back to the room and, standing firmly on my little legs, announced, "What I really want is a water pistol."

I got it, and a ring, too, which I promptly lost in the toilet bowl.

Since there wasn't much parental presence in my daily life, my brother was at the center of my small universe. He was tyrannical, but in his company I never knew boredom or loneliness. With the enthusiasm of the very young, Aimery was endlessly inventive. He conceived every kind of device that could roll, fly, float, or swing. He gave out the orders for the building of the contraptions, and I executed them. I was also the test pilot. Once, for instance, he built a little wooden platform set on four wheels, ready to go down the steep street in Saint-Cloud. Aimery said, "Go ahead" and off I went, fearlessly. A car coming up around the corner just missed me.

Our pockets were always full of the indispensable marbles, strings, rubber bands, sticks, and stones. In Neuilly, which was not built up, as it is today, there were two empty lots next to our house, facing the river. The neighborhood boys would join us in our playground, our Sherwood Forest, our unknown continent where adventures and dangers lurked. The terrain was rough with trees, weeds, and wild brush. Cowboys and Indians, cops and robbers, as seen in my brother's comic books, were our usual games. The guns were made out of sticks, the bows were sticks with a string attached to both ends. We also climbed a particular tree with low branches and played Tarzan. There never was any other girl with us, and I always dreamed that my favorite boy would be wounded; blood would flow, so that I could play the devoted nurse. I was never out of love throughout my whole childhood.

Both my brother and I still bear scars on our knees from roller-skating behind cars. Automobiles were scarce in our neighborhood, but the whole gang of four or five would hook on to whatever ones passed by—we would bend low so that the driver couldn't see us in his rear window. The game was fine when going uphill or on flat ground, but invariably one of us would let go and fall going downhill. As I was considered "just a girl," I was last in the long snake that swayed to avoid potholes. The first victim was always me.

Alive still is the memory of an impure little girl who followed a man into a wooded area of the Bois de Boulogne where our nanny had taken us. The man was trying to relieve himself discreetly. I kept trailing him until finally he shooed me away angrily. Little girls aren't always innocent.

I have no memory of playing with dolls. In any case, I don't think we were given as many toys as children are given nowadays. It may have been considered an irrational waste of money. One Christmas, when asked, I voiced a yearning for a scooter with a pedal but never got it. (At long last my son gave me one—alas, without pedal—for my seventieth birthday.) I may have owned a teddy bear, but my adored brother probably didn't approve, so I'm sure I discarded the silly thing.

I was an obedient child when treated with fairness and kindness. I wanted above all the love and approval of my mother and of the brother I worshipped. I quickly acquired the younger child's expertise at being lovable. Inevitably, cultivating this childlike charm had its consequences. My mother nicknamed me "Minnie Mouse," and to this day some friends still call me "*la petite* Leslie." Grace Kelly, shortly before becoming Princess Grace of Monaco, once said to me, "Hello, little one!" I could have strangled her. Despite the image people had of me, I could be rebellious and willful if treated unfairly. I have been known to blow up in violent outbursts, surprising everyone who thought me sweet and accommodating. The French director Jean Renoir used to say there was a Joan of Arc in me. I may be shy, but I do not hesitate to face potential blows. As a child, if Aimery had done some mischief, I would step in front of him and blurt out to my parents, "Don't you touch Aimery. He's my brother!" as if I had some legal authority over him. But I also didn't hesitate to oppose him, so I suffered the inevitable dragging by the hair, pounding in the stomach, trip-ups, and slaps that all brothers inflict on their sisters. I learned how to scream and scratch like a cat in the hands of my tormentor. I was at times refused entry to the boys' games with the insulting "Go away, you're just a girl!" This provoked a nightmare that I still remember: A dark forest, at night—I'm lost, and I can see my brother disappearing ahead of me among the trees. . . . "Wait for me!" I plead. "Wait for me!" But my voice is lost in the darkness. He never turns around, and terror wakes me.

Although I was basically healthy, my health did break down, like that of all children, I guess, as the result of emotional trauma and later, during the war, from food privations. At age five I went on a hunger strike. I suspect that the reason was the departure of Greta, my beloved nanny, and I refused to eat anything except yogurt. Why yogurt? I don't know, but for me to swallow any food it had to be buried under a coat of yogurt. I was losing weight rapidly, doctors were consulted, and the method of the day among the well-to-do was adopted: I was sent to a boarding school, in Caux, near Vevey in Switzerland. "The fresh air will make her hungry," said the doctor. My cousin Françoise Caron was already enrolled there, a sharp and caustic girl, six or seven years older than me. Rather than smooth the introduction to boarding-school life, she took great pleasure in describing the penitentiary methods that prevailed. A cat-o'-nine-tails was depicted in detail, not omitting the lead weight at the end of each leather thong. "It is used quite regularly," she warned, and God help the victim.

The headmistress was given full authority over me and left to her own devices to make me gain weight. At first she sat me next to her at mealtime and tried to force-feed me, but as that plan proved ineffectual, she would lock me in the smelly toilet, my cheeks swollen with food, and give me strict orders to swallow, or else. The vision of fried eggs, burned at the bottom and gelatinous on top, nauseates me to this day.

While I was in boarding school, I caught scarlet fever. My head was shaved ignominiously, and I spent days and nights in quarantine, alone in the infirmary. One night, when the fever ran high, I watched in terror until daybreak the wolf at the foot of my bed, in case he pounced on me. A dark, lonely room and a high temperature can play awful tricks with a bolster. I was freed from this penitentiary after my mother finally came to visit and noticed the lumps in my cheeks. She pried open my mouth and saw old food that I hadn't dared to spit out. My revelation of having been locked up in the toilet for whole afternoons was decisive. Horrified, my mother took me back home immediately.

2

Paradise Is Called Goyetchéa

During Easter and the summer holidays, my grandparents' estate in the Pyrenees, Goyetchéa ("The House of the Sun" in the Basque language), became the focal meeting place of the extended family, friends, colleagues, and assorted friends of friends. The crowd of family members, sometimes so far removed that we didn't know if there was a blood connection at all, were nevertheless called aunts, uncles, and cousins. My immediate cousins were Philippe Caron, his sister Françoise, and Teddy Culbert—Lucette's son and also my godfather in a wicked sort of way. Less closely related were Hubert, and let's not forget cousin Annie, my godmother. Annie was plump and fresh-looking, which didn't save her from committing suicide at a very young age, inconsolable at the early death of her fiancé from polio, or so I was told.

On the departure date, Lalo drove the long road from Paris down to the Pyrenees in a single day. There were no freeways then, but also far fewer cars. It was always a major expedition. Car doors slammed at 7:00 A.M., and then it was onward until very late in the day when we would reach Goyetchéa. The large Hotchkiss would be crowded with Odilia and our nanny in the front seats next to Lalo, then behind the partition were we two children on jump seats. Mamy and her dog, Marmot—a Pyrenean shepherd dog with long golden hair—and her pet canary, Mickey (who could peel apple seeds with his beak), sat in the backseat. The silverware chest traveled safely in the trunk. My grandfather sometimes came with us and sat next to Mamy in the back, unless he drove his own Rosengart. We drove and drove with only a one-hour stop for lunch at Châtellrault, and God help the child who asked for an extra stop to relieve himself. Papy had principles: children had to have endurance and discipline. We had to be as quiet in the car as at the table, and we had to control ourselves.

Goyetchéa was simply paradise. The young people and the family all stayed in what was called "the farmhouse," although the real farm was behind, where the farmers, cows, pigs, rabbits, and chickens were raised and—most thrilling of all—where the ponies' stalls were located. A feeling of rapture still seizes me when I recall the first dinner after the long day's drive. Smells and colors come rushing in, bringing back the same intense emotions as they did then. As soon as we stepped out of the car, the farm dog—alas, I don't remember his name—gave us a boisterous reception. His rustic charm was in the disparity of his eyes—one was pale while the other was dark—and in his patchy dark gray fur. He respected Marmot's superior position as the mistress's dog and never overstepped the limits of his territory. The fresh fragrance of fern from the hill mixed with the farm smells still overcomes me when I think back to those days.

We were quickly whisked off to the large dinner table, which was set with a Basque tablecloth. I was particularly fond of the table service from Lunéville—wild splashes of hand-painted roosters, flowers, and leaves in vivid reds, greens, and blues. Our napkins slipped into pink, green, or blue linen folders in the shape of envelopes, the flaps of which were embroidered by Odilia in white cotton thread with the names of the Olympian gods and goddesses. My scant knowledge of the Greek deities dates from those napkin folders. Papy was Zeus, Mamy was Juno; when they were there, my father was Apollo and I remember well that my mother was always Terpsichore, goddess of dancing, because she had been a ballerina. There was Hermes, Pomona, Hercules, Pluto, and Bacchus. Aimery and I, being the youngest of all the grandchildren, were Ares and Ganymede. The flattering Aphrodite and Leda were probably given to less regular female "cousins." Papy, who sported a large mustache, like that of President George Clemenceau or Theodore Roosevelt, was in the habit of wiping his mouth with a large rub, holding his napkin by the edges, right and left, and again left and right, just as one rubs one's back after the bath. It looked as if the napkin was never large enough.

At the table we were cautioned by Mamy never to mention where

the meat on our plates came from, especially when it was a product
of our own farm. We often ate chicken that my grandmother assured
our tenderhearted grandfather had been bought from the market, and
also rabbit, when Mamy would inevitably advise, "Watch out for little
bones," recalling how an aunt of hers had choked to death on a rabbit bone. The cheese tray was something extravagant. My grandfather
was a connoisseur. When he became diabetic in his later years, Mamy
would shake her finger. But he knew how to finesse her: "I think I need
a little cheese to finish my bread," followed by, "I need a little bread to
finish my cheese," and then, "Alban, I would like some wine to finish
my bread and cheese." My grandmother would scold, but he grumbled
a sound argument: "I don't like to waste food."

At bedtime, according to my grandmother's recommendations, we
were rubbed with freshly picked chamomile flowers and leaves, to ward
off mosquitoes, and sleep would envelop me suddenly, with the promise of all the discoveries awaiting us with the coming of daylight at the
rooster's crow.

The first day was spent in reconnaissance of the realm—had anything changed? The cry of the white peacocks, "Leon! Leon!" would
draw us—"Quick! Hurry up!"—toward the aviaries and the flower garden. Two aviaries filled with birds of every size—an endless spectacle!
The one for the smaller birds was the one for me. The fire crest! The
sweetest little creature!

Had the fir trees grown, trained to form arcades behind Mamy's little basin where her statue of Pan played the flute? Yes, they now formed
perfect arches, and the red fish flaunted their silky fins as they swam
gracefully in their shallow pond. Then the wild hill covered with ferns
called us toward the mysterious cave where smugglers had spent the
night after crossing from Spain to France and back. Often at night, snug
in our beds, we'd shudder at the plaintive call of an ox horn used to
signal that the passage was clear or, conversely, that the carabiniers were
on the lookout. In the mornings, leftovers of bread or animal bones and
forgotten cartridges were proof of their passage.

On mornings when the weather was fine, one of the ponies would
be harnessed to the cart, and Adrien the gardener would take us on a
trot along the road to the beach at Saint-Jean-de-Luz. We would pass
the slow oxen carts, the animals paired off under their heavy wooden

yokes and gaily covered with the red and white Basque cloth that kept flies away from their eyes. After Paris the rustic accents of the Basque country thrilled me intensely.

On the beach a tent was rented from the Club Neptune, supervised by Mr. Charles, where the attendant spread towels and deck chairs for the ladies and the elderly. The smell of the ocean air, the sun, and that particular wind blowing in the Pays Basque resurrected all the thrills I had forgotten during the winter months. The beach was my kingdom, the place where I showed off my physical skills. I was a champion at the horizontal bar and hoped everyone's eyes were fixed on my exploits. With shrieks and barbaric cries, my brother and I would rush toward the explosive waves, where swimming filled me with rapturous excitement. We came back to the house for lunch, after which we were made to nap for an hour.

Often in the afternoons, we were invited to take part in a two- to three-hour trek in the surrounding hills, led by our grandfather. Complaints were not welcome, and cousins and guests trailed along under Papy's leadership. Turned out as we were in the classic Basque uniform—white trousers and shirt for my grandfather, red or black beret, espadrilles, and a carved wooden stick with a steel point—we had to trudge on to the halfway point, a farm where milk or water was offered for refreshment. I still remember the cool fountain carved in the rock, nearly hidden under lush vegetation.

At Goyetchéa important guests stayed at the "the big house." Flanking it were a pool that faced Spain on the edge of the hill and, on the other side, facing France, a cascade that gurgled down the mosaic-colored steps to a second pool, where, dressed in sailor suits, we children were allowed to sail our little boats. These pools were not deep enough for swimming but freshened the air and reflected the splendor of the big house. I remember only the large drawing room with oversize beige seats, a card table where the currently fashionable game of mah-jongg was always ready for use. I never went into any of the bedrooms, since they were grown-up territory, and I never knew where the kitchen was. A detail remains: At the grown-ups' table, just before the war, I ate my first corn on the cob and found it very strange. Under the encouragements of the grown-ups, I learned my first lesson in tolerance: "Just try it. . . ."

In the "big house" Mamy held grand receptions. Family legend has it that the most memorable event was the "royalty dinner" attended by three deposed kings: Alphonse XIII of Spain, Constantine I of Greece, and Carol II of Romania. Is it even true? I wonder. And what could they possibly have talked about? In its archives the "big house" also boasted of its being the setting for Julien Duvivier's prestigious 1937 film *Un Carnet de Bal* with Danielle Darrieux.

The estate was built along the route taken by Napoleon's armies retreating after the disastrous war in Spain. A serious battle must have been fought on these grounds—every time Aimery and I scratched the earth, we would find lead bullets. While digging went on for the big house's foundations, two little cannons were unearthed. These were placed facing Spain on either side of the Spanish pool. We were so close to the border that when the civil war started in 1936, the cannons had to be removed or we would have been shelled as a partisan bastion. Papy had a fence erected for our safety. Photographers and journalists came to watch the bloody Battle of Irún from our vantage point, near the river Bidasoa.

I also remember a path of pink hydrangeas leading to a little mount in the back of this house, crowned by a proud obelisk, at the foot of which was buried the skeleton of our own "unknown soldier." But most of all I have a vivid recollection of Mamy explaining with religious fervor the significance of the passionflowers that climbed along the railing, on either side of the steps leading to the main entrance:

"Here are the three nails hammered in Jesus's hands and feet," she would point out. "This is the crown of thorns, this is the lance that pierced His flank. . . ." I have never forgotten her words and now reflect how odd it is that passionflowers are used in homeopathy to induce peace and sleep.

A huge, heavy linen tent with double roof for better sun and rain protection was regularly set up near the entrance of the property. A truck and half a dozen able-bodied men were required for the operation. Was this a nostalgic reminder of Mamy's camel trip in the Moroccan desert when she was a young woman? Whatever the inspiration, it now served for picnics and outdoor meals prepared over a campfire. My brother Aimery remembers being taught to flip his first crepes at one of these occasions.

Papy was fond of new mechanical inventions. One summer we discovered with amazement, at the bottom of the wild hill behind the farm, a miniature red two-seater convertible tank, made by Rosengart. Papy had a team of six men remove rocks to build a trail up the nearby mountain to climb the Pyrenean hill in style. Lalo and Adrien were mobilized to make the toy work. The poor underpowered thing climbed valiantly a few yards until it heated up and melted the bearings, at which point it would move no more. After a few tries, it was ignominiously carted away by a pair of oxen and definitively scrapped.

What worked beautifully, however, were the large hot-air balloons (*montgolfières*) that Papy was fond of sending over the mountains, to be followed by guests sent off in their cars with baskets of food in their trunks. But first, all able hands were required to hold the ropes that held down the air-filled sphere, while my grandfather ignited with the help of a long stick an enormous cotton wad soaked in alcohol. The air warmed up slowly, and the balloon, released at Papy's call, would surge gracefully in the air. A run for the cars—the slam of the doors and the chase was on. A trophy was given to the winner who could bring back the deflated striped cloth and its wicker gondola.

My cousin Hubert fondled me awkwardly one summer. He was fourteen, perhaps, to my young seven years, and he drew me into shady spots to "make love." He was blond and smelled of soap. The memory of those shameful and forbidden gestures lingered in my thoughts throughout my adolescence. Hubert was chemistry-mad that summer. He melted pink gelatin wafers that exploded when mixed with other ingredients. Mamy always referred to his mother as *"la pauvre tante Margot,"* her pity mixed with contempt. Margot and her son had been abandoned by her husband, Paul Jouve—famous for his wild-animal paintings and sculptures. Quite obviously, a boy raised without a father became wayward.

I saw my first film at Goyetchéa, *The Jungle Book.* I was enthralled and fell deeply in love with Mowgli, fascinated by his easy complicity with wild animals. My second cinema experience was less successful. For some foolish reason, I was taken to see *The Great Chicago Fire.* Being, I guess, excessively emotional, I was terrified by the film. I was literally engulfed by this great fire; my fear and my anguish for the burned victims, people, and animals were immense. I cried, wouldn't go to sleep, and had nightmares when I finally dropped off.

Around that time, too—it must have been near the summer of 1939, because my memory links them with the dramatic events of that September—my cousins decided to celebrate Halloween, not a French custom, but with several Franco-American marriages in the family the folk tradition had crossed the ocean. Two ghosts in white sheets with pumpkins for heads, cut into grotesque faces and lit inside by candles, moved toward me howling and shrieking as I sat at the dinner table with Aimery and our nanny. It took several hours to calm me down, even after my cousins appeared from under the sheets. What seemed like inoffensive boys' games triggered reactions out of all proportion. Was there dissent between my father and mother at that time? Very possibly. To me it is clear that I had inherited my mother's excessive sensibility. Every time she went through a crisis, it had repercussions on my health.

3

The War

On September 3, 1939, the world as I knew it collapsed. It was dinnertime at Goyetchéa, and the family was sitting in the farmhouse at the end of the large dining table, listening in dead silence to the radio. Some dramatic event was being announced, which I didn't understand. The only thing I remember is the solemn tone of the voice on the wireless, and all at once my grandfather took me on his knees, hugged me, tears brimming in his eyes. He then said, "My poor children, the war has started!"

I tried hard to understand why Papy seemed so upset. To this little girl of eight, romantic visions of a white nurse's uniform promised a new heroic role. An exciting game was about to start, much like the games we played in the vacant lots next to our house in Neuilly.

The next day, life at the house took on an abnormal rhythm. Grownups were in a state of shock and frenzy—tears, silent hugs, hasty orders, and urgent recommendations shouted in feverish voices. And suddenly the corridors were crowded with trunks, guests and family members rushed away in their cars, and all at once the male staff was gone. I remember, in the tumult of hasty departures, my grandmother standing in the kitchen, a desolate expression on her face, scolding what was left of the staff for having forgotten the basket of food meant for my cousin Teddy, who'd gone off to enlist in the American reserve. "Too many cooks!" she murmured for the last time. For the last days at Goyetchéa, Mamy served us moldy chocolate at teatime. Rationing had started. I didn't see my beloved Alban and Odilia again until years later, when they became concierges in a fancy Parisian apartment house on the avenue du Bois, which is now avenue Foch. Lalo, who cried on departing, spent the next four years in a German prison camp.

Our beloved Goyetchéa disappeared from our lives forever, like Xanadu after one stepped out of its portals. It was sold and split up into several estates. I heard that the army requisitioned the Shetland ponies. What for? I always wondered.

My father was drafted at the rank of lieutenant and was assigned to a hospital train. We did not go back to Paris, because the German army was marching throughout northern France, and most of the French people were fleeing toward the south in terror of the advancing enemy—by any means they could, in cars, on bicycles, or pushcarts, or baby buggies, or simply on foot, while being strafed by the German Luftwaffe, who were perfectly aware that these were civilians. We were very lucky to already be in the south.

My mother rented a little cottage near Saint-Jean-de-Luz, at walking distance from the local school where Aimery and I were enrolled. There were rough boys and girls in that school, and we were mercilessly teased for having Parisian accents. I became ashamed of my name and developed a fear of hearing it called out by the teacher. One day after class, some boys followed us on the way back home, jeering and baiting my brother. For once our mother was walking with us. Turning to Aimery, she said impatiently, "What are you waiting for? Go and fight them!" My brother turned on them with clenched fists and gave a few kicks and blows as I watched, terrified. The enemy disbanded, he came back to us with a victorious smile. As fast as we could, Aimery and I acquired the proper southern accent. We started to learn the lessons of a harsher reality.

One afternoon as we were playing in the street in front of our little house, there was suddenly a thunderous roar, louder than anything I'd ever heard. A huge, dark metallic object shadowed the sun and shaved the top of the houses, low enough to make us crouch to the ground in terror. It was an intimation of the violence of a war that we were going to live through for nearly five years.

The house we occupied was the smallest I'd ever seen, set in a street with many others. We had a cook/housekeeper, a Burgundian farm girl. She taught us country wisdom that filled me with admiration. She said that on her father's farm they washed the sheets, towels, and napkins only once a year, at the village washhouse. It took the women two or three days of soaping and beating the coarse linen with paddles. The thing that amazed my mother was their having enough sheets in their tall cupboards to use for a whole year!

That first winter of war there were food restrictions immediately, and our mother tried to feed us with seaweed she picked on the beach and dandelions from the railroad tracks. The seaweed was inedible—a disaster. The bitter dandelion, cooked to pass for spinach, was a daring novelty but actually quite healthy. Our modest meals were also enriched by the Burgundian maid, who caught snails and knew how to prepare them. We had a little cage suspended on the outside wall of the house. The snails were picked on rainy days—we knew how to find them hidden under leaves. The maid would line the cage with flour to make them disgorge their spit for eight to ten days of slow agony. Then, after washing them, she would throw them quickly into boiling water. After less than a minute, they were ready to be prepared with garlic butter and parsley for cooking in the oven.

That winter also marked the end of our childhood. I was eight, Aimery was nine, the last nanny had been dismissed, and we were now responsible for ourselves, with our mother our only authority. For a while at least, she tried to see that we brushed our teeth, cut and cleaned our nails, changed clothes, had shoes large enough for our growing feet. Finally, she became a mother. My first real memories of her presence date from that Christmas in 1939. With our father away at the front, she must have felt sorry for her two children. A week before Christmas, the door to the little front room was closed and there were mysterious whispers in the kitchen. "Never you mind," was the only answer in response to, "Why can't we go in?"

Then, on Christmas morning, she opened wide the drawing-room door to let us discover the glittering tree, alight with candles reflected in the colored glass balls. We stared in wonder and screamed and giggled. The presents that year were not luxurious, just small tokens. In all my childhood years, there had always been a Christmas tree at Papy and Mamy's, but this one is the one I remember most vividly. My mother had decorated it.

She left us briefly to go see our father, who was on his hospital train, which was passing through Pau, I believe, somewhat close to Saint-Jean-de-Luz. When she came back, she described endless delays due to trains that stopped for hours in the middle of nowhere and the difficulties of getting food or drink during the trip. Then suddenly, a few months later, my father returned, demobilized as of June 22, 1940, from our very short war—they called it an armistice, which was just another word for capitulation. Nevertheless, he was a hero to us children and was brimming with anecdotes, the most awesome of which was about a bomb that had landed on the roof of his train. Seconds of terror passed while medics and patients alike held their breath waiting for the explosion to annihilate them. Nothing. There wasn't time to evacuate the wounded. As all eyes strained toward the ceiling, a brave young orderly swiftly climbed onto the roof, took the bomb in his arms, and with infinite care climbed down to the ground to throw it farther afield. One of those incredible miracles!

Now that my father was back, we returned to Paris so that he could reopen his pharmacy. German soldiers were occupying the city, but apart from their unpleasant presence they didn't rape women or eat little children, as was feared at first. My grandfather's fortune vanished when he became the scapegoat in an imbroglio involving the sale of the chain of Pathé-Nathan cinemas, which he had transacted. The buyer, immediately after the purchase, made a very profitable if illegal turnaround sale before escaping to the United States. Needless to say, Papy had nothing to do with the second sale, but in the absence of the real villain, justice, in need of a culprit, turned to my grandfather. After several years of trying to build up his case to prove his innocence, the guilty sentence with its enormous fines and pending prison term later caused him to have a stroke. Papy was forced to resign from all the advisory boards and partnerships he held. He didn't live long enough to learn of his rehabilitation by President Charles de Gaulle.

My grandparents' houses in Neuilly and Goyetchéa had been sold in a hurry, and they now lived in a rented house in Saint-Cloud, their staff considerably reduced to a cook and a maid. Cars, liveried chauffeur, grand balls, and sumptuous dinners were a thing of the past. The only vestige of these splendors salvaged by my grandfather was his remarkable collection of eighteenth-century mechanical toys, which he used to restore and keep in running order. Metal rolls played music when set in motion. The most banal was perhaps a Swiss landscape with a waterfall and a working clock on the belfry, timing the church bells with a perfect little train crossing the mountainous landscape, smoke puffing through the chimney. The most amusing one represented a plump nanny in frilly bonnet, giving a milk bottle to the baby in her arms while a young soldier tried to steal a kiss. There was also a smoking sailor with real smoke coming from his mouth when he pulled out his pipe. Another was a magician with the face of a monkey, lifting cups from a fringed table, each time revealing a ball of a different color. A circus scene had a big bear with a ring in his nose, turning and dancing while a dog ran endlessly on a barrel. But my all-time favorite was a tightrope dancer holding a large balancing pole, accomplishing perfect *ronds de jambes* and then kneeling on her rope, one knee after the other, in tune to the music. Years later Dame Margot Fonteyn, the great ballerina who became a friend when I lived in London, after viewing the little acrobat observed, "One leg works better than the other—just like me!"

My parents had to find lodgings for the first time. Our mother, who always came through in times of emergency, located an apartment in the Latin Quarter, 155 boulevard Saint-Germain, nearly above the renowned Brasserie Lipp. By the time we settled in, the Germans had already taken away the tram to use the rails for war armament, which dates our move after March 1941.

Saint-Germain-des-Prés was an austere neighborhood at that time. The local shops reflected its origin as church land where monasteries and convents had been built. Merchants selling religious ornaments and vestments were at every corner, and ivory objects as well as gold and silver reliquaries could be repaired in dingy little ateliers. The few cafés—Le Café de Flore, Les Deux Magots, Lipp, and, farther away, La Closerie des Lilas—were occupied mostly by Germans in uniform, as the French avoided mixing. However, there were a few writers—Jean-Paul Sartre, who lived above Les Deux Magots, and Simone de Beauvoir, who had settled in a hotel close by (La Louisiane), were a permanent fixture, allowed by the staff to remain and write all day long, as close to the stove as possible, over just a single cup of coffee.

At the corner of Saint-Germain-des-Prés and boulevard Saint-Germain a large store displayed in its windows the evils of alcohol in three colorful tableaux. In the first window, a happy family sits around the dinner table—the plates are full, parents and children are well dressed and smiling as father serves himself a glass of wine. In the second window, the father thunders while finishing his second bottle. The frightened family stares at him, with nothing to eat on their plates—the lights are definitely dimmer. In the third window, the furniture has disappeared, mother and children are lying on the floor in rags, while father, in a blind rage, shakes a stick at them. The floor is strewn with empty bottles, and rats are running freely. Today an expensive fashion shop has replaced this edifying parable.

At first we had a general maid—I remember a country woman called Blanche Pesé—but as the occupation dragged on and finances became meager, we had to fend for ourselves. One of the last girls to work for us was a Polish refugee; she had so few clothes that she begged my mother for a pair of my father's socks. Another, a rather pretty, buxom girl from Normandy, was encouraged by my mother to present herself to the Folies-Bergères, where, the clients being German officers, she would at least get a good salary and enough to eat. My mother, who was no prude, commented, "Better nude than hungry." The girl listened to her. I was going to school in a convent and was profoundly shocked. The nuns had turned me into a priggish little girl.

When we lived in Neuilly before the war, a seamstress came once or twice a year and stayed for about a week to make dresses for my mother and myself. Her name was Rose. I loved her for her pink cheeks and the perfume she wore that matched her name. In my childhood my preference was for well-groomed women—I was particularly fond of rose powder on round, healthy cheeks. At some point during the war, I noticed that Rose had stopped coming. To my questions about her absence, my father gave me a vague answer about Rose's being Jewish and the "difficulties" she had met. I didn't get more details than that. I hate to think of what happened to her. I didn't make the connection, but suddenly in the winter of 1941 there were a lot of yellow stars with the word *Juif* sewn on people's left breast, and then, around the summer of 1942, they disappeared altogether. Nothing was ever mentioned in front of me—at home, at school, or at church. Did my parents know anything? It is too late to ask. But an extensive anti-Semitic propaganda campaign was afoot in France. There were posters with caricatures in the streets, we were bombarded with vilifying comments on the radio, and the newspapers carried vile headlines about the Jews' being the source of every ill in the country. A horrible documentary was shown in the cinemas before the main feature, where Jews in Orthodox headdress and white blouse were slowly bleeding a wailing cow. I blocked my eyes and ears, but the memory is still vivid. The Nazis were corrupting our minds, and for a lot of people it worked.

There began to be a shortage of everything: food, clothes, heat, water—hot or cold. Gas and electricity were turned off at certain times of the day. We had to plan our baths and rush our meals so that we could wash the dishes while the water was available. Taking a bath became so difficult that we began going to the public bath once a week, bringing our soap, as this, too, was severely rationed. My mother saved wafer-thin slices of soap in a glass, adding water to bind the leftovers together. Long after the war, I kept up this salvage operation. Even today, when I stay in a grand hotel, soap has such value for me that I can't help snitching the perfumed bar from the bathroom when I know that the maids will throw it away after my departure.

On weekdays we washed in the cold bathroom with a saucepan full of water heated on the coal-and-wood stove; the bathtub fell into disuse for several years. My father's shirts were boiled in a big pan, and the ironing job was painfully long, with the three heavy irons heated up on the stove. Blanche, our maid, taught me with professional skill to iron men's shirts, starting with the back and finishing with the collar and cuffs.

At night the town had to become invisible, for fear of bombing. Bathroom windows were lined with black paper, and curtains had to be drawn early. Beware of the inspector's whistle—or worse, a visit from an angry inspector, or worse still, a shot through the window. Streetlights were off, and during early nightfall in winter you walked in pitch-dark with your own flashlight. There was a curfew at midnight. Very few cars roamed the streets, except for German Mercedeses. We went about in the Métro or on buses propelled by coal combustion or some strange kind of gas that exploded like gunshots. There were bicycles for the young, and my father had a little motor scooter.

The Métro was always crowded, and the tight and smelly bodily contact offered a temptation for some men who tried to squeeze next to young girls or women. From time to time, a woman would exclaim sharply, *"Salaud!"* at a man who slid away quickly. On the whole, passengers were indifferent, hostile, and selfish. There were two classes in the Métro. First class was more expensive, of course. Although clothes showed their wear, there was an effort at keeping a look of elegance and respectability. Women wore hats, furs, jewelry, and gloves. Men wore a tie around a frayed shirt collar and a hat in the winter. Suits were buttoned up and belted tightly around waists kept slim due to food restrictions. Stockings drew a straight line up the calves of women to reinforce the right principles. The second-class passengers took their example from the first and copied them with lesser means. Yet together with this display of decorum, scenes of moral and physical degradation occurred often. Were they the result of hunger, frustration, alcohol? In the Métro or in the streets, you would sometimes see a man beating up a woman or a child. Women, as well, were given to beating children in public. The victim screamed, the molester hit harder. People who tried to interfere were brutalized, too, until "everyone for himself" became the de facto motto. You couldn't ask for directions in the streets or the time of day without being insulted. In broad daylight on avenue Marceau, I saw a woman lift up her skirts and crouch down on the sidewalk to urinate.

In strange contrast, German soldiers had orders to be courteous. In the Métro they stood up to give their seats to pregnant women or older people. Sometimes the situation was gently humorous. One day in the Métro, my grandmother started sneezing in a fit of hay fever. A German officer seated in front of her half lifted himself from his seat to murmur "Gesundheit!" Mamy nodded a polite thank-you. But her allergic disorder had just started, and every time she sneezed—and she must have exploded at least five times—the officer felt obliged to repeat his wishes.

And I remember, too, this homage to the beauty of Paris: on any given Sunday, soldiers sitting in front of easels, painting the place de la Concorde, the place des Vosges, or the bridges of Paris. Apart from this touching tribute, the German soldiers were extremely unappealing due to their smell. They wore heavy boots which were polished with fish oil—revolting!

Paris was desperately gray. The "palace" hotels were camouflaged. The George V, the Plaza-Athénée, and especially the Meurice, requisitioned for the German Kommandantura, were painted all shades of khaki, like bush uniforms. Some buildings with antiaircraft guns on their roofs even had nets covering them in different hues of green, to make them look like a clump of trees from the air. That was the case with the George V. A menacing-looking soldier with a machine gun stood in a sentry box at the corner of rue Pierre 1er de Serbie and avenue George V, right around the corner from the hotel. Street signs appeared in German pointing to every landmark. Paris became a foreign town to the Parisians. There were no lit-up window displays, just empty cardboard boxes piled in symmetrical harmony with nothing in them. Time was suspended in a sort of purgatory—between us children, and among the adults, too, from the start of the war and for the next four years, conversations started with, "Before the war . . ." or "After the war. . . ." Years seemed to drag on at a slower pace.

Holidays at our Basque estate were gone forever, so one summer my brother and I were sent to a summer camp, where we learned sailor songs around a campfire. The camp was near the Loire River, where we were taken to swim; a boy in the group drowned, although we had been warned not to wander off because of the strong currents. My sweater was used by the staff when they tried to resuscitate him, but his lips remained blue in the waxy little face. He looked asleep.

A bicycle holiday to the Burgundy town of Vézelay was organized one Easter. We traveled a little part of the way by train, and then my mother, my father, Aimery, and I climbed onto our bicycles. I remember a sort of black oilskin tent with a hood, to protect ourselves from the persistent rain. It was hard going for my little legs. My mother, who hadn't ridden since she was a child, took a bad fall going down a hill while trying to avoid a car coming up. There she lay on the side of the road, stretched out on the grass, with blood pearling on her grazed leg. The bicycle idea was a disaster.

Vézelay was a beautiful medieval town with nothing for us to do, so my mother encouraged me to draw the cathedral and complimented me on the result. Those praises were honey to my ears.

The best holidays, though, were on a private island, Les Ebiens, off the northern coast of Brittany, occupied since the seventeenth century by a family who descended from pirates; they took children in for the summer. Our crossing to the island was on foot, at low tide, in the dead of night, with just a little flashlight to avoid the rocks or slimy fish across the large stretch of sand. We were instructed to maintain total silence in order to dodge the German patrols, who kept a keen eye on these heavily defended shores. What an adventure! For a month Aimery, myself, and the three Peynaud girls played at being Robinson Crusoe and his good man, Friday. Water had to be drawn from the well, potatoes and vegetables dug up from the garden patch, and fishing was from a three-hundred-foot-long net, beached at low tide during the predawn hours. If the catch had been plentiful, we would be required to clean the mackerels and string them on a line to dry in the sun. The island had a tower, of course, built by the great Vauban, military engineer to Louis XIV; we dug around unsuccessfully to try to find the entrance to the dungeon and the oubliettes. For a few weeks, the war was on the other side of the bay, and we felt safe and carefree.

The winters during the war seemed colder than any we'd ever known, perhaps because of the long lines under snow or under rain. As there were no supermarkets in those years, we had to go to a different shop for every foodstuff. You lined up for vegetables and fruit in one shop, milk and cheese and hoped-for butter in another, and then again you went to the bakery for bread, to the butcher's for meat, or to the fish-monger's for fish. Of course there were lines at the cinema and even to buy the newspaper. You had to line up at the cobbler's and at the cleaner's—lining up just became a debilitating French reflex, a sort of fatalism that took political intervention to reverse, years later. Nothing could ever be done while you stood by; it became a question of pride to make people wait, a week if possible. A revenge against the harshness of life, perhaps.

Blanche, the maid, and sometimes my mother and I would split up the chore. Once when my mother came back to my line, I pointed discreetly to a woman who had moved ahead of me. Forgetting all rules of polite society, my mother made a violent scene—right there on the sidewalk—berating her for cheating a child, as people murmured *"Resquilleuse!"* The crowd took sides and timidly defended me against the cheater.

We were warned not to let on that our mother had been born an American. There were camps for foreigners. At night my parents listened to the BBC with the sound turned low—*"Les Français parlent aux Français . . ."*—messages barely heard over German jamming, spoken by Jacques Duchesne, nom de guerre of theater director Michel St. Denis.

Years later Michel became a friend at the Royal Shakespeare Theatre, Stratford-upon-Avon, where Peter Hall, my future husband, invited him to be co-director and teacher, together with Peter Brook. Several times the sirens howled at night and we rushed down to the damp and moldy cellar with the other tenants—most of us in robes, slippers, scarves, wool bonnets and gloves, hugging a bag with a little money and identity papers, just in case, and carrying a blanket to sit or lie upon on the damp earth. People whispered foreboding words of disaster, a child cried because the cat had been left upstairs. . . . We listened for the advancing sound of airplanes rumbling. All heads tilted up, trying to guess how many planes and what damage the antiaircraft guns could do. Where were the bombs going to drop? The railways or the factories, most probably. . . . All the cellars in the neighborhood had been connected, so that in case of a direct hit you could hack your way through from cellar to cellar until you reached a clear street. Finally the all-clear siren would wail. We would later hear on the radio where the bombs had fallen.

My brother and I watched, in broad daylight, the bombing of the Citroën factories from the balcony of Tante Margot's flat, on the hill of Saint-Cloud—250 yards away as the bird flies. An amazing fireworks display, detonating with deafening explosions. Unaware of the danger, we were simply mesmerized by the Technicolor spectacle.

Once, at mealtime, our father told us how he had seen a gentleman caught in a store for stealing. "What did he look like?" I asked. "He looked . . . he looked like *un monsieur*—a hat, a tie, nicely dressed." "Oh . . . and then what happened?" "I don't know," said my father. "The director took him in his office and closed the door." "Tell it anyway," was my urgent retort. The family laughed at my "simplicity."

You occasionally heard of men of honor committing suicide because they had gone bankrupt, but morals were breaking down. Corruption, theft, lies were creeping in. Standards were changing. Hushed tones were used to discuss a lead for obtaining precious black-market food. Many farmers made fortunes by selling food illegally at extortionate prices. We called them the BOFs: *beurre-oeufs-fromage* (butter-eggs-cheese). In our household we took to hoarding eggs in salted water; dry goods such as white beans, flour, and dried peas were hidden in a false cupboard. A new strain of moths and maggots developed, to which we got accustomed. We simply picked them out of the food! Because I loved children so, I took to giving his nightly bath to a sweet little boy of three from the second floor, named Jo, whose parents had German friends. They had a box of chocolate on the coffee table in their living room. The newest tunes were played on the record player, and Jo's mother wore gold jewelry and elegant clothes that seemed new. It was warm in their flat. The parents had an air of good living, with the pink and healthy skin that comes from eating well. "Collaborators" was the term used to describe them. Who said that? The concierge? My parents? Neighbors? I don't know, maybe those things became clear only at the end of the war when the time of reckoning came. They found themselves in trouble when the purge started.

As Aimery and I were growing fast, we were dressed in hand-me-downs, cut to size or elongated with a strip of material. Sweaters were unraveled and reknitted in multicolored stripes—three old ones made one new one. It was so cold in the winter that I went to bed fully dressed and undressed only when my body had unfrozen the sheets. We wore woolen scarves in the house, and at school, too. The classrooms were barely heated. In the food shops, where the door to the street was constantly opened, shopkeepers wore coats under their white cotton smocks, and the standard shoes were wooden clogs lined with rabbit fur and woven hemp to cover the wood. They usually wore mittens, as did usherettes in the cinema and the priest at church. Entertainment was so vital that movie theaters were assaulted with the same desperation as food stores. Once, Aimery and I were very nearly smothered to death in the line for *The Good Earth.* Wartime conditions did not abate after the liberation; they went on—food coupons and all—until after I left for Hollywood in June 1950.

My father and I prepared our breakfast together, in the cold kitchen—I remember jokes about ersatz coffee, ersatz butter, and ersatz jam, and to make it more fun, our conversation was always spoken in foreign accents. Swiss, Russian, or German, anything to avoid serious subjects, such as why my mother, who had resumed her favorite pastime, studying, never got up in the mornings. Sometimes she would try to dress just before my father returned home, but otherwise she let herself go. The war had destroyed her dream of a rich and pleasant social life—she wanted none of this hardship.

I remember endless hachis parmentier (shepherd's pie, or hash and mash). For vegetables we were down to animal fodder: salsify, ruta-baga, Jerusalem artichoke, all three previously unknown to Parisians, though potatoes were still available. Fruit was as rare and expensive as tobacco. Children had one glass of milk a day. We were each given an ever-shrinking ration of butter; it eventually amounted to an eggcup-ful per person, per week. By the end of the war, bread was down to one slice a day per person—two-thirds flour, one-third wood shavings. Meat was also extremely scarce: about two hundred grams a week each. Cats and dogs disappeared—they were stolen and eaten. As a pharma-cist, my father received cocoa butter to make suppositories, and it be-came the substitute for butter and oil in our cooking. Everything at our table had a faint cocoa flavor, which I for one didn't find unpleasant. At school each child was given a vitamin biscuit around eleven o'clock. Ev-erything foreign or exotic vanished, including chocolate and bananas. I was laughed at for the rest of my childhood for asking innocently enough, "When is the banana season?"

Because of malnutrition I caught several childhood diseases; many of my teeth needed fillings. Finally, my bottom covered with boils, I was sent to an old-fashioned doctor who gave me a dose of ether and lanced the painful things. I vomited, of course, and could easily have choked while passed out. After such an experience, I refused to go anymore, preferring the abscess to the torture of the lancet. I still remember the foul taste of the horse's blood I was made to drink a few spoonfuls of a day, to fortify me.

But children will be children. My best friends in the convent school where I was enrolled were a pair of identical twins, Corsican by birth, jolly and mischievous by nature—Toutoune and Dédé Batistelli—each pretending to be the other when it suited their pranks. The nuns were always mystified. Of course we were dying to find out how the nuns wore their hair under their veils. Did they have long hair, or were they shaved like convicts? We watched in turn at the bottom of the stairs for a glimpse of their underwear.

Since my mother didn't encourage social life, I found it in the warmth of my friends. Toutoune and Dédé had a hospitable home,

where the maid said *tu* to them and ate at the table. The twins studied the cello, and the sight of those diminutive girls, with braids rolled
into medieval macaroons on each side of their round faces, tackling
the enormous instruments between their legs, impressed me endlessly.
I was always welcome there, and I was in love with their eldest brother,
Michel, who later became a physician. We played "theater" every single
night of the week except for Sundays, when my brother and I went off
to the Luxembourg Gardens to sail his boat on the pond. The play we
performed was loosely based on *Le Cid* by Corneille, which we had
studied at school—there were always a king and a queen, and all three
of us vied to be the queen. Costumes were made out of rags and tinsel
jewelry. Only the advancing hour would send me back to my cold and
silent home. A cloud of depression overcame me as I climbed up to
the third-floor apartment, where my mother would barely emerge from
reading on her bed to fix dinner.

She was fond of playing bridge, however, and from time to time
pulled herself together to go play at a club. Later, when I started to
study ballet, she gave me her winnings to buy ballet shoes. One of her
bridge friends was the couturier Christian Dior. He was a calm, smiling
gentleman. Perhaps twice in all the war years, she gave bridge parties. It
must be said again that everything was rationed.

After a couple of years, my mother decided that the neighborhood of
Saint-Germain-des-Prés was too dull, which it certainly was in those
days. During the war there was ample choice of flats in Paris. You
could buy or rent anywhere if you had the money. The thousands
of Jews who had been arrested or escaped, as well as Parisians who
had gone to live in the country where food was more readily available, had left empty apartments. My mother's preference was for the
rue de Rivoli, facing the Tuileries gardens, but the rents were expensive. She found a rare opportunity at 48 avenue Marceau, next to the
Champs-Élysées.

We were now on the fifth floor, facing southwest, in a handsome
nineteenth-century building with an elevator. A balcony ran the length
of the building, with six French windows where sun poured in during the summer. At first my parents took pains to decorate our large
new flat. A black Venetian soubrette, holding an oval mirror, graced

the entrance, which was painted white and lined with shelves where an amusing collection of popular glass bottles—shaped as a portrait of President Edgar Faure, as the Eiffel tower, a gun, a dancer, Bacchus astride a barrel, and other artifacts—were displayed, filled with colored water. Indirect lights brought a shimmer to this colorful show. By the time I left for Hollywood, after years of neglect by my bedridden mother, dust had settled on them and their colors were faded. The drawing room was furnished in Napoleon III (Edwardian) armchairs and seats, all covered in white moire. Since the walls were also white, the effect was one of icy elegance. A semi–grand piano stood in the back corner, and from time to time my mother played airs from the Diaghilev ballets she had so loved—*Les Biches* by Poulenc comes to mind. She played timidly and sang in an uncertain voice. She was fond of all ballet music and sometimes played recordings of Stravinsky's *Firebird* or *Petrushka* and also *The Rite of Spring.* When I joined Roland Petit's Ballet des Champs-Élysées in 1947, I was fully acquainted with the great Russian composer's music. To my young ears, he was humorous and melodic. His music, which created such a scandal when first played in Paris in 1913, made perfect sense to a child's ears.

The kitchen gave onto the inner courtyard, where street singers performed regularly—as Edith Piaf had at the beginning of her career. We would throw coins from the kitchen window, wrapped in a piece of newspaper. The dining room was spacious enough for my brother and I and our friends to give a little performance, using the large dining table as a stage. We pushed it against the mirror, and I experienced my first pangs of stage fright. Quite bossy during rehearsals, I kept correcting my colleagues as only the worst dictator/director can. I was so full of myself and concerned with what everybody else was doing that I didn't study my lines well enough. During the performance I suddenly went blank. Cold shivers overtook me when I found myself in front of "the public." My brother, quite rightly, teased me for years, until I was nominated for an Oscar.

Very early in the morning, when the clear air carries sound with predawn definition, I could hear from my bed the milk train chucking slowly into Paris. During the day you could also hear the long cry of the glazier, sheets of glass on his back, offering to replace your broken windowpanes: *"vitrierrrrr!"* And announcing himself with a handbell, the knife sharpener, pulling his wheelbarrow contraption, on which a revolving whetstone turned to sharpen your knives and scissors. Most delightful of all, after the end of the war, a goatherd in his traditional blue country blouse and wooden clogs would walk down the avenue Marceau followed by a herd of some ten goats and a sheepdog—brass bells tinkling, like they do in the mountains—to sell his cheese. He announced himself with a Pan flute, and I would hurry to the balcony to see the parade. Ladies rushed out to the street to buy the authentic fresh goat cheese, slowing down this pastoral procession.

One of the five bedrooms became my mother's library—lined with books, from floor to ceiling, on three walls, the fourth having a mantelpiece and a daybed. The guest room never received any guests except for my American grandmother, who came from New York for a short visit at the end of the war. It served mainly as a storeroom for dry goods. When the eggs we kept in brine became rotten, my brother and I thought nothing could be more fun than to throw them onto the roofs of passing buses, in hopes that the passengers would smell the foul things. Nasty adolescent games . . .

And on rainy days: calling people randomly out of the phone book, using a German accent and announcing ourselves as "the Gestapo." People's first reaction was fear, though they quickly realized that this was just a childish prank. We thought it was really funny. I'm not proud of these wicked games. War corrupts children's minds, too.

My mother didn't have any close friends, except for one man, whom I called "the Lion Tamer," because of the center parting in his lacquered hair and the double row of gold buttons on his jacket. On freezing winter days, only my mother's bedroom was heated, and I had to do my homework there. One unforgettable afternoon she confided to her friend the kind of escapade that is unfit for a young girl's ears, unaware that while my eyes stared at my book, my ears were eagerly recording every word.

I was now going to a different convent school, L'Assomption de la rue de Lubeck, much grander on the social scale, where all the young ladies from the aristocracy were enrolled. On the entrance papers, you were asked to list your name, your surname, and your parents' titles. I wrote impudently, *"Pharmacien de Première Classe."* Here the nuns were not called sisters but mothers, and they were dressed in the most royal aubergine purple. I didn't learn anything more than I had in the previous school and didn't have any better grades, except for one exam where I tried for once and to my surprise found myself ranked third in the class. It had not occurred to me that I had any brains at all. The curriculum leaned strongly toward religion. It was prayers, genuflections, and chapel services all day long. Adultery was among the deadly sins hammered into us. Added to other unwise behavior on my mother's part, her indiscretion in this area sparked off a great turmoil in me. The difference between the morals I was taught at school and her behavior disturbed me profoundly.

My phase of religious zeal dates back to that event. I decided I wanted to become a nun. A long talk with the head sister of the local convent (dressed in demure gray, these) cooled my fervor. The feeling of pettiness in the description of a day in the life of . . . deflated my enthusiasm. My spiritual aspirations went no further than that first meeting.

In a great surge of compassion, I gave away my second shirt to a homeless woman, sitting on a bench down in the street, and I took on the care of an impoverished old woman, Antoinette, who couldn't manage the six floors to her minuscule maid's room. I regularly brought her groceries, washed her feet, and cut her nails, as Jesus had done for the poor. Instead of thanking me for my time and efforts, she would lift her eyes to her little skylight and cry out with fervor, "Oh, thank you, Jesus, for sending me this nice girl!"

We were now close enough to the Champs-Élysées to hear and see every Sunday morning the Germans' goose-step military parade, banners and martial music in the lead. Those blue-eyed robots sang their marching songs full-throated, flaunting their domination over our defeated country. We turned our eyes away, humiliated. Since those days I hate any such display of military precision. I'm suspicious of Busby Berkeley's numbers with girls kicking their legs in time, and the cheerleaders at American sporting events give me a shiver. Truly.

In 1942 Aimery was sent to a boarding school—the Stella Matutina—in the Vercors, in the northern Alps, a region that became the heart of the French Resistance. In the spring of 1944, the retreating German army was fighting ferociously those young men in the hills around his school.

Just as in Louis Malle's film *Au Revoir les Enfants,* Aimery's school, like many others, was implicated in the Resistance movement. Fearing for the safety of the young students and unable to feed them any longer, the school directed the boys to go back home. With no train or bus available, my brother, who had just turned fourteen, knowing we were near Grasse, simply took off on his bicycle with a little bundle on the back rail. He made his way to Grenoble, some forty kilometers away, hiding in the bushes whenever he heard a car, a truck, or marching soldiers. He fed himself on fruit stolen in the fields. In Grenoble he managed to find an electric train that took him farther north to Lyon, where our Aunt Lucette was staying. Several days later a friend's car was going to the south of France, scuttling away to safety. Aimery was crowded on board.

I was standing near the front door of the small farm that my grandparents had recently bought for summer vacations when I saw coming through the gate at the bottom of the garden what appeared to be a tramp. I could tell that this human being was young, tall, and very thin; he was also blackened by sun and dirt. He was walking wearily toward the house. He carried no bag, and his feet seemed to hurt. He looked vaguely familiar. I stood still and stared for a while, squinting in the sun, as the form approached. It finally struck me that this gawky youth resembled my brother. I seemed to recognize the skinny knees, protruding like bolts on a rod. He was now some thirty yards away from me.

"Aimery?" I questioned with a shaking voice.

"Oui, c'est moi!" He chuckled awkwardly.

I rushed toward him and hugged him—he could hardly stand the shock of my embrace. I screamed toward the house, "Mamy! Mamy! It's Aimery!" The scene following resembled the ones featured in every war movie, where laughter mixes with tears, and Aimery offered endless descriptions of every detail of his trip while gulping down whatever there was to eat and drink. Except for my cousin Teddy, Aunt Lucette's son, who had enlisted in the American army, everyone in my family was now accounted for. We were lucky.

Soon afterward, on the fourteenth of August, 1944, the hill facing our farmhouse was shelled for several hours by the American warships anchored at the Sainte-Maxime Bay. Somehow they knew that the hill was an ammunition dump. We were in the garden when I heard the first bomb whistling, right above our heads, closer and closer, until the whistling stopped. Then silence! I pulled Aimery by the collar and yelled, "Get down!" Just then the bomb exploded on the hill across from us. We rushed to our underground shelter in the garden until the shelling stopped, about an hour later. One day Aimery and I were sent along a country lane to the baker for our daily ration of bread. Suddenly, from the path, we saw a pair of German legs with boots, lying very still in the grass. The rest of the body was hidden by the brush. We stared at this pair of boots for an endless minute, too frightened to come closer and look.

The next day, August 15, 1944, the first American GIs came marching in, along the road to Grasse, friendly, relaxed, and smiling. They were distributing Hershey bars to the children who were lining the road, giggling, waving, and crying out whatever English exclamation they had heard, such as "Hi!" and "Hello!" and shouting *"Bonjour! Les Américains!"* The women cried, *"Bravo! Vive les Américains!"* and threw flowers, kissing the boys as they trooped along. The men raised high a bottle of wine kept all the war years for this grand moment when it would be over, and poured a drink to those boy soldiers. I particularly recall a young trooper sitting on the side of the road attending to his regulation crew cut with a broken comb and a broken piece of mirror. I smiled, thinking, *I must always remember this.*

The enormous dark lead weight had lifted from our lives after four years of distress and shame. The war was over.

4

First Ballet Classes

*D*uring the war, eager to have my mother's approval—she always talked with adoration of Anna Pavlova and Nijinsky—I started taking ballet classes once a week at Madame Preobrajenska's. I was then eleven. Years later I realized that I was working in the very room where Zelda Fitzgerald had studied and used to change in the dressing room described in her book *Save Me the Waltz*. The building—the historic Studio Wacker—was permeated with the acrid smell of years of sweating bodies. The whole place thumped and creaked—discordant bars of Chopin and Schumann and sometimes Tchaikovsky were heard, overlapping a bad soprano's vocal exercises. The floor was gray and uneven. Madame sprayed the oak floorboards with a little watering can to settle the dust before doing the "middle."

Olga Preobrajenska was a legendary figure, a prima ballerina at the Maryinsky Theater who had escaped the Russian revolution with her *prince*. (Every Russian ballet dancer seemed to have fled accompanied by a prince.) She was very small indeed—probably no more than five feet high—and wore a little kerchief around her neck to hide the wrinkles. She demonstrated the steps mainly with her hands, but sometimes she jumped and twirled like a young girl. She liked the boys best and did not hesitate to touch them to redress a faulty posture. The greatest dancers in France came to this class and did incredible turns and leaps, even though the room was not large and the ceiling was low compared to those in modern rehearsal rooms. A few mothers clustered around the piano, but my mother seldom came. I took the Métro alone or went by bicycle. My teacher was good, and it was up to me to get on with it. I progressed slowly.

* * *

In those financially difficult war years, my mother sensed that my future did not necessarily include the rich bourgeois marriage that she would have liked for me. With the Caron fortune depleted, she now completely reversed her tactical plan: "You must depend only on yourself! You must have a professional career," she insisted, concluding with bitter nostalgia, "And don't give it up for any man." My love of and aptitude for dancing were genuine, added to which my mother's constant reminiscences of Diaghilev's Ballets Russes clearly pointed me in the direction of a ballet career.

My mother encouraged me to announce my ambitions to the patriarchs of our family while they were gathered for a Sunday lunch. We were seated in the library, and after coffee was poured, my mother said that I had something to say.

"I want to become a professional ballet dancer," I declared with as firm a voice as I could.

After a few seconds' silence, revealing the shock and consternation I had created, my grandfather turned to my mother and asked in a hoarse whisper, "Margaret! Do you want your daughter to become a whore?"

Of course, my grandfather was born in the nineteenth century, and to men of his generation a ballet dancer was a woman of easy virtue—which goes a long way to describing how the family felt about my mother. My grandfather, like other men in his social class, "kept" dancers. The Opéra Garnier even has a salon, called "Le Foyer," where young dancers, accompanied by their mothers, met possible "protectors" to discuss and conclude discreet negotiations for the young ladies' "future."

My mother jumped to my defense. "Times have changed. There are girls from good families who start a career on the stage as dancers, as actresses. . . . Leslie loves dancing, and she is gifted." She concluded with a decisive argument, "Leslie can't rely on a dowry anymore. It is therefore essential for her to have a career." My father, rather embarrassed, only held his breath as she then expounded on the practical side of the plan. "If Leslie is to become a professional, she must take ballet classes every day. She must give up school. It is perfectly possible for her to pursue her studies with a private teacher."

The battle was won. I stopped going to L'Assomption de la rue de Lubeck in order to study at home with a young teacher who proved utterly ineffectual; she was timid and bored, and my brain went to sleep. I learned absolutely nothing from this poor young lady. We ended the relationship by mutual agreement after a few months of misery for both of us.

What I did do with enthusiasm, though, was to ride my bicycle furiously across half of Paris to take my daily ballet class. I loved the class, but I wasn't strong physically—malnutrition was partly the reason. Some days my feet wouldn't hold me, my ankles would twist, and I would simply collapse on the floor.

On the way back from Pigalle, the little hill of the avenue Malesherbes seemed as steep as a mountain—a stopover for an ice-cream cone was my reward—and I would spend the rest of the day lying on my bed with a book, trying to recover from the exhaustion of class. Absentmindedly, my mother would hand down from her library shelves whatever happened to fall into her hand—often quite unusual reading material. She was fond of gothic horror tales where the bride is married to the devil—a red necklace of blood reveals the poor young woman's bondage. She also gave me some novels by Dickens, which I went through without understanding English. She gave me all the Beaumarchais plays, which I found repetitious. Wishing to share what interested her, she lent me *Venus in Furs* by Sacher-Masoch—a rather exotic choice, I thought, even then. In an ultimate effort to offer me something more appropriate to my age, she started to read aloud the English version of *Pinocchio*. My floods of uncontrollable tears—too emotional again—at the passage where poor Geppetto sells his coat to buy his son schoolbooks—marked the end of the English lessons for good. There was also a small book called *Croquemitaine,* the terror of naughty children, who turned out to be a poor hunchback with a heart of gold. At my grandparents' house in Saint-Cloud for the weekend, I grabbed the forbidden Émile Zola novels and went through *La Terre* and *Nana,* and then, at fifteen, moved on to Dostoyevsky. So much for my eclectic education.

At fourteen I entered the national ballet school, Le Conservatoire, and did quite well. Out of some fifty girls who auditioned, I was one of the six or so who were accepted. So was a small girl with black curly hair who became my lifelong friend, Simone Mostovoy, later Simone Hormel, when we became sisters-in-law. Every year I ascended to the next echelon. My mother also enrolled me in a children's theater, with the intention of providing me with early stage experience. The Conservatoire didn't allow its pupils to perform, so I took a stage name: Madge (a deformation of my mother's name) Aimery (after my beloved brother). In a play called *The Pearl Divers,* I was a pearl diver, acting the part of a little boy, and received very good notices. I also danced a variation in the first act before intermission, wearing the silk dress my mother had made me. I was becoming a professional.

I also took classes with the great Russian teacher Alexandre Volin-ine, a gentle and charming man in his seventies who had been partner to Anna Pavlova. On the walls were pictures of the two of them danc-ing together; it gave me wings and filled my heart with dreams. But I found it hard to withstand the pace of this heavy schedule and became anemic.

In 1945 an incident took place that I have never forgotten. Like ev-eryone else I felt strongly the deprivations inflicted by the Germans. In those days when I was very thin, there was at the Conservatoire a rather hefty girl who seemed quite a bit stronger than me. Somehow during a conversation in the dressing room the word "Gestapo" came up, as it was often mentioned, in jest. The girl stopped the chat and said, "Look!" Pulling up her sleeve, she revealed her forearm, where about six large numbers were tattooed from elbow to wrist. "I was in a concentration camp," she said simply. An awesome sight that reduced us to silence. I thought later that her family must have tried to compensate the camp's restrictions with very rich food.

With the end-of-year exams approaching, we were studiously re-hearsing dance variations. Tutus and hairstyles were imposed by Made-moiselle Jeanne Schwartz, our headmistress. She favored a short tutu, exposing our thighs and barely covering the ruffled panties—just like a bunny rabbit, I thought—and our hair was to be gathered in a bun perched nearly on top of the head. I, on the other hand, had a vision of myself as Anna Pavlova: knee-length tutu and a romantic bun at the nape of the neck. I was very firm in my tastes and convictions. What was I to do? I couldn't compromise on this issue, and so, without further consultation, I resigned just before the exams. Mademoiselle Schwartz was appalled. She called me to her office after class, where I arrived trembling but determined.

"Leslie, what is this I hear? You want to leave the school?"

"Yes, mademoiselle," I said succinctly. How could I explain that I didn't approve of the style of the tutu?

"But why? Just before the exams? Your whole career? The Opéra House?"

The silence lasted and lasted. Finally the stern mademoiselle said with a sigh, "Too bad. I thought, my dear, I really thought you might have a future."

She offered her hand, and I curtsied. I left with despair in my heart.

Back home I unburdened my heavy heart. "Mama, I've ruined my life! I think I made a fatal mistake. Mademoiselle said that I could have become someone, and now my future is ruined. . . ."

My mother's reaction was surprisingly calm. "No, no, Minnie Mouse. You've done the right thing. In any case, I don't think you want to enter the Paris Opéra House. I tell you what, let's find out where Roland Petit and his company go to class when they are in Paris—that's the school you want to go to."

I now started going to Madame Rozanne's class, back at the Studio Wacker. Crowded and stifling, the school was very popular. The teaching was basic, simple, and very efficient. Barely a few months after I had joined, with a ripple of excitement announcing his arrival, the great Roland Petit made his appearance. Madame Rozanne didn't hide her adoration for her famous pupil, which she expressed by fussing over him. Roland was her favorite son, and he played it to the hilt.

After the barre the great master came toward me and asked point-blank, "What's your name?"

I had previously decided on the professional name "Caronova" to rhyme with "Pavlova," but the bluntness of his question took me aback, and I blurted out the truth. "Leslie Caron."

"Would you like to be part of my company, Les Ballets des Champs-Élysées?"

Speechless, all I could do was nod. I think he was enjoying the moment.

"I want to hire you for the next season. We start rehearsals next week. Come and see me at my office, at the Théâtre des Champs-Élysées."

The Ballets des Champs-Élysées confirmed the resurrection of Paris. Its home was the most prestigious of all the Paris theaters, Le Théâtre des Champs-Élysées, built in 1913 by August Perret in the purest art deco style. The elite of French society fought for tickets to this new ballet company's premieres, events that were bursting with bold innovations, full of joy, youth, and elegance. The new genius choreographer and dancer Roland Petit galvanized the artistic scene. Modern composers like Henri Sauguet, Henri Dutilleux, and Vladimir Cosma wrote the scores. Jean Cocteau, Jacques Prévert, and a number of avant-garde writers created the most daring story lines. The sets and costumes, designed by the great Christian Bérard, were innovative and glamorous. It was the Renaissance of Paris. It was September 1947, I was sixteen years old, and I felt on top of the world!

In the opening ballet, *13 Danses,* Roland Petit gave me a solo, lasting one long minute—alone on that mythical stage where Diaghilev and Nijinsky had first presented *The Rite of Spring!* I was wearing the most adorable clown's outfit in orange satin, designed by Christian Dior, who had just invented "the New Look." As soon as I stepped onto the stage, vibrations of warmth, excitement, expectation enveloped me. So that's what it's like! The thrill of it! All these eyes on me! I was nervous and intense, but I felt bold, too, and very thrilled. Near the end of the number—here come my double turns—I wobbled! *Oh, dear, dear! Oh, dear me! What have I done? I've ruined the evening! I've dishonored Roland Petit! I've ruined my career! My life! What shall I do? I must go off and disappear forever. I'm not fit to be on this stage!* But to my surprise the music continued. I thought, *Perhaps I'd better go on. . . .* I finished the number. *But . . . what is this thunder? Applause? Applause! The public is applauding! My God! It's lucky I continued.*

I was also given the part of the little girl in *Les Forains,* music by Henri Sauguet, a part that had been created in 1945 by Ethery Pagava, the ballerina prodigy, who had been only twelve at the time. One of the most successful ballets choreographed by Roland Petit, its story narrates the arrival of a rather shabby traveling circus—a motley group who walk onstage pulling a cart loaded with their set and all their belongings. They start to shed overcoats, hats, and scarves, apply circus makeup, dress up the tent and roll the drums to attract customers, who slowly gather around the stage to watch the spectacle. Every night one could discover in the little crowd of extras fashionable personalities of the stage, movies, or literature—all friends of one or other member of the company. This became the Parisian thing to do. Jean Cocteau, Jean

Marais, Albert Camus, and others took their place in the group. The numbers performed were touchingly picturesque: the magician with his disappearing assistant, the Siamese twins, the dance of the veils, the clown, the bearded lady, the acrobats, and finally my number, the little girl with a twirling chair. When the show is finished, a hat is passed around to collect a few coins—most passersby turn away rather than pay anything; the tent is taken down with resigned lassitude, and the company pulls the cart off. Then a brief gap while the stage is empty, until the little girl rushes in, looking for her birdcage, forgotten in a corner. She picks it up and skips away, caressing her beloved birdcage.

Nellie Guillerm, later known at the New York City Ballet as Violette Verdy, and I were the two babies of the company. She was only fourteen, while I was sixteen. Already a remarkable technician, she later developed through George Balanchine into an assertive, brilliant personality and became one of the world's greatest ballerinas. For the time being, we shared roles, and on the road we roomed together under the surveillance of her ferocious mother, Madame Guillerm. Simone Mostovoy, my colleague from the conservatory school, was already in the company dancing a complicated pas de deux with the great Jean Babilée. Another very young dancer, lazy but very promising, with a pretty face and a slim figure, joined the company for the 1947 Paris season. She was only in the corps de ballet, but with a lot of work she could have become excellent. She chose another road and did quite well. We called her "Bichette" (Little Doe), but her name was Brigitte Bardot.

After the Paris season, we went on the road. Egypt first—the Egypt of decadent King Farouk. We were told to be careful. There were tales of girls being kidnapped and disappearing in the palace labyrinth for good. King Farouk did come backstage before the show, but we had been briefed. As soon as the word of his presence spread, all the girls locked themselves in the toilets until the all-clear. He met only male dancers in the corridors.

We had a close call, Nellie and I, when we ventured, unchaperoned, into the Arab quarter, where men were seated in front of their doorsteps, smoking or drinking tea. I was unwisely wearing a pair of red cotton trousers, a gift from my American grandmother, very far from the local female attire: the black burka with a little gold spring running down the nose. When we heard men heckle us and try to get close to us, we turned around and started running in the direction of the city center, where lit-up streets and European shops were safer. Luckily, we were in such athletic condition that not even a young man could match our running speed. In those years there was terrible poverty in Egypt. You could count the ribs of any dog, horse, or cow. In the crowded streets, it was common to see children maimed by their parents to become beggars. The worst case I saw was a boy who was an armless trunk, managing to propel himself forward on short stumps, his head barely reaching people's knees.

The French embassy's cultural attachés were our escorts and daily providers of Oriental sweets. In Cairo they took us for an hour's ride out of town to see the awesome and mysterious Sphinx, still buried up to its neck in the sand and just a camel ride away from the amazing pyramids. Begging children followed us everywhere, dressed in indescribably dirty rags. We were also taken to the underfinanced, badly lit Cairo Museum, where stacks of mummies, stripped of their royal status, had to suffer the ignominy of our bored glances.

In Alexandria we were crowded onto a small ship on our way to Beirut, for our next date. During the roughest of crossings, Nellie's mother, who received direct messages from God, predicted imminent shipwreck—she knew we were all going to be engulfed in the deep. All night long Madame Guillerm prayed loudly and fervently to the Virgin Mary to save her and her daughter. She blamed the director of the company, wicked Jean Babilée, and all the sinners in the troupe for our impending death—until we disembarked safely. But another disaster awaited us: The company manager ran out of money and failed to pay the two principals, Jean Babilée and Nathalie Philippart, his wife. Babilée, *"l'enfant terrible,"* expressed his discontent by throwing his left shoe into the auditorium where the president of the Republic sat with madame and their retinue. Babilée then finished his variation with hand movements rather than with his feet. The scandal hit the press the next day and nearly created a diplomatic incident.

Our "theater" was nothing but a small cinema, and during one ballet, the last girl in line was still in the wings while the first was in place—there was no room for her on the stage. We giggled a lot while performing a cut-down version of this ballet. We had arrived two days before our opening and were eager to catch the previous show. A belly dancer with her orchestra in the background was shaking her generous contours in rhythm to the drums and a multitude of gold pieces sewn onto her costume. All this sexual exuberance seemed to be for the benefit of one small boy sitting in the middle of the front row, his mouth open with admiration. The men sitting around him laughed, approved, and encouraged the performer. I think it was in Beirut that the rake of the stage was such that every effort had to be taken not to fall forward. A satirical cartoon in the local newspaper showed a dancer crawling up a steep incline to reach his partner. These were the hazards of being on the road—all part of the great adventure.

Athens was our next theatrical date. On opening night I was chosen to curtsy and give the inevitable bouquet of flowers to Queen Frederica in her royal box. Her young son, Crown Prince Constantine, who could not have been more than seven, stood at her elbow; as he wasn't reacting to my smile, the queen nudged him discreetly, and he extended his hand. A civil war seemed to be taking place in the country while we were there—something quite frequent, I hear—with no other visible effect than water cuts. I was taught the Greek for "A glass of hot water, please," which seemed to be all I could obtain in the small hotel where we were lodged, for washing morning and evening. If attending to teeth and body were essential in the morning, it seemed possible to do without evening ablutions once in a while in order to freshen my ballet tights. I must have boosted my health during my stay in Athens. Mutton, chickpeas, and salads were on the menu of every café in our neighborhood, where large pans full of rich yogurt, my favorite food, were exhibited in the window. The top cream, cracked by the sun, attracted flies that no one seemed to chase away in those unhygienic days. I suspect that yogurt produces its own form of penicillin. We went in groups to visit the Parthenon, where I concluded that ruins upset me; these days I observe with great satisfaction the progress of restoration that has been achieved over the sixty years since that first visit. It is indeed starting to look again like a temple with magnificent proportions. We filed past countless beheaded statues and noseless stone heads in the museum, where again I mourned the ephemeral life of human endeavors, be they carved in stone. Small things seem to survive best—I still have my Tanagra head of a goddess, intact with its headdress and nose.

A year later we participated in the second year of the Edinburgh Festival. The British Royal family gave their gracious support to the event. Stretched out on the floor, we kids lifted the fringed bottom of the curtain to peek at King George VI and Queen Elizabeth arriving in fanfare with the two princesses, Elizabeth and Margaret, while the patrons in the whole theater stood up, turned toward the royal box, and clapped! The queen saw our faces and smiled. What heaven for a girl of seventeen!

In Edinburgh we stayed in digs where the first-floor bedroom advanced like the prow of a ship onto a square, light pouring in through three large, curtainless windows. The exposure was fun during the day, but we felt like goldfish in a bowl at night. To preserve our privacy, we devised a technique of spreading out our nightclothes on our beds, then turning off the lights, undressing quickly by the lights of the square, and diving into our cold beds.

I saw a number of remarkable performances at this festival: the Brandenburg Concertos by Bach, heard for the first time; the cinematic debut of a tall and lean Federico Fellini, acting a Jesus Christ character in the short film *Il Miracolo,* by Roberto Rossellini, with the unforgettable Anna Magnani playing the simple-minded shepherdess. We were so moved after seeing this poignant film that, once outside the cinema, we parted without a word.

I don't remember how, but after our near shipwreck on the Mediterranean Sea I had managed to shake off the oppressive supervision of Madame Guillerm. Danielle Darmance, the company's acrobat, was now my "little mother." I roomed with her from then on, and became very fond of her. A married woman, she had experience and good advice to give. She warned me about the constant attention Babilée was paying me, as indeed I was invited daily to share Jean and Nathalie's meals, to the point that it must have looked suspicious to the rest of the company. In their presence I felt bathed in a haze of warmth and charm, amazed by their sophistication and talent. My religious education forbade any thoughts of intimacy, and Babilée respected this unspoken prohibition.

The rest of the company was very protective of my youth and ignorance. I remember once on the beach of the Belgian town of Knokke-le-Zoute describing a young bather's muscles as *bandés,* which means taut but also "erect." There was an embarrassed silence and some stifled giggles. No one cared to explain, and I felt foolish. At that time I didn't know what a homosexual was, and the term had to be explained to me. But we were like brothers and sisters, and later, in Paris, those of us who lived at home would share their pay with someone who needed a knee operation. As there was no national health care then, such sharing was normal. Members of the company took little Tania Constantine to the doctor when they found her shivering with fever outside her parents' hotel room. Eddie and Helene Constantine were Christian Scientists and didn't believe in medical intervention. I think her colleagues may have saved Tania's life.

In London at the Shaftesbury Theatre we were a huge success and came to appreciate the best audience in the world—the British public. Educated, passionate, and faithful, Londoners filled the theater at every performance. They knew when a dancer had accomplished a tour de force and clapped. We kept up our strength by eating, without any qualms, horse-meat steaks down in the basement of a little Greek café on Shaftesbury Avenue.

Years of bliss! And yet I felt that time was of the essence—a gnawing anxiety convinced me I was late in achieving my destiny. I remember crossing place Vendôme with Roland Petit and telling him of the dramatic urgency of time. My inadequacies caused me deeper pangs than can be imagined. I was seventeen, and I wasn't a perfect prima ballerina yet! Surely I was late for my years, even though I was also aware of the absurdity of my reasoning. I blame my mother for this deep-seated anxiety. The fear of time passing fast, much too fast, without my having accomplished anything significant, became worse as I grew older. I cannot call it ambition. It wasn't that at all—the contest was not against others, and later it wasn't medals or honors that I was seeking, or even money, it was an inordinate sense of duty and guilt that drove me on. The devil was on my tail. I felt I should improve my technique and nearly gave up the tours in order to concentrate on the basics. Babilée gave me a few private lessons and impressed upon me the importance of continuous movement, sustained even at standstill.

In 1949 we were invited for one exceptional performance to . . . was it Leipzig or Frankfurt? I honestly don't remember which German town it was. Jean Babilée was to perform the most remarkable ballet in our repertory, *Le Jeune Homme et la Mort*. His wife and partner, Nathalie Philippart, was ill, and I was asked to replace her. Each time and wherever that ballet was performed, the event sparked off mass emotion on a scale I have never seen since. Designed by Jean Cocteau, choreographed by Roland Petit on the music of Bach's Passacaglia in C minor, the ballet's story takes place in a painter's studio and describes the last rendezvous of an amorous young man with a cruel girl who laughingly shows him a noose hanging from the rafters and tells him to go hang himself. Babilée leaped high with steps that only he could do—he expressed his despair with such realistic violence that the public feared, every night, that he had actually hanged himself.

I was extremely thrilled to be chosen to dance this grandiose pas de deux, but what awaited me was unforgettable. We arrived from France by train to discover that there was no town left. Hardly a whole house standing. Ruins and rubble stretched as far as the eye could see, but here and there half a wall, towered over by a chimney. Bits of buildings torn open like tragic dollhouses revealed the remains of what had once been a home. A scene of utter desolation. We went outside of town to a hotel that had been spared. We dropped our luggage and were driven by bus to the theater. On the way I saw the survivors arrive to attend our performance. I have the vivid memory of ghostly thin people, impeccably dressed in black—hat, scarf, and gloves—brushed down so that not a speck of dust remained on threadbare clothes, in contrast to the rubble they were walking through. They appeared from cellars, from the ruins, from holes in the ground, and walked, serious and eager, toward the only remaining building: the theater! It was simply miraculous—the theater had survived!

We danced before a public holding its breath in sacred silence. We could feel waves of emotion soar as the drama unfolded relentlessly, almost to the breaking point, until finally the curtain fell and freed the audience. Howls of enthusiasm swept the people to their feet. The applause lasted as long as the ballet had. Twenty minutes! For twenty minutes they stood on their feet and clapped to express their gratitude for the shared emotion, their release from the horrors of the war, for the French ballet coming over to start civilization again.

5

The Phone Call

*T*he voice on the phone said, "You're hired! MGM wants you! You're leaving for Hollywood in three days!" I remember catching sight in the mirror of my drained face with hollowed cheeks, quite exhausted from ballet classes and performances, as my mother gave me serious advice about my future career. "You look a bit like Gene Tierney," she said sententiously. "There is something exotic about you. Be careful they don't put you in a sarong—I mean it. Look at what happened to poor Dorothy Lamour! And whatever you do, don't marry Mickey Rooney!"

The voice on the phone had been that of David Stein, younger brother of the all-powerful president of MCA, Jules Stein. The agency, Music Corporation of America, was the most influential talent agency in Hollywood—New York as well, for that matter. David, who had chosen to live in Paris because he was a playboy at heart, had made me sign a unilateral contract, just in case MGM decided to hire me, after the test that Gene Kelly had shot with me some two or three weeks earlier.

Gene had seen me dance at the Ballets des Champs-Élysées the previous year, on the opening night of *La Rencontre,* the ballet I starred in with Jean Babilée. He had come to meet me at the end of the evening, but, inexperienced as I was with backstage protocol, I had already gone home. A year later, though, a meeting was arranged, and I met Gene in his suite at the Hôtel Plaza Athénée. He was gentle and respectful and spoke of doing a film test.

"I'm going to do a film called *An American in Paris,* which is the story of a young American painter in Paris who meets a French working girl who seems to slip away every time he wants to declare his love for her. He discovers she is engaged to marry one of his best friends. There is a twenty-minute ballet at the end of the film. I want to test you for the part of my leading lady. I might get fired for doing this—the studio only gave me permission to test Odile Versois. I know you can dance, but I want to see how you photograph and if you can act."

I had projected my future in a serious classical ballet career. To tell the truth, when the phone rang, I had all but forgotten the film test with Gene Kelly. I had gone through with it to please my mother, who thought there was more future and longevity in a film career than in ballet. A variation from *Les Sylphides* on the music of Chopin, for the annual reunion of my father and my brother's old school, was my immediate concern. While still under contract to the Ballets des Champs-Élysées I'd been approached by quite a few filmmakers since the opening of *La Rencontre*. J. Arthur Rank had invited me for a three-day test in England; other important producers and directors, Marcel Carné among them (for *Juliette ou la Clé des Songes*), had tested and passed me over, but frankly I didn't care. Ballet, Anna Pavlova, Nijinsky, Les Ballets Russes, Bach, Mozart, and Stravinsky were my idols. Most of all I was in the flush of my first passionate love. I was completely, profoundly, breathlessly in love with my partner, Jean Babilée. He was married—in fact, he had married only two years previously—and I was a fervent Catholic. The pain and conflict of this situation were already taking a toll on me, and I began to see Hollywood as the way out of this intolerable situation.

"You're leaving for Hollywood in three days!" I was really taken by surprise. The words reverberated in my head in a loop. "You're leaving for Hollywood in three days!"

What do you do when you only have three days left of life as you know it? First I cut my hair short. Off with my long tail of hair! What was the symbolism of this act? A proclamation of independence? I usually cut my hair to celebrate important events. I went to ballet class as usual and, with extreme embarrassment and self-deprecation, told the news to a few of the kids. I don't think I ate or slept much during those three days, I was in such turmoil. After buying a length of blue cloth at Boussac, the fabric shop on the Champs-Élysées, I sewed, on a child's toy sewing machine that worked with a little wheel, a two-piece suit and matching blouse to travel in. We were still on ration coupons in 1950 and my wardrobe was miserably limited.

My first publicity assignment was organized by MGM's offices in

Paris, the premiere of *Gone With the Wind,* the most prestigious production MGM had ever made. Released in 1939, just at the onset of
the war in Europe, the masterpiece was finally coming to Paris. A formal Parisian event! I wore my only adolescent party dress. The press
photographers crowded me, embarrassed me to no end. I smiled and
smiled, just because I didn't know what else to do in front of the flashing bulbs.

And finally I said good-bye to Jean Babilée, good-bye to the pleni-
tude of my heart, to the exhilarating, the all-enveloping joy I felt in his
presence, his animal beauty, the hours of poetry he recited so well, the
perfect grace of his body when he danced, his knowledge and sense of
music, the surprise of his mercurial moods. Good-bye to the love we
shared. We were lovers in all except in the flesh. It has remained this
way throughout our lives. It never was the right moment. Time has now
quenched the ardor of our passion to leave us the closest of friends—
almost an old couple. Life is like that sometimes, unresolved. . . .

We formed a little group at the airport of Le Bourget, the only Paris
airport in those days, when flying to America was a rare and thrilling adventure. An MGM photographer was there to record the event.
My mother—who was flying with me because I was still underage according to movie rules and needed parental supervision—my father,
my brother Aimery, and . . . Eddie Constantine. An American crooner
with a pockmarked face, a sometime nightclub singer, always penniless
and wandering backstage in search of a few francs for a cup of coffee
and a sandwich, Eddie was soon to become a very famous star in the
French cinema. His wife, Helene Constantine, was a solo dancer in our
company and shared a dressing room with me. When Gene Kelly, who
didn't know how to contact me, had asked Eddie, his American pal, to
bring us together, Constantine had arranged the meeting, after which
he felt that the subsequent wondrous developments in my life were his
achievement. Right there at the airport, he named his fee: He wanted a
white suit as payment—a white suit to perform in. Soon after my arrival
in Hollywood, the news broke in all the papers that he had become the
new protégé of Edith Piaf, that his name was up in lights at the Olympia
Theatre, singing with her, that he had film offers, et cetera. I was very
pleased for him but didn't think he'd want to be reminded of the days
when a white suit meant a chance on the billboards, so I didn't send it.

Eddie never forgave me. In the winter of 1991, when I was in Berlin doing *Grand Hotel* on the stage of the Theater des Westens, I bumped into an old and frail Eddie Constantine, nostalgic about his heyday. He sat with me at the Café de Paris, where I was having dinner before the show, and reminded me with lingering resentment of the white suit I had not sent him. I confess that I remain, to this day, beholden to him.

The trip to Los Angeles in this spring of 1950 took some thirty-six hours. The plane stopped in London, then in Shannon to refuel, and again in Newfoundland, until we finally landed at La Guardia Airport in New York. Along the way—London, it was—the glamorous star Joan Bennett boarded the plane, to the intense curiosity of my mother. Later, at La Guardia, where we changed planes, I ordered my first banana split, a vow I had made after hearing my mother's descriptions of her birthplace. A banana split epitomized America and all its rich, exotic bounty. Inevitably, after ten years of undernourishment, I was violently sick in midair.

I only have a very blurred recollection of our arrival at the L.A. airport. Thirty-six hours of flying will do that, not counting the nine-hour time difference. We were whisked away to the Beverly Wilshire, at that time an unpretentious, middle-range hotel, with a clothes shop and a bookstore (Doubleday) on either side of its Wilshire Boulevard entrance. A soda fountain stood unpretentiously on the side street. We were given, against my mother's signature, a check for $150, our pay for the week: $75 each. We went to sleep exhausted.

I was assigned an agent, much as the court automatically assigns a lawyer to the accused. With the intolerance of youth, I immediately sized him up: Howard Herty was an old man, slightly suspicious because he was kind and accommodating. In Paris during the war years, you had to be on your guard, as no one was this kind. He can't have been more than fifty, but was like an old dog with no fight left in him. Like all agents in the studio-system days, he was assigned to me primarily to ensure I would toe the line.

My mother bought herself a white three-quarter-length spring coat from the shop down below, explaining, "Darling, you're young, you don't need elegant clothes to look good. But I do." Mr. Herty had invited us to La Rue on the Sunset strip, the restaurant where the stars were to be seen. During the dinner I think he described in glowing terms to my distrustful mother what my future would be like. I understood very little English, but I could see that she wasn't buying it. Like a good French girl, I ordered pâté for the first course, quite enough to feed my thin frame, really, then for the main course a steak. A slab of meat arrived so huge that it covered the whole plate, defeating me altogether. They called it a "T-bone." I had never seen such a large piece of meat. At that point I became aware of the gulf separating me from these gratified, contented people who had not known hunger, cold, or fear of an enemy in boots and uniform with a gun slung over the shoulder.

Later, on the sidewalk, while we were waiting for Howard Herty's Cadillac, there stood a tall, lean man who looked down and smiled at me with benevolence. Gregory Peck! I gazed up as if he were Santa Claus!

I was awakened around six by my mother, ready for action. She had done the accounts and calculated, what with the purchase of the white coat, the rates of this hotel, plus the necessary meals and occasional taxis, that we were not going to last the week. "Quick, let's pack up and get out of here."

We stole away before eight, almost like thieves. I felt humiliated in front of the surprised cashier. I think my mother did, too. We asked the taxi driver to find a cheap hotel near the MGM studios, and he did. There was then, and still is, I believe, a large, traveling-salesman kind of place, five stories high, between two noisy avenues, called the Culver Hotel.

My heart sank at the sight and smell of the room we were going to share—a filthy carpet, thin faded curtains, an open sink in the bedroom. . . . This was as bad as digs in Beirut. Finding a diner, a launderette, a neighborhood grocery store, and the public library took a day or two. On the third day, my mother called Gene Kelly. The voice exploding in the receiver was so loud I could hear it from the other side of the room.

"Where have you been? Where are you? The studio has been looking for you for two days! . . . The Culver Hotel! I don't believe it! . . . But, Margaret, that is where assistants bring showgirls during their lunch hour! Wait till Hedda Hopper hears this! Margaret, take a taxi and come over to my house. I'll explain a thing or two about Hollywood. . . ."

Notwithstanding the ten-page contract in our hands, we still didn't earn enough money to rent a real apartment, so we moved to a motel behind the MGM studios. Slightly more comfortable than the Culver Hotel. Every morning I walked to work with the crews into the rear entrance, where the impressive electrical works that supplied the studio took a whole acre. Stars usually entered through the front gate, guarded—and this is true—by Sergeant Don Hollywood. With very few exceptions, actors left their cars in the executive parking lot and walked in the front gate on foot. There was a third entrance where day actors, extras, and office employees were clocked in. The hierarchy was respected in Hollywood.

6

Metro-Goldwyn-Mayer

*T*he Metro-Goldwyn-Mayer studio was as vast as a town. MGM had streets and back alleys, bungalows, offices, dressing rooms, rehearsal halls, recording studios, printers, several furniture and costume warehouses, workshops for plasterers, carpenters, and painters, and around thirty-one soundproof stages. There was also a school, a hospital, and a dentist's bungalow. Just outside the studio entrance, on the alley leading to the administration building, was, to MGM's intense irritation, a mortician who not only refused to sell his property, but advertised his specialty in bold letters, ever reminding his powerful, rich, and famous neighbors of the frailty of their pretensions.

Black limousines were readily available to drive leading actors and important visitors from one set to another, to fittings, to makeup and hair departments, or to lunch at the commissary. The second assistant recorded your every move in a great book and gave instructions for all the rendezvous. That was how the factory functioned.

MGM had an executive dining room on the uppermost floor, where only the top brass went. Male and elitist, with the prettiest waitresses to serve them, they very seldom invited actors into this sanctum sanctorum. Actors and actresses were expected to take their meals in the commissary, which was a sort of casting ground. Directors, producers, and mostly agents thought it important to go and be seen there. It was a combination of the Roman marketplace and the gossip lounge.

Everyone turned around when a star came in and discussed the latest rumors: Who came late to the set this morning and held up production. Who had gained weight and who was seen at Mocambo's last night with What's-Her-Name's husband. . . . Did you read the trades this morning? Bette Davis took out an ad in the trades where she said,

"Twice Academy Award winner seeks work! Contact Bette Davis at . . ." What a shock!

I took only half an hour to eat lunch—every day the same, half a pound of hamburger steak and a salad, Jell-O for something sweet, and a cup of coffee. I usually went to the workmen's cafeteria counter, where another actress was already perched on her stool—Ava Gardner, who preferred to eat with the fellows. More friendly. I would rush back to my trailer and steal a half-hour nap.

Gene Kelly, who kept his car in front of his bungalow, very democratically walked to and from rehearsals. He was saluted with familiarity by one and all: "Hi, Geno! How you doing?" "See ya!" He wore the same kind of informal clothes every day—beige cotton pants, a Lacoste polo shirt hanging out, white socks and brown loafers, and, on his head, what was then called a beanie—a baseball cap to cover his baldness. Until Sean Connery came along, every bald star wore a toupee when performing: Gene Kelly, Fred Astaire, and David Niven (who called his toupee his Aubusson) wore them to film, to do publicity, and also to go to parties, which were in fact performances. Stars were careful of their image then.

On the morning of our first day of rehearsing, Gene had me booked in one of the private projection rooms in the basement of the executive building—where the producers and execs viewed the rushes every night. He wanted to show me a montage of all the numbers he had choreographed and danced in his MGM career: around forty-five minutes of remarkable skill, precision, and invention performed with cocky charm and apparent facility. I was really impressed. A black limousine drove me back to the rehearsal hall, where I expressed my admiration with perhaps the wrong words. "What tremendous fun you must have had!" "Fun!" he retorted, and I received five minutes of dressing-down as he pointed out the hard work all this represented. I stood corrected. That was lesson number one.

I started every morning by doing my ballet warm-up, about a half hour alone, as every dancer does before rehearsing or performing. Gene Kelly's two assistants—Carol Haney, who would later star on Broadway in *The Pajama Game* and was a remarkable Jack Cole dancer, and lovely Jeannie Coin, freshly divorced from director Stanley Donen and later to become the second Mrs. Gene Kelly—were watching my exercises to give Gene ideas for my introductory solos. Putting a book in my hands, Gene very cleverly used my stretching barre movements for the "studious" solo number. There is no doubt that Gene was a great partner, strong, skillful, and with a perfect sense of rhythm. But more than a dancer, he was also smart, a born leader, and liked to take command. He could assess the qualities of his partners and knew how to make the most of them. Gifted with a sense of space on the screen—camera moves held no secrets for him—he was interested in the technical side of camera equipment—lenses and filters, tracking and support equipment. As a choreographer, he was inventive, daring, and more of an athlete than a dancer. Gracefulness wasn't his thing; you felt he was after strength—a modern man's physical expression. As a dance director, he was exacting, very much so, but he also had a sense of fair play and would indicate, in measured tones, his approval. His disapproval was sharp, straightforward, and didn't allow for any excuses. His rebukes were feared by one and all in the studio. At first, thank God, most of my rehearsing was with Gene's two assistants; although he was very encouraging, I could lose my confidence in front of him.

What sustained me in this new adventure was that I adored working to the syncopated music of George Gershwin. When we filmed to the playback, I was thrilled beyond words by Gershwin's own orchestration, so humorous and sophisticated. And for me the great novelty was learning to do "modern dance" on jazz. Because I was trained in classical ballet, I kept reverting to the formal movements automatically. Hour after hour the two girls, Jeannie and Carol, had to restrain me, saying, "Bend your knees, Leslie! Keep your feet forward! Forget your second position! Loosen up your arms!" I kept trying to copy Carol Haney, who danced with powerful, voluptuous grace.

As the summer was advancing, the sun beat relentlessly on the corrugated roof of the rehearsal hall. No air-conditioning in those days; the vast room was a furnace. We had to be present for our eight hours, like factory workers. When I felt that I had done my work and was ready to go home, Gene would explain, "They clock us in . . . they clock us out. Eight hours. That's how the studio works."

One morning I came in late. Gene wasn't pleased.

"What's the matter? Didn't hear your alarm?"

"Sorry, I . . . I don't have an alarm clock."

"You don't? Well, let me tell you something, the war is over, kid. You can buy one now—in any drugstore."

That simple phrase introduced a new concept. The possibilities were infinite—I realized with wonder that I now lived in a country where I could buy an alarm clock, and perhaps even a pair of shoes once in a while. There was food in the shops, and soap and Kleenex! The banana season at last! For years, whenever I received my weekly check, I would quickly calculate how many pairs of shoes that sum meant.

While an alarm clock, a belt, or a pair of shoes might be within my reach, I still couldn't look as far as whole outfits. My pathetic wardrobe—so scant that I even knitted my own underwear—embarrassed the studio, which wanted to do publicity with their new star. I was invited to the wardrobe department and outfitted with some of Elizabeth Taylor's clothes from *Father of the Bride*. We were the same size, and her outfits fit me perfectly. A beautifully made tweed skirt was my favorite, with a couple of twinset sweaters to complete the ensemble. This was indeed opulence!

Right from the beginning, MGM assigned me a publicity assistant who was present every time a journalist interviewed me. The pretext was to help me in case there were difficult questions, when the English language was still a problem. She was a kind person, but nevertheless I was being censored. The usual collection of seasonal glamour photos—cheesecakes, they were called—also started soon after my arrival. The very first one had me bursting through paper stretched across a hoop on which the words A STAR IS BORN were printed. I was wearing Vera-Ellen's tutu—not a very good fit, too long at the waist. There followed a series of spring pictures, taken as I was dipping my foot into a brook or lying in the grass in a seductively dreamy pose. Easter had me holding a basket full of eggs and looking puckishly at a stuffed bunny. The summer one featured a basket of juicy strawberries. In the autumn, of course, Leslie was reading a book by the fire while lying on a fur rug, and Christmas was the ideal moment to wear those red bobbles on my ears while putting the finishing touch to a ready-made Christmas tree. I felt acutely embarrassed at those inane photo shoots and positively refused to pose for them after a couple of years.

The publicity department also took me to make the rounds of all the stars who were on call in the summer of 1950. Among the men were Howard Keel, very handsome and affable; Van Johnson, jovial and genuinely nice; Peter Lawford, dead handsome and sophisticated. Among the girls was June Allyson, America's little sweetheart. My response to her was, she's a phony! No one could be that nice. It was only some thirty years later, when I met her on a talk show, that I came to appreciate her down-to-earth simplicity and real friendliness. In 1950, after living through the war, I was incapable of appreciating these qualities. I also met Box Office Star Number One, the queen of MGM's musicals, Esther Williams, openly, arrogantly claiming her status, wet or dry. She was competitive and didn't try to be friendly—she didn't see the point. She was also as foul-mouthed as a sailor and didn't pretend to be a lady. I liked her—but at arm's length. Judy Garland was the one who gave me the simplest, warmest welcome of all the players. She grabbed me in her arms and planted two warm kisses: "Good luck, honey!" I was hers for life.

My mother left after three months, around the beginning of filming. According to the law for working children, I was now officially of age, nineteen—after a birthday that had passed quite unnoticed. Exceedingly bored in Culver City, my mother couldn't wait to leave, and I don't blame her. Just as she had in Paris, she lay on her bed all day, reading or writing. It must be said that Culver City didn't have a lot to offer, as it was a transient neighborhood where Mexican immigrants and studio crews lived until they could afford better. My mother never came to rehearsals or to the studio. She knew that Gene wouldn't have liked it, and neither would I. Every night, returning to our motel, I found myself describing the work in progress in positive terms, hoping for her approval, just as my father used to when coming home from the pharmacy. I realize now that for the rest of her life, whenever I wrote my mother, I automatically avoided mentioning the setbacks and reported only the successes, in fear of her sharp disapproval. After her departure I mentally cast off my moorings. I felt I had no more roots, no more links to any continent, country, or family. I had emerged through some effect of spontaneous birth. This mental surgery was necessary to face the vast unknown that now faced me. I had to gather my strength; I couldn't afford to be nostalgic.

In my neighborhood I made the acquaintance of a few locals. Three or four Mexican children with the most delightful giggles would come to visit me at the end of my film day. There was LaReine, Lynn, and Celeste. LaReine was fond of flies and would call them by name and encourage them to rest on her hands. "Here, Pedro . . . Pedro . . . don't fly away, Pedro!"

I started taking driving lessons and bought myself a Hillman Minx, which gave me mobility. We worked a six-day week in the fifties.

Gene and Betsy Kelly offered the warmth of a few dinners at home, en famille with their daughter, Cary, "brighter than you" would tease Gene, and he was right. I remember how surprised I was by the simplicity of their home. There was no domestic help that I could remember, but a new invention, the electric dishwasher, which seemed to elevate the kitchen to a sort of domestic factory. I also saw an amusing contraption in the dining room called a lazy Susan. Instead of a maid passing the dishes, as was the custom in Europe, the round dining table had a second smaller shelf on ball bearings, where dishes were placed and for you to turn at will so that you could serve yourself. Their front door opened straight into the living room, simply furnished with a long L-shaped sofa ending with a baby grand piano in front of the large street window. At the back of the living room was the bar, a serious affair with barstools, professional enough for the real Irishman that Gene was. The back wall was all glass and gave onto the garden, with a volleyball court taking all the space. A game was held every Sunday afternoon.

Saturday night was the night to unwind at the Kellys' home, on North Rodeo Drive in Beverly Hills. From sundown on, the front door was open to all actors, singers, entertainers, scriptwriters, and directors from Broadway or Europe. There were no locks on the front door—you just walked in—and you never locked your car either. This was long before the horrors of the Manson murders. Gene told you to help yourself at the bar, and you did a turn if you felt like performing. Saul Chaplin, our musical director, was at the piano, and everyone knew the words to the songs by Gershwin, Cole Porter, Jerome Kern, Rodgers & Hart or Hammerstein, Irving Berlin. Betsy Blair sang enthusiastically but completely out of tune. It didn't seem to disturb anyone. Gene did the Irish thing—drink whiskey and talk. Surprisingly enough, Stanley Donen slept soundly on the sofa, undisturbed by the din. Lena Horne was there regularly with her husband, Lennie Hayton. Their interracial marriage had created quite a stir in those intolerant days. She did not do Saturday-night improvisations.

Oscar Levant, who played Adam Cook, the prodigy, penniless pianist in *An American in Paris,* was a fine, amusing fellow as long as the word "death," to which he was allergic, wasn't mentioned. His comment about me still amuses me: "She looks too much like me, as far as I'm concerned!" We did have a round face, slanted eyes, and very full, pouty lips in common. There was a quote in the film script that was supposed to have been said by Oscar to George Gershwin: "Tell me, George, if you had to do it all over, would you fall in love with yourself again?" Adolph Green and Betty Comden were regular guests, and all the sketches that became part of their New York show were tried out on us. I remember their weekly complaints about the difficulties of creating a plot around that tiresome song "Singin' in the Rain," with lyrics written by our producer, Arthur Freed. We had all been brought to Hollywood by him, we loved and respected him, but there were constant jokes about his uncommunicativeness. A shy man, he didn't mingle easily. His secret passion was not for tall Texan showgirls but for orchids. He possessed vast greenhouses and was America's foremost orchid grower.

Judy Garland and her husband, Vincente Minnelli—Vincent to me, Vince to Gene and the others—came from time to time. Judy sang, and oh, could she sing! On her twenty-ninth birthday, everyone from the film was invited to the Ira Gershwins'. The dinner was fine, with crystal, silverware, and starched servants, but the evening became memorable when Judy announced, "This is my night, and I'm warning you, I'm going to sing as long as I please!"

Ira hit the piano, and Judy started to sing every song in her repertoire. She sang for several hours, her eyes locked to Vincent's. No one could foresee that the marriage would soon break up. She sang "The Trolley Song" and "Over the Rainbow," but I particularly remember her poignant interpretation of "Someone to Watch over Me." In effect, she was trying out what she soon performed on the stage with huge success, her one-woman show. Her voice came straight from the heart. There was in her a feverish intensity; she seemed to be living at a pace that burned her, with her brown eyes wide open, revealing her extreme vulnerability. The words "a delicate balance" applied to her. Soon after this party, she tried to slit her wrists on an airplane when she was due to film *Annie Get Your Gun.* It seems that once at home she locked herself in her bathroom and tried again to open her veins. The studio took fright and recast the film with Betty Hutton.

But Judy, who had a wicked sense of humor, could also be the life of the party. She told a story about the very short Louis B. Mayer, who had a chiropractor in the executive building. This doctor had devised a contraption on which the boss lay down, held by the ankles and by the neck. The machine would slowly pull the two extremities apart. The method was effective, and Louis B. would walk out of the office delighted to have grown an inch. Of course, an hour later he was back to his normal size. And no one dared to tell him that this contraption was called "the rack"!

My first date was with a young prodigy of European descent: André Previn, who was then the protégé of Johnny Green, musical director at MGM. His family had escaped Nazism by coming to the States. At seven-thirty one evening, he rang the doorbell of my motel suite. In lieu of a corsage, he had brought me a French camembert. I was won over by his charm and intelligence, but my inexperience was all too visible. Shirley Temple at eight knew more about life than I did. The camembert evening was the last. He didn't follow up on the relationship.

With time, I started to learn my way around Los Angeles. In the fifties even the shopping center of Beverly Hills was very provincial, a series of cement shacks—ground floor only—like shoeboxes with more-or-less ornate fronts. Valentino, Gucci, and Chanel were not even heard of on Rodeo or Bedford or Beverly Drive, but you could be fitted with the perfect cowboy equipment—western boots, shirts, and saddles. You parked your car for five cents an hour and browsed in the best hardware shop in town—double frontage and a window display of hammers, saws, and other household tools. There was, of course, the inevitable ice-cream parlor, and Nate 'n Al, the delicatessen, was already open for Sunday brunch. Old World nostalgia gathered dust in an antique dealer's shop that exhibited the kind of ornate Viennese stuff that most Beverly Hills citizens had left behind in the old continent. Brooks Brothers came later and was the chicest shop in the street. You had to go to Saks or Magnin's on Wilshire Boulevard to find French,

Italian, or even New York fashions. The day Cartier and Tiffany finally had a little stand in the two prestigious department stores marked a step toward international sophistication. In the residential section of North Rodeo Drive, where Gene and Betsy Kelly's house was, the locals rode their horses on the bridle path in the center of the road, just as they did on Sunset Boulevard on Sunday mornings. There were plenty of lots for sale for ten thousand dollars or under.

Many aspiring stars, writers, and producers lived in the Valley, where the land was even cheaper. As soon as they advanced—with a larger salary or their name above the title—they changed neighborhoods and took their house along. That is how one fine Saturday night, leaving Gene and Betsy's party around eleven, I found myself face-to-face with a two-story house blocking the street! Was I going mad? I was seized with irrational terror. I then discovered the gang of grips who were maneuvering the tottering edifice, pulled inch by inch behind a tractor; the men were shouting and whistling warning signals to avoid the curbs and the branches that had to be sawed off from time to time. Raised on a platform, the house was rolling very slowly from its neighborhood of origin to the more elegant section on the flats of Beverly Hills. On Monday morning when I told the story at rehearsal, no one seemed surprised. Everyone in Hollywood was in transit. You were either rising or slipping.

7

The Making of An American in Paris

After several months of rehearsals, we were ready to start filming. The makeup tests were a torture. In the French ballet company, my face was my own, and I designed my own makeup and hair, but here William Tuttle and his staff were in charge. They wanted me to adopt the fashionable look of the day. Suddenly my eyebrows were threatened by a pair of tweezers! "No! Please don't! Don't touch my eyebrows!" An agreement was reached. Now for the hair. The great stars—Lana Turner, Ava Gardner, Esther Williams, and Elizabeth Taylor—all had a crown of tight little curls, so of course I should have the same. I tried to explain to Sydney Guilaroff, head of the hairdressing department, my idea of a modern French girl's hairdo—as short as a boy's and straight. In Paris I had seen the most-photographed French model, Jacques Fath's Bettina, wearing this revolutionary hairdo, and I wanted the same. I met with some resistance. They didn't seem to understand what I meant. I was going to show them.

In front of my little bathroom mirror, leaning forward to get a glimpse of the back of my head, I cut my hair with a pair of nail scissors. "I am sure they will see what I mean now. . . ."

They saw only too well. At seven in the morning when I arrived at makeup, everything stopped in the department until the executive hierarchy could be summoned. There were frantic phone calls from Culver City to Beverly Hills and Bel Air. I found myself back against the outside wall of the building, facing the firing squad. They stood in a line, staring at the disaster, shaking their heads in disbelief: Benny Thau, head of production; Arthur Freed, the producer; Vincente Minnelli, the director; William Tuttle, head of makeup; Sydney Guilaroff, head of hairdressing; and Gene Kelly. After a brief debate, I was sent home.

The first day was rescheduled, as were the next three weeks, to allow for my hair to grow. Three weeks off, and no scissors near the foolish girl! Gene Kelly had the final word: "They fire girls for less than that, you know!" The three-week postponement was not such a bad thing. It gave me the opportunity to improve my English.

I finally made it to my first day of filming. We were starting with what in musical-comedy terms is called "the book." My hair had grown a little; my hairdresser kept pulling and brushing it. I was still disappointed, but the look I wanted was made fashionable a few months later by Shirley MacLaine in *The Trouble With Harry*. I would have been the first.

Gene (not Minnelli—I was Gene's protégée) guided me in front of the camera with patience and good humor. I spoke my first lines phonetically. He would say to me, "Lester"—that was his affectionate nickname for me, "Lester de pester," as he liked the rhyme and was a tease—"Lester, if you want your grandmother to see you in this scene, you had better turn toward the camera when you speak your line." I wasn't used to expressing myself with words and definitely not in English; inhibitions were seriously blocking me. I remember the following lines, spoken in the waterfront scene, to Gene, who was already running up the stairway, ten yards away from me: "Jerry! If it means anything to you, I love you!" I was of a deep red hue under my makeup and had broken into a sweat out of fear of being ridiculous.

The camera seemed cold and forbidding. I missed the warm presence of the public. With time I became attuned to the presence of Vincente Minnelli, who sat right under the camera—most of all, I wanted to please him because he called me "Angel," and who could resist that? I came to know Minnelli well later, when we grew close on *Gigi*. More than most men, Minnelli had an understanding of women. Although he married three times, there definitely was a feminine side to his nature. Working with him was an easy meeting of imagination and taste. He could express poignancy in dramatic situations but was never cloying, and he always respected the limits of elegance. He also had what I call the great Hollywood sense of humor, which was in fact a blend of New York and Hollywood humor. He was, however, quite inarticulate when it came to giving directions on the set and found it difficult to voice his desiderata. His lips would form soundless vowels, his big brown eyes became pleading, and after a while he would end this soundless discussion with a short, "Do it again, Angel," but I had understood him. There was a quality in him that pushed you to surpass yourself in order to surprise him. The best was a matter of course; he confidently expected the miracle.

His daughter, Liza, came on the set with her nanny one day—she was four years old then, a beautiful child with the same huge, soulful eyes as her father, and her mother, too, for that matter—while Gene and Vincent were kidding around and pretending to have an argument. The child went into hysterics, started to cry and scream, "Don't fight! Don't fight!" until her nanny and her father calmed her down. She obviously was a very highly strung child who had witnessed scenes that were too emotional for her age.

Minnelli and Kelly treated each other with love and respect. They both allowed for each other's sensibilities. If Gene tended to take over, Vincent had a way of circumventing opposition and eventually getting his way. Vincent would back down happily so long as things were on the right track, but he was categorical if he felt there were aesthetic mistakes.

In 1950, Hollywood was entirely under the dictatorship of the self-imposed code of morality—the Hays Office morality code had been endorsed by all the major studios in 1930, after scandals endangered the movie industry's box office. For a musical comedy, especially, it was imperative to have the Hays Office certificate of approval.

In my introductory number, my solo with a chair was filmed twice because of "censorship difficulties." A lady with a very plunging neckline came from the Hays Office to watch rehearsals. She was particularly taken with Gene Kelly's charm, while he did his wicked best to make her feel welcome. The following week, after shooting this particular solo, I was told I had to shoot it again. I wondered which of the specific twelve rules this number was violating:

1. Nudity?
2. Ridiculing of religion?
3. Depicting scenes of illegal drug use?
4. Showing methods of crime, like safecracking, arson, or smuggling?
5. Sexual perversion, such as homosexuality? (Could dancing with a chair be considered perverse?)

6. Bad language?
7. Imitation of real-life murder?
8. Attacking the sanctity of marriage? Adultery?
9. Miscegenation? (The dictionary told me that this had to do with race mixing. The chair was not even painted black!)
10. Excessive and lustful kissing? Scenes of passion? (What mischief can you do with a chair?)
11. Disrespectful treatment of the U.S. flag?
12. Vulgarity? Low, disgusting, unpleasant scenes such as capital punishment, cruelty to children or animals, prostitution, surgical operations?

Whichever rule I was breaking, I reshot the number and moderated my relationship with the chair. Colonel Hays and the lady with the low décolletage were satisfied.

Filming conditions were punishing, especially for musicals. During the long hours of waiting while setting up the lights, the crew amused themselves with numbers, playing the races, and listening to the games on little radios kept near the coffee corner. Every Saturday—payday at the studio—a jeweler would turn up on the set with a special pass. He'd open his Pandora's box, and lots of guys, from the director to the grips, would buy gold trinkets. I still have a little gold angel given me by Jean Negulesco on *Daddy Long Legs,* just as I still wear the first ring I bought when I finished *An American in Paris.* If the work was hard, MGM crews were well paid. The downside was the long days and the intense heat while shooting. The bigger the set, the more spotlights (which were called 10Ks) were necessary to light it. When the carbons wore down and needed to be renewed, the sparks would call for a pause to change the carbon sticks. A moment of respite. The crew stood way up there on the catwalks, one man for two or three 10Ks, and from time to time, when the heat became too ferocious, they would yell, "Open the doors!" The director of photography would immediately call out, "Kill the broads! Open the doors!" and after the click of one light switch after another, a welcome darkness would engulf the huge hangar while the large doors were rolled open. Accidents had happened. An electrician had fainted from the heat and fallen to his death.

The physical pressure of filming began to tell on me. I came down with strange, insidious symptoms—low-grade fever, swollen glands throughout my body (mostly in the groin), unbelievable exhaustion, a feeling of insurmountable lethargy, incapacity to lift my legs, as if they were made of lead. A broken leg is visible, but you can't see the exhaustion of glandular fever. The studio doctor, Dr. Blank, was called in. He diagnosed mononucleosis. My mother was not sympathetic. "Vivien Leigh goes on filming with tuberculosis. You can carry on." But Gene Kelly, my protector, arranged for a lighter filming schedule: one day on, one day off. I spent a lot of time in bed. Dr. Blank gave me three shots twice a week—vitamin C, the B vitamins, and iron. Slowly, slowly, the disease left me. I became painfully aware that I wasn't strong and must find ways to cope with this exhausting profession. I learned about proteins, vitamins, and minerals to improve my diet. A young man with the prestigious name of Loew (a major studio shareholder—his family owned the chain of Loews-MGM cinemas) took me out to dinner one night. I ordered a New York steak and ate with the appetite of a working girl. When presented with the dessert menu, to the amazement of my dinner partner, I asked politely for a second New York steak. He never asked me out again.

A full company of dancers had been hired, and some became friends. Michael Panaieff, our dancemaster, gave class in the morning to the sound of a piano, after which we rehearsed all day long—one sequence after another, working in small groups first, then all together. Gene did not always attend. Extremely busy, in charge of the choreography, he was everywhere—with models of the sets, making sure the sets and the choreography were coordinated, present at costume fittings with Minnelli. Near shooting date we went through the final ballet in front of everyone involved: Minnelli; John Alton, the director of photography, with whom they discussed camera angles, lenses, and cranes; Johnny Green, Saul Chaplin, and André Previn, when the music and tempi were discussed. The music was prerecorded, and we filmed to playbacks. During this time the huge sets were being built in the workshops, one set at a time, and wheeled in on platforms to be assembled. An army of painters would come into those hangars, big enough to hold an airplane, followed by the set dressers. Finally we were asked to find our bearings on floors that were always painted in shining colors and were too slippery for my satin toe shoes. I invariably asked to have them repainted, with sand added to the paint. Furthermore, the hard cement was painful for calf muscles, as I was used to dancing on wooden floors. I had to adapt. My body-makeup woman, an American Indian, would massage my painful ankles, calves, and feet. She used to tell me about her people. I came to rely on her stoic, faithful presence.

Slowly, ponderously, the shooting advanced, one dance number at a time. The great undertaking of filming the seventeen-minute ballet to Gershwin's symphonic poem *An American in Paris* (arranged for the film by Johnny Green) started. Gershwin is supposed to have brought a few car horns from Paris for its first performance in 1928—I'm not sure whether real taxi horns were used in our interpretation.

Important visitors dropped in to watch when we started filming the numbers—presidents, queens, and princesses who were keen to visit the set. To pilot them around, the studio had hired one of the legendary "Four Musketeers" tennis champions, "Toto" Brugnon. Always genial, he would turn up with his guests, and everything stopped while we stood and smiled graciously for a few pictures. The film sets were seldom closed—there were no nude scenes in those days, and cooperation when it came to publicity was part of our job.

Several months later, after our film was cut and edited by the first and only female editor in Hollywood, Adrienne Fazan (nominated for an Academy Award for her work), the studio organized what was called a sneak preview.

Before opening an important film to the general public, it was considered wise to test audience reactions. Not only did the public fill in questionnaires, but studio representatives took note of the emotional temperature during the projection. Were they bored during a scene? Did they fidget? Did they cough? The scene was probably too long; it needed tightening. Did they laugh during a love scene instead of at the jokes? The disappointing reactions were recorded and solutions discussed with the appropriate technicians. Reshoots were often programmed. I recall with admiration the humbling discipline that this demanded.

Culver City had a tramway line on its main avenue that was still operational in 1951, and I remember the special train that all the studio executives took, together with the heads of departments and leading actors. On March 21, 1951, we boarded the tram to go to the Crown Theatre in Pasadena, an hour out of Culver City, where the owner had simply pasted a strip across the posters announcing, SNEAK PREVIEW TO-NIGHT. With that you could be sure of a full house.

The first preview of *An American in Paris* was considered a disaster—there were sound problems, and work was undertaken immediately afterward to remedy this. The second preview, at the Bay Theatre in Pacific Palisades, was very successful. One hundred and five patrons rated the film "Outstanding!" "One of the best musicals ever," and so forth. Arthur Freed, Vincente Minnelli, and Gene Kelly had won their bet. Before the sneak preview, gossip around the studio had been quite negative. A seventeen-minute ballet so near the end of a film couldn't possibly work. But it did work. There was an enthusiastic round of applause at the end of the ballet and again at the end of the film. The responses on the cards were superlative. They were good for me, too—the newcomer—with 141 cards rating me "Excellent."

As I came out of the cinema, dazed after two hours in the dark, reeling with what I thought was fever, my cranium throbbing from a headache, Gene asked me how I was feeling.

"Gene, I think I caught the flu."

He looked at me and laughed. "Honey, you don't have the flu. You've just seen yourself on the screen for the first time!"

Everything about the premiere on Hollywood Boulevard terrified me. The howling crowds shrieking in the bleachers, the photographers, Army Archerd and Louella Parsons interviewing the shyest of all stars who could hardly put two words together in the microphone—it all seemed like a frightening chore to me. The studio later told me the film was a hit, a very big hit. I felt nothing of that; it didn't change anything in my life. I certainly didn't feel any different. I wasn't used to reading the trade papers, which gave all the box-office figures but remained mysteries to me.

By the early 1950s, rumors of a political cancer had spread over the country and had even reached the protected movie kingdom. Communism! A senator by the name of Joseph McCarthy was creating a reign of suspicion and denunciation in a country hitherto free and trusting in its integrity. One morning word went through the studio that Mr. Louis B. Mayer, the boss himself, wanted to talk to all the employees. At twelve o'clock sharp, everyone was to assemble in front of the Irving Thalberg Building, also known as the administration building. So there we were. After a short wait, the mythical little man I had heard so much about but had never met came through the large double doors, followed by an assistant or two. He was quite dapper, dressed in dark blue pinstripes with matching vest and silk tie. While he spoke, he strutted from left to right on the front stoop, satisfied that the five steps above his audience enhanced his stature. I thought rather wickedly that he looked like a little pigeon, generously convex at the waist. He started by telling us about his love for America, his deep gratitude for the country that had welcomed him with open arms and given him a life he hadn't even dreamed of. And now his dear country of adoption was threatened by enemies within—here his voice faltered with emotion. The dangerous enemy called "Communism" had infiltrated the good people of America to destabilize and overthrow the government. His voice now became severe. He wanted everyone in the studio to be fully aware of the danger and to pledge allegiance to the flag of the U.S. of A. He expected everyone's full cooperation. There was polite patriotic applause, and we disbanded in thoughtful silence.

The witch hunt that followed destroyed a lot of careers. As late as 1961, I personally called Jack Warner to ask him to let us employ Zero Mostel in *Guns of Darkness*. Mostel had been blacklisted, and no amount of cajoling could make Warner agree. While writers could and did work under assumed names, actors and directors really suffered.

In Hollywood, employees followed the guidelines of the studio for Academy Award voting, but intelligent and enlightened writers, directors, producers, and a few actors felt these enforced guidelines infringed on their constitutional rights. As for me, at that time I had no notion of politics—my mother's education had been successful in these matters, convincing me that politics were best left to men. However, the German occupation did teach me to question and distrust imposed codes of behavior. I was shocked to hear that "the corporation" expected its employees to follow its line of opinion. That attitude made me very uncomfortable.

8

This New Life

My life up to then had gone through such a quick professional development that it didn't really amount to growing up. A hard-driven ballet training and initiation to Hollywood stardom came at the expense of my emotional maturity. MGM cultivated in its young players an infantilism that took me years to get over. During all interviews with the press, my publicity "assistant" stood by to censor any embarrassing questions. Topics and behaviors were dictated and controlled. Dates with suitable male escorts were organized by the studio. Etiquette lectures were held once a week by the new big boss, Mr. Dore Schary himself. All aspects of "real life" were supervised or carried out by the studio. I never learned any of the elementary duties of a citizen. The studio took care of my working papers and would have arranged my American naturalization had I wanted it. Although tax was withheld at the source by the studio, my agent recommended a tax lawyer and a business lawyer. An assistant agent came with me to help me buy a car and find an apartment to rent if I wanted to. Studio people took their driving tests at a special office in Culver City, accompanied by a production assistant, and the rules were easy. If you transgressed the traffic laws in Beverly Hills, the police would give you a gentle warning and ask for your autograph. I had no idea you needed something called insurance, for either my person or my property, until I turned fifty. To this day I have never taken the subway in New York; there was always a chauffeured limousine and a suite at the Plaza when I traveled for the release of a film.

The contradiction was that MGM in its wisdom gave twelve weeks' unpaid holiday a year—they called it layoff—to all its contract players. As most actors lived above their weekly paycheck, the studio loved to loan them money—a good way to keep pressure on rebellious players. With my wartime psychology, I had managed to live within my modest salary and thus I maintained my freedom during all those years.

After *An American in Paris,* I felt what everyone in Los Angeles always feels after finishing a film: out in the cold. In Hollywood you learned to live in your car—the distances are so long that going from one place to another always takes a minimum of forty-five minutes. Los Angeles has no center. There were no theaters then except in downtown L.A.—the Biltmore—and no museums. After you had a good look at the tar pit—a roped-off section on Wilshire Boulevard at La Brea, where thick petroleum bubbling up on the sidewalk was brought to your attention by a life-size plaster mammoth—Los Angeles was a cultural desert. With nostalgia in my heart, I learned to search through the newspapers for foreign films. There were two cinemas—only two!—that showed them, my favorite one being the Los Feliz, the so-called art-house cinema, in a remote outpost of Los Angeles, at least an hour's drive from Beverly Hills before freeways were built. Two members of the film community were fervent customers: Marlon Brando and myself. European films were then considered a minor form of expression, from a spent continent. Hollywood was sufficient unto itself. It was at the Los Feliz cinema that I saw the classic German expressionist films, as well as the films of Ingmar Bergman and Federico Fellini.

My days became a succession of lessons. To pay the rent during "layoff," I taught dancing at Michael Panaieff's American Ballet School on Hollywood Boulevard. I liked teaching and learned a lot, passing on to others the training I'd received in Paris.

I felt I must learn to speak English fluently, and as fast as possible to be ready for the next film; so I took an English lesson every day, paid for by the studio, with a lovely lady from New England, Gertrude Fogler (who had also been hired to rid Ava Gardner of her southern accent). At the onset she asked me how I wanted to proceed. Grammar? Conversation? I chose a third possibility: through reading the greatest play in the world, *Hamlet,* by William Shakespeare. I had seen, some months previously, the film made by Laurence Olivier and was under the spell of his romantic interpretation of the character. I also wished I could have a small, delightful mouth like Jean Simmons, so like that of my idol, Vivien Leigh. It took me about six months to get through *Hamlet.*

In the end my vocabulary was a little archaic, but I was never bored. I also learned, as children do, by listening to people talk, by going to the movies, and by reading English or American literature. Finding a French bookstore took me some time, but I finally found one on Little Santa Monica Boulevard in Beverly Hills.

Betsy Blair, Gene Kelly's wife, noticed that I had a great interest in acting. She suggested that I take lessons with her teacher, George Shdanoff, a Russian coach who had learned the craft in Moscow, at the legendary Stanislavski School. He had met the great master in Moscow, where his family lived, before escaping the Bolsheviks' secret service, and now, having landed in Hollywood via Berlin, France, and England, he taught the real Stanislavski technique. He also transmitted—and this was invaluable for the newcomer that I was—something rare in Hollywood in those years: the notion that acting was a craft that could be taught and ought to be learned. Hollywood had a deep distrust of New York stage actors—"too arty" was the term used for them—a stereotype that survived until very recently. A beautiful face with no acting experience was infinitely preferable in films; technique only got in the way. The result was intolerance and prejudice from both East and West Coasts, mixed in with the usual envy. Movie Star versus Legitimate Stage Actor. Personally, I was grateful for anyone who could teach me what to feel in a part, how to feel it, and how to express what I felt. I started to work with Shdanoff up to three times a week.

After a few months of exercises to develop concentration came exercises in improvisation. Later I learned how to dissect a script to determine the arc of the plot, the main scenes, the climaxes, followed by the character's mental and physical particularities—her walk, her stance, her rhythm. Finally I was allowed to start acting, and we tackled *Saint Joan* by George Bernard Shaw. I must confess I'm still waiting for someone to discover how perfect I would be as the uncompromising French shepherdess. George Shdanoff used to call me "the Professor" because I would arrive at his studio so concentrated on the lesson to come that I walked staring at the ground.

Shdanoff and his wife, Elsa, were very kind and protective toward me. I was, to them and to other Hollywood couples, the deserving little French girl who had gone through the war and must be cared for. George's narrow escapes from Bolshevik Russia and Nazi Berlin and my own wartime experiences were bonds that united us. In fact, all Hollywood inhabitants with a European background had this displaced-person nostalgia about them. In the Hollywood of the fifties, the movie community still consisted of first-generation immigrants who were living in splendor but remained immigrants at heart. They retained their accents; they adopted a meticulous style of dressing—an important detail when you want to erase all traces of an impoverished childhood—and in their homes there were lingering traces of furnishings and eating habits from the old country they had left behind. During my lessons, when George knew that I had just come from a dancing class or from filming, he would offer coffee and Austrian biscuits, served on polished Austrian silver. For ten minutes our hearts were transported to the Europe of his youth.

Shdanoff also opened my eyes to the Jewish situation in Nazi-occupied Germany and France. I became aware of the immense talent, intelligence, and survival force of the Jews, who were a majority in Hollywood. I appreciated most particularly the solidarity that binds them together wherever they are. I was ever in search of family ties.

From a cosmopolitan education, George had retained the habit of taking evening walks after his work, but in the rich neighborhood of Beverly Hills, unless you were black or Mexican and wore a uniform, which identified you as a domestic, you were automatically asked questions by the roving police patrol. George, who had a splendid head of wavy black hair and dark, brooding Boris Karloff looks, was routinely stopped. He always took his passport when out walking to avoid ending up in the police station.

My social life was practically nil. I considered myself a pupil who had to learn everything. Tooting around Hollywood in my little Hillman Minx, entirely focused on my work, I was at a loss in my heart. Plucked from the dark years of war and dropped into the civilization of plenty I now lived in, I found no matching soul in my immediate circle. Because these rich Americans hadn't known the war, I found it difficult to form attachments. My religious upbringing was not strong enough to bear me up in my solitude. With detached premeditation I took the decision to get rid of my burdensome virginity—I didn't find the first experience pleasant. This taught me to become much more selective. Luckily, the chosen young man was quickly drafted into the army. Blond and conventional, he had quickly become tyrannical. (I don't blame him, I'm sure he was hurt by my indifference.) I decided it was more rewarding to get to know, one at a time, the fascinating people who made up this rich and remarkable community.

I met Jack Larson very soon after being brought to MGM—the only native Angeleno I met in all my years in Hollywood. Jack was at the time suffering the typical fate of good-looking young actors of short stature—he was offered clean adolescents' parts when he longed for much more rewarding dramas. Jack did attain film immortality when the studio cast him as the cub reporter Jimmy Olsen in the original TV version of *Superman*. After his last performance in the series, he quickly moved on to become an original poet, playwright, and librettist (especially notable for the libretto to Virgil Thomson's opera *Lord Byron*) and a producer of some major Hollywood films. He now administers the foundation he set up in memory of his companion, James Bridges, for UCLA film students.

Jack and I met by a swimming pool, of course—where else do you meet in Hollywood? A young player at Warner Bros., Debbie Reynolds, had achieved a nice success with a song that the radio stations played in a loop, "Aba-Daba Honeymoon." With the royalties Debbie ordered a swimming pool for the backyard of her family's house in Burbank. Somehow Jack Larson and I were both invited to the poolwarming barbecue, and a long friendship ensued, still close to this day.

Jack introduced me to odd and grotesque places in Hollywood. I remember a huge white-elephant property, now destroyed, called the Green Goddess estate, the dream of some megalomaniacal star of the silent era; of course a murder had taken place in the sinister park surrounding it. Jack knew where the Frank Lloyd Wright houses were and has since bought one for himself. He also possessed the huge rubber wrench that Charlie Chaplin used in *Modern Times*. He could tell you every Hollywood legend, myth, and recent item of gossip. And soon a cherubic young actor, James Bridges—who became a scriptwriter/director of many remarkable films—joined our escapades. We became bonded for life the day we tracked down my idol, Stan Laurel, near the end of his life on the second floor of a small apartment house in Pacific Palisades. We arrived at the janitor's office with four dozen roses in our arms and hearts full of gratitude for all the pleasure he'd given us in our childhoods. Mr. Laurel excused himself on the intercom, said he was too old and didn't want his fans to see him the way he was now. We assured him of our undying love and respect and left the roses in the hands of the janitor.

Eager to move out of the volleyball-on-the-beach crowd of young players, Jack cultivated a lot of interesting people in Hollywood. Many had been invited to L.A. by the movie studios to escape the Nazi regime and had remained for the sunshine and the allure of cinema. In particular Jack introduced me to Salka Viertel, intellectual movie royalty, kind, generous, and worldly, noted for the scripts she wrote for Greta Garbo, whose closest friend she was. Salka was a rallying point for all Europeans; she ruined herself financially by opening her house and her table to producers, directors, and writers who were passing through. Her parties in Santa Monica Canyon were a Sunday must. A lot of European intellectuals lived in that neighborhood, more so than in Beverly Hills. Charles Laughton and Elsa Lanchester had their weekend home there, their main one being in the Hollywood Hills. Christopher Isherwood lived on Adelaide Drive, in Santa Monica, with his protégé, the young painter Don Bachardy and, for a while, a houseguest—Tennessee Williams, who seemed to Chris a nice enough young man but a mediocre poet, until Chris discovered to his amazement that the nice young man had written, right there under his roof, a masterpiece called *The Glass Menagerie*. The producer John Houseman—nicknamed "Puff, the Magic Dragon" by my friends Jack Larson and James Bridges, perfect description of his imposing persona—took over Salka's house when she went back to Europe. From then on, the New York intelligentsia joined the Europeans on Sunday afternoons.

John Houseman in turn sold the house to Gordon Davidson, the bright director of the Ahmanson Theatre and Mark Taper Forum, at the Los Angeles Music Center. During a visit he showed me something Salka Viertel had forgotten in the attic when she moved out, which John Houseman had left undisturbed and Gordon himself had no intention of removing from its dusty and peaceful repose—a death mask of the great silent film director Friedrich Wilhelm Murnau's face, taken immediately after his death. Murnau and Salka had been friends. Murnau was in a car accident on the Pacific Coast Highway—distracted, the legend says, by what the French call "voluptuous driving." His front-seat companion, unscathed, called Salka's house, where Garbo, a guest at the time, had enough presence of mind in the panic and drama that ensued to insist that a cast be taken of the great man's face. It is very probably still there in the attic.

Salka and Bertolt Brecht were friends and decided, since the big blockbuster films were made from rather conventional scripts, that they, too, could come up with a successful scenario. They started one Monday, quite sure that in a couple of weeks they could produce a winner. They got so involved with their script that the two weeks became a month, which spilled into several, and pretty soon they had a script no studio would touch, probably much too left-wing for the times. Somewhere in the basement of one of Hollywood's majors sleeps that script.

Roland Petit's new company, Les Ballets de Paris, came to perform in Los Angeles in 1951—an emotional reunion with my beloved colleagues. Proud of my newly purchased Hillman Minx, with a quickie driver's license in my pocket, I appointed myself the ballet company's chauffeur. Almost immediately I had a little collision on the Pacific Coast Highway—though not for the same reasons as Murnau. There were no seat belts then, and the accident scarred Roland Petit's face. He very generously claimed that the gash in his cheek gave him an attractive "rough trade" look. He bore me no grudge.

In a town where fabulous personalities clustered within a small periphery, one of the most intriguing was Howard Hughes, who owned RKO Pictures. I met him one afternoon through Zizi Jeanmaire, who wasn't yet married to Roland Petit. She was under contract to Hughes, together with Petit and the whole ballet company. Howard Hughes controlled things and people in a lavish way, mostly through generous salaries. From what Zizi said, their only meetings took place at night, on the phone, but as with many women he fancied, he kept Zizi a virtual prisoner in her glamorous Beverly Hills apartment. After having filmed *Hans Christian Andersen,* both Roland and Zizi wanted to get out of this golden contract—dancers in the company were growing fat and bored with nothing to do. I drove my two friends on the Sunset Strip to the house of Robert Maheu, Hughes's man when it came to dealing with women. Howard Hughes was already there when we arrived. He first shook our hands politely but then went to sit in a dark corner at the back of the living room. He was a striking-looking man, with hair and eyebrows black as jet and burning eyes deeply embedded in their sockets. I can only describe him as a Francis Bacon character, haunted. He seemed very tall and more than lean, quite gaunt. Somehow I could well understand his success with beautiful women—he presented a strong draw to the maternal instinct. Back in his corner, he never smiled, never spoke, let Robert Maheu do all the negotiating. We were there about an hour, and all was resolved to Roland and Zizi's satisfaction.

One day my ballet-school friend Simone Mostovoy, who was now a leading dancer in the Ballets de Paris, met a charming family—one, two, three six-foot-tall boys with a French mother. The Hormels! The boys' fantasy and spontaneity gave rhythm to their days, with a light-hearted background of jazz. The two older boys were amateur musicians, while the last one, "little Jimmy," was still in college. The Hormel home in old Bel Air was a meeting point for young people in the film world. Merv Griffin, a popular young singer then, was around, as was Debbie Reynolds. French charm operated fast, and in no time Simone found herself married to the second son, Thomas. In a great burst of laughter, Thomas asked me to marry his elder brother, Geordie. When a handsome young man with a French mother asks you to marry him, and you are twenty and desperately lonely, you can't seem to think of a reason to refuse. The Hormels were wealthy and fun, the father seemed as wise as he was charming, and this marriage seemed the solution I had been searching for. As a prank, I was introduced to my future father-in-law, Mr. Jay Hormel, one morning at nine o'clock, dressed in a frilly white apron—the new French maid—to serve him his bacon and eggs. I think that following the good old American tradition, our decision to marry was made midweek with the ceremony to be held the following weekend. Why not do something crazy?

The chauffeur drove the Hormel limousine to Las Vegas for the wedding, which took all of ten minutes. After dragging Germaine Hormel away from the roulette table and waking up the minister at the "Little Church of the West" sometime around midnight, I heard myself murmur, "I do." Grotesque old ladies pulling endlessly on one-armed bandits in a city where sunshine is replaced with electric lights—vice, vulgarity, decadence hit me straight in the face. Has anyone cried like a little girl when visiting Las Vegas for the first time? I confess that I did.

I was in a state of shock. I wasn't jaded enough for Las Vegas or foolish enough to call this a marriage.

As soon as we moved out of the Hormel house, the charm of irresponsible days ended and reality hit me hard. I tried seriously to adapt to my new situation and be the perfect housewife. I took cooking lessons from the Hormels' French chef, Pierre, and was up until two in the morning trying, yet again, to succeed in making my profiteroles. I learned to bake meat pâtés and to whip up a mayonnaise from the *Good Housekeeping* cookbook, and I took the trouble to mark our clothes with name tags. (What for? I wonder, as we weren't going to college.) I took in a stray cat for company because Geordie was out all day cutting a record, "I'm the Sheik of Araby," and I hoped that I might become pregnant. What was happening? This much-acclaimed state of marriage was in fact painful to the point of being intolerable. At first the thrill of sexual awakening had dazzled me into believing in lasting happiness. But how could a young man's ardor vanish so rapidly? Why did I feel abandoned? There was so little communication between us. Surprised, I realized I had nothing in common with the man I had married, morose and silent as he was, with sudden explosions of anger. We rented a brown wooden shack in Topanga Canyon, where hardly any light reached the small, dark rooms. This was so removed from the cut-stone elegance of Paris and its classical parks, its curling river with bridges spanning the centuries, that slowly, inexorably, I plunged into desolation.

I didn't become pregnant, but my little cat did. Trusting in my affection, she woke me up one morning with urgent meowing to inform me that she had selected my sweater drawer for her delivery room. I followed her and obeyed her persistent cries, commanding me to rub her flanks until she had the last of her litter of three. Very unusual for a cat . . .

And then one day Geordie brought a young woman to stay in our house—a country-and-western singer. My mother-in-law wondered why I accepted this ambiguous situation, but frankly, I was grateful that a voice, even a rival female voice, was breaking the heavy silence in this household—and perhaps, in a perverse sort of way, I saw an escape route. To the movie magazines who ran articles about us, we presented the image of a perfectly happy young couple. I wore my wedding ring throughout the next film I made, *The Man with a Cloak,* but I felt trapped. Escape became imperative.

Soon enough Geordie bought a house, an old mansion aspiring to be a Normandy castle. For the first time, I started to restore a house—building in order to fill the inner void. I worked to exhaustion at making it colorful and welcoming, but as soon as it was finished, I made my getaway to New York, where I wanted to train for a world tour with Roland Petit and his company. I was through with what I came to call "my childhood marriage." It had lasted less than three years.

And then suddenly, while I was in New York attending ballet classes every day, the news splashed across the press, radio, and television: Geordie Hormel, son of the great industrial millionaire who had fed the American GI with Spam during World War II and served morning bacon in every American home since, had been caught in a drug scandal! Everything suddenly became clear to me. Why hadn't I seen it? His remoteness, his uncommunicativeness, those long hours he spent lying about with eyes staring into space: Geordie was a drug addict!

Thankfully, *An American in Paris* had come out and was nominated for all sorts of Academy Awards; the studio kept me busy with press interviews. The Hormel lawyers, afraid lest I claim alimony, used the pretext of my staying in the flat of an old friend, Michael Mindlin, who was himself staying at his girlfriend's, to attack me on the grounds of infidelity. I felt the injury to my reputation very acutely. In those days, apart from the fact that I was innocent, a woman was never charged with infidelity in a divorce; it was considered most discourteous. In such cases the injured husband would gallantly stage a situation in order to take the blame, assuming the guilt through a totally fictitious scenario. Ironically, at the same time, my husband and his family were trying desperately to win me back. They need not have feared, as alimony has always been an alien concept to me. In fact, I have given generous parting gifts, but I have never claimed any financial compensation from a man.

I didn't see Geordie again except once, thirty years later, in the eighties. Glancing through the front window of a shop in Beverly Hills, I caught sight of an old man with long, straggly hair and a white beard spread on his chest, a ghostly figure of himself. I fled. My former brother-in-law, "little Jimmy," though, has become a good friend. He pursued his studies and went on to a very distinguished career as U.S. delegate to the United Nations General Assembly and the UN Commission on Human Rights. President Clinton chose him to be ambassador to Luxembourg.

Everyone around the world remembers where he or she was when President Kennedy was assassinated, and for the Hollywood crowd the same sort of heightened memory took hold when the news hit us that James Dean had been killed in his Porsche. The milestone date was the thirtieth of September, 1955, and all Hollywood was at the Annual Hairdressers' Ball. This event was extremely popular with the community for several reasons. Actors and stars made a point of being present to express their gratitude and affection to their personal crews, but it also was the one party of the year where you could, quite literally, let your hair down. James Dean wasn't particularly popular with the profession—he was often late, often rude and surly, and his lack of personal hygiene annoyed some—but everyone agreed about his immense talent. He was the most brilliant young actor since Montgomery Clift and Marlon Brando. The news was a shock that considerably dampened the party. Many of us went home with heavy hearts.

I was contacted a few days later by his best friend, a young man whose name I can't remember but who seemed very affected by Dean's death. He went straight into offering me information about the funeral, which was to be held back home, in Fairmont, Indiana, including the times and how to get there.

I was very surprised by his call and said, "Thank you for calling and for giving me all these details, but . . . why me?"

"Because you were so close to him," he replied. "I'm sure you'll want to be there."

"I'm very sorry but I have never met Jimmy. I didn't know him."

The friend couldn't believe me. "But every time I saw Jimmy—as recently as a few days ago—he told me what you had done together, the film you'd seen, what you had said, where you had gone to eat. . . ."

I repeated, "Oh, dear . . . I'm so very sorry, but I never met Jimmy Dean. I would have liked him as a friend. . . ."

The young man didn't know what to say. He finally proposed, "I'll send you Jimmy's favorite portrait of himself. It is a profile, just like the most famous portrait of John Barrymore."

I received the picture, framed. This portrait of James Dean, totally unlike any other, has stood on my bookshelf for over fifty years. Few people recognize the legendary icon.

9

Under Contract

*A*lthough I was beginning to adapt to the life of Los Angeles and to MGM studios, I desperately wanted another assignment—another film—to focus my energies. Howard Herty, my agent, was my only link to the studio executives, who, remote and apparently indifferent, never made direct contact. You learned the news concerning your career either through the trade papers (*Hollywood Reporter* or *Variety*), through your agent, or most often in my case, through friends who had read the trades. The waiting seemed endless. It was in fact only a few months.

One day the phone rang—Howard Herty with some great news: "You've been cast in a film opposite Barbara Stanwyck and Joseph Cotten. The script is on its way, and the costume department expects you Monday at two-thirty. Hairdressing an hour later. They want to take your measurements for a wig."

My questions were urgent. "A wig? What kind of film? What part do I play? When does it start?"

His answers were vague and laconic. "I think it is a period film, honey. It's called *The Man with a Cloak*."

"What period?"

"Well . . . long dresses, you know. I think it's a detective mystery. Read the script. Barbara Stanwyck is a great star. And Joseph Cotten, you know, Orson Welles's friend . . . The director is Fletcher Markle, who used to be an actor."

A brown envelope arrived in the mail, I tore it open feverishly. THE MAN WITH A CLOAK was printed in bold black, suggesting mystery and danger. The preface mentioned *Edgar Allan Poe,* a dark and tortured poet, to be played by Joseph Cotten. I was thrilled to be offered a dra-

matic script, not a musical, and with such great actors as partners. I set
to work with my coach, George Shdanoff.

The experience was exciting. During the year of hard work with
Shdanoff and Gertrude Fogler, I had acquired a little ease both with
acting and with the English language. I conscientiously used every new
tool at my disposal. Acting was becoming a game, a thrilling exercise in
perception and psychology. I learned that minute details build a character and that listening can be more expressive than speaking. But I still
felt very much the newcomer next to Academy Award players.

Stanwyck was a great pro of the old school. She told me that she
got up around five-thirty and turned up at the studio around six-thirty
to go through the rigorous routine of makeup and hair and probably
also brushing up her lines and getting mentally ready for the serious
business of being a star. She was first on the set, ready to start work.
She never faltered in anything and never fluffed her lines; she didn't
kid around but stayed concentrated. And in order to stay focused, she
knitted—never stopped between the scenes. You could see she'd done
that throughout her career, because if the set was a little cold, she'd
wear a hand-knitted sweater, each time of a different color; she said she
had many. Her maid came with her on the set and brought her coffee
and anything she might need. Stanwyck, however, was not a bit stuck
up or capricious, just the opposite. She was simple, almost rustic in her
manner, straightforward and generous. The crew loved her and called
her "Missy." One day we were playing a scene together, and suddenly
she stopped, something actors must never do. It's against the rules for
an actor to stop short in the middle of a scene; only the director can say
"cut." Fletcher Markle asked, "What's the trouble?" She answered, "A
shadow on the kid's face, I stepped in front of her light."

Joseph Cotten was in person just as he was on the screen, a relaxed
southern gentleman. There was an aura about him that nothing could
shake. He acted so smoothly that it always looked as if it were his own
persona he was playing. Before one of our scenes, I was brooding in a
corner, getting myself in the mood. He looked worried and asked me,
"What's the matter, not feeling good?" I answered, "No, no, I'm fine,
I'm getting ready for the scene." He hadn't heard of the Stanislavski
method, or if he had, he didn't think much of it.

My closest friend on the set was Louis Calhern, who was in almost every MGM film in those days. He was a ham, and everyone loved his overacting. Legend had it that he'd been John Barrymore's best friend and drinking buddy. He never failed to encourage me with extravagant comments about my charm and talent. I loved him.

I viewed the film recently—the young actress up there is doing fine; she courageously attacks her part in the story. There is not an ounce of self-consciousness, and all her energies are focused on the problems of Madeline Minot, the girl in peril, come to America to ask her lover's rich grandfather for financial support for the French revolutionary cause of 1848. Perhaps only one major quality is missing: womanliness. Madeline represents her companion, an engaged revolutionary. Leslie Caron acts like a very young girl, not an adult woman.

At around this time I started to receive scripts in which the description of the main character always started with the words: "She's not beautiful, but . . ." Slightly irritated, I used to think, *If I ever write my memoirs, the title will be, "Not Beautiful, But . . ."* What were the canons of beauty in those days? Obvious sex appeal that asserted itself through a well-padded bra, aggressive makeup, and a very controlled hairdo, but all of them belonging to a docile, submissive, infantile personality, quite opposite to the real personality of the American woman, who was, underneath it all, an independent individual. The women's movement was just around the corner.

The next film I did in 1952 was *Glory Alley,* with the director every French film buff worships like a god: Raoul Walsh. The plot was a dismal pile of clichés, and we were ripped to shreds by Bosley Crowther in the *New York Times.* I don't blame him; the story was an improbable tearjerker about a prizefighter (Ralph Meeker) in love with a bar dancer named Angela (me) who has a blind father (Kurt Kasznar). Socks Barbarrosa, the prizefighter, leaves the ring to enlist in the Korean War, and frankly I don't remember how the story ends. . . . But I am pleased to think that I shared credits with Louis Armstrong and Jack Teagarden. Yes, I really did sing "St. Louis Blues" in a baby voice, swinging from a chandelier, wearing black mesh stockings.

Incidentally, I was made to take great risks dancing, on toe, on top of a U-shaped bar with the elbows of men and their whiskey tumblers resting on it. During the filming, Raoul Walsh, ever mindful of his one eye (he'd lost the other in an accident while driving his convertible to Las

Vegas when a bird flew in), was seldom near the camera. From way back at the coffee corner, his voice would call to the camera operator, "Were they all in the frame, buddy?" "Yep, they were." "Okay. Print!" I would ask, "How can you tell?" The answer came, laconic, "Pace sounded good. Next!" *Glory Alley* was what my friend Jack Larson called "Hollywood product," to fill up the Loews theater chain. What was I doing in such a film? MGM was trying to define my particular qualities. Why not try the sexy angle? Let's see what we can do with the girl.

The answer came soon after. Someone who read the trades called and said, "Leslie, congratulations, you've been cast in a musical called *Lili,* written by Helen Deutsch from a novel by Paul Gallico, *The Love of Seven Dolls.*" I discovered years later to my dismay that the project had been developed for the young Italian actress Pier Angeli, but that Helen Deutsch had seen a private viewing of *An American in Paris* and proclaimed, "I want that girl!" Anna Maria (Anna Maria Pierangeli was her real name) was a friend of mine, and her being passed over upset me.

Luckily I had about three months ahead of me in which to prepare. The part of Lili suited me well, as I could express in it all the angst I couldn't share with anyone. It is the story of an orphan who finds the end of the road in a fairground where, because of her naïve charm, she is engaged to give a show with puppets. The puppeteer with a sarcastic personality is Mel Ferrer; his friend, the fairground Adonis, is Jean-Pierre Aumont; and his coquettish wife is Zsa Zsa Gabor. George Shdanoff and I first started work on the body center. The Stanislavski method teaches that in every human being there is a center. (Examples: the forehead in the case of an intellectual, the tip of the nose for someone whimsical, the rump or the breast for the voluptuous, and so forth.) We located Lili's center in her knees. Lili never straightened her knees, which gave her an awkward, ducklike walk. She was a rough-hewn country girl. A little stutter here and there to indicate her bewilderment, her slow mental and physical reactions—a childlike view of the world around her. Building this character was pure joy. For a few months, I became Lili. I was so concentrated in my work that the cast and especially the director, Charles Walters, mistook me for her. "But you can be fun!" he exclaimed when he saw me joking around after filming was over.

Mel Ferrer was excellent in *Lili*, because his own personality was moody and hypersensitive, like that of the character he played. There came an explosive moment when Chuck Walters, the director, who couldn't stand Mel's temperamental act anymore, cleared the stage to have it out with him. "Everyone take five!" he shouted with authority. Lights were switched off, and we all slid away, as far as possible from the trailer/dressing room where both men confronted each other. The walls of the trailer were soon vibrating like in a Tom and Jerry cartoon. After some fifteen minutes, all went quiet, and Chuck came out with satisfaction written all over his face. Mel was a lamb for the rest of the film.

Dear Zsa Zsa Gabor was a generous colleague. One day I admired the blouse she was wearing; the next day she brought it to me, washed and ironed. But I don't think she ever understood the concept of schedules, for either shooting or rehearsing. Her mentality was essentially that of a glamour girl. After picking up her poodle from the grooming parlor and finishing her shopping, she was quite amenable to rehearsing, if darling Chuck really wanted her to. She preferred brief rehearsals; everybody knew that exertion could line the face. But she was fun and believed in getting the best out of life—and men. She played the role with the discipline of a pro. Frivolity was the essence of the persona she presented with great success; all Hollywood discussed her extravagances. She declared—and advised me to follow her example—that acquiring a diamond ring was essential for a girl's reputation, and why not exchange the last one you've received for a new one, from time to time? To remain in fashion, she also recommended borrowing a new mink, then trading in last year's and paying the difference. But despite her gold digger's philosophy, she was in fact quite maternal with her men. Though she had several husbands after him, the real love of her life was the actor George Sanders, who was not rich and must have given her plenty of somber moments to deal with. However, on the day the news broke that Sanders had left a suicide note on his bedside table saying, "Dear World, I am leaving you because I am bored," the professional in her took over. That day, in April 1972, Vincente Minnelli's memoir, *I Remember It Well,* was being presented to the press at the American Film Institute and both Zsa Zsa and I were invited. Zsa Zsa made a beeline for me and the line of press photographers; she blew a sideways kiss in my direction and, without disturbing the smiling contours of her carmine lips, murmured, "Did you hear, darling, my poor George killed himself!" Flash! Flash! Smile! Smile!

My heart was wide open to my co-star, the puppet "Carrot Top." I could read expressive nuances and thoughts in the carved wood of his little face. Separated by the puppeteer's curtain, Mel and I played a very sensitive duet that moved the world and still rings true.

During filming, someone among the executives did not think that *Lili* was fulfilling MGM's standards of glamour. One morning at seven o'clock, as I sat in the makeup chair, I was suddenly told, "Today we are going to make you glamorous." "What? Change my look? Why?" "Orders, honey." A fierce battle took place inside me—frustration, anger, pain. . . . I didn't have enough authority to refuse categorically, so I tried pleading, arguing. The head of the department was deaf to my arguments. "Orders from the producer," he said. "I want to see him and discuss this," I retorted aggressively. This early in the morning, Edwin Knopf was still in his Beverly Hills mansion. He was called on the phone. Shrill and stuttering, I tried to explain that this character could never wear false eyelashes, curls, and high-heeled shoes.

Meekly, Mr. Knopf finally admitted, "I can't help you, honey, orders from above."

"Above? Who is this above?"

After some hesitation, the voice, now really annoyed, said, "Dore Schary, my dear." The big boss since Louis B. Mayer had been eased out.

"I want to go and explain to him that he's wrong." After further negotiations, the tone rising on both sides, I still wasn't budging. Finally a limousine was put at my disposal while the technicians and crew waited in exasperation.

I arrived at the executive building, trembling with cold, sweating palms, and short of breath. I took the elevator up to the top floor, where God Himself lived. I had never met him. I was first ushered into a waiting room, where a minute later the door was opened by an assistant, and the private secretary welcomed me from behind her vast desk.

"Yes, Miss Caron [pronounced *Car-rown*]. What can I do for you?"

"I want to see Mr. Schary," said I, both meek and belligerent.

She looked at me for a few seconds and then decided to humor me. "I'll see if he can meet you." Discreet phone conversation. "Please go in. Mr. Schary will see you."

The door opened, and there he stood, Big Boss smiling with both arms outstretched. "Yes, my dear. What can I do for you?"

I took a deep breath and threw myself into the argument, spinning out the details of the carefully structured character I had built with Shdanoff.

Dore Schary looked at me, more and more puzzled. Finally he asked, "Tell me, darling, what film are you making?"

"*Lili* . . . Mr. Schary."

"I see, I see." I could tell he had no idea what I was talking about, hadn't even heard of it. "Well, my dear," and a broad smile spread on his face, "you can do whatever your little heart desires. Good-bye, my dear. Come and see me again if you have any more problems."

I was speechless. I finished the film in peace, looking like a genuine orphan.

Halfway through the film, Arthur Freed, the producer who had brought me to MGM to do *An American in Paris,* came to the set for a surprise visit. This was not his usual behavior. He was a very discreet person. His inability to communicate was legendary, but he nevertheless managed to make it clear that he was upset by what was happening to me. He was tactful enough to put the blame on "the studio." "They" were destroying the glamorous image he had worked so hard to build. He would like to do another film with me to give me back the allure that *Lili* was destroying. Did I have any ideas? he asked. Was I interested in a story—any story?

I was so convinced about the quality of *Lili* that I dismissed his worries, but I did pay attention to his offer of doing another film. After one or two bad ideas, I finally came up with *Gigi.* Audrey Hepburn was doing the play on Broadway, and I certainly knew and loved Colette's novella. He paused, looking thoughtful. "I'll get back to you on that," was his comment as he walked away.

It took him a year and a half to get the rights and have the first script written—not as a musical but as a straight comedy. Before the film itself was even started, I would meet the British director, Peter Hall, fall head

over heels in love, marry him, and have my first child. But I shall return
to that later. Back to *Lili*.

Here is the story that Benny Thau, one of MGM's top executives, told
me years later.

When *Lili* was finished, the studio paused to consider what they
had: a hybrid little movie that looked more like a neorealist European
film than an MGM musical. What on earth could they do with it? Dore
Schary was seriously thinking of shelving it. Before consigning the cans
to oblivion, the boss decided to ask his wife to view it. A screening was
organized for Mrs. Schary, who afterward went to her husband's office
and announced, "I cried. I think the film is very touching." And so the
film was released, thanks to the sensitivities of Mrs. Dore Schary.

The distribution department devised a new form of release that had
never been done at MGM: Every major city in the States featured it in
an art-house cinema, as if it were a foreign film. YOU'LL LOVE LILI, the
posters said. Timidly the public went to see it, because of the reputation of De Sica, Fellini, or Bergman, whose films were usually shown in
these theaters. They came once, then came again with their children—
they talked about it to their friends and came again with them. The film
remained for up to two years in the same cinemas. One theater in New
York boasted of itself as "The cinema Lili built!" For quite a while I was
a household name. The phone operator at the Plaza Hotel in New York
would call to wake me, "Good morning, Lili!" (A few years later, that
became, "Good morning, Gigi!") Women stopped me in the streets to
kiss me—mothers put their babies in my arms to snap a picture. One
mother said to her daughter, "You see, my darling, Lili is all right." She
explained that her daughter had been worried about my fate. I found
this recognition surprising, touching, but sometimes a heavy burden; I
wasn't sure I deserved so much love and admiration.

The film received six nominations at the Oscars, including two for
the composer, Bronislau Kaper, who won Best Score and Best Song. I
was nominated for Best Actress (Audrey Hepburn won for *Roman Holiday*), and Charles Walters was nominated for Best Director. I won the
BAFTA (British Academy of Film and Television Arts) as Best Foreign
Actress, Charles Walters won Best Director at the Cannes Film Festival,
Helen Deutsch won the Golden Globe for Best Writer as well as the

Writers Guild award for Best Writing in a Musical. From time to time, I still receive $8.75 from the annual sale of the recorded song "Hi-Lili, Hi-Lo."

Four years had passed since I'd arrived in Hollywood, and MGM was now reflecting on how to follow up the unexpected success of *Lili* while also being aware that rebellion was brewing. "Why not give the girl a break." They had been informed by my agent that I was desperate to escape the parochial boredom of Los Angeles. Oh, to go back to Europe! It was at that point that I was invited by Roland Petit to join his Ballets de Paris on a world tour. My heart longed to return to the warm atmosphere of the ballet company, the best family life I'd known. MGM gave me their blessing. I was once again happy on the road, as we worked together, ate together, were feted by the press, were invited to parties by French embassies everywhere we went, met adoring fans, and got up to childish pranks. While in London we appeared at the Shaftesbury Theatre and stayed at the very sedate Brown's Hotel. One night, coming back from supper after the show, we switched the shoes left out for the shoe-shining service. First we mismatched and moved them from one door to another and then, gathering momentum, from one floor to another. Around seven in the morning, pandemonium broke out in the corridors of the hotel—loud, angry cries from guests missing their trains, their planes, their appointments. Just like pupils in a boarding school, we were severely reprimanded by the manager of the hotel.

Disaster awaited us at the Broadway Theatre in New York. On opening night we were presenting three ballets with three set changes in each—these were opulent days. The New York crew hadn't had the necessary rehearsal time—one afternoon instead of the three days required. The curtain finally went down around one-thirty in the morning to a near-empty auditorium. The press kindly wrote, "We'll come back when they've finished rehearsing!" Of course they never returned.

In Washington, D.C., I came down with a high fever. The doctor diagnosed flu and gave me firm orders to stay in bed for several days. True to his mischievous self, Roland Petit climbed up the drainpipe outside the hotel walls with his colleague Robert to appear, giggling, at my window. They hoped with this prank to convince me to go onstage that night. "You have to perform," they said. "Ambassadors, senators, and socialites are invited, together with the world press! The rest of the tour is at risk! Our reputation! The reputation of France itself! Come on, get up and dance!"

I went to the theater three hours before the show and did my warm-up exercises, slowly, slowly, with aching limbs. During the performance—I was giddy with fever—every time I did my pirouettes, my heavy per-spiration sprayed the first three rows with a shower of fine drops that glittered in the lights like diamonds. By the end of the evening, I was totally cured.

After Washington we went straight to Hollywood. Knowing that my next studio assignment was *The Glass Slipper,* with Chuck Walters again directing, Roland Petit, who was always short of cash, had asked me if I couldn't get the producer, Edwin Knopf, to hire the entire ballet company to appear in the film, with him as the choreographer. The idea thrilled everyone, myself most of all. I thought the world of Roland Pe-tit's choreography, and besides, it meant that I wouldn't be parted from my dear friends. Roland's concept for the film was delightfully original. In her dreams, instead of imagining the ballet numbers in the ornate ballroom, which Cinderella, being a simple girl, couldn't likely visual-ize, they take place in the depth of the palace kitchens—Cinderella's world. Pots and pans steam in rhythm, while lovely kitchen maids and scullions brandish wooden spoons and huge ladles. Two of the tweenies became famous later on—the remarkable Violette Verdy, soon to be Balanchine's prima ballerina, and Liliane Montevecchi, who became the toast of Las Vegas and Broadway. The pas de quatre between four cooks and me is a very witty takeoff on the *Rose Adagio* in the ballet *Sleeping Beauty.* As for my performance, I was in very good training after all those months on the stage, and I think that I did my best clas-sical dancing in this film and in *Daddy Long Legs,* which was to follow immediately after.

I was very pleased to be working with Chuck Walters again, as our affection and complicity during *Lili* continued where we had left off, and it was certainly a great treat to play with the two magical ladies Estelle Winwood and Elsa Lanchester, who were both so rich in expe-rience and originality. You never forget these professional encounters. Michael Wilding, my Prince Charming in *The Glass Slipper,* was the most pleasant partner one could dream of. He was no dancer and had to have a double for the ballet sequences—slightly humiliating for a romantic British actor who had been brought from England for his resemblance to Leslie Howard. More to the point, he didn't like his colorless part. Early during rehearsals we were having lunch in the commissary when he begged me to stage a star tantrum and insist on having him replaced. I didn't comply. Michael Wilding was then married to Elizabeth Taylor, whom I saw quite a few times during the filming. One evening, during a dinner at my flat, the conversation angled toward acting—I talked enthusiastically about my training with Shdanoff and elaborated on it. Elizabeth then asked a question that absolutely baffled me: "What do you learn? What is there to learn?" In view of her remarkable performances throughout her career, I am astounded to think that she was never taught even the basics of acting. She was a natural. Her beauty had me enthralled. Her violet eyes surrounded by black eyelashes were a wonder. Even in black and white, her beauty was thrilling. But most of all I think it was her unaffected sweetness that touched me.

One amusing note on my creation of the character of Cinderella: I was, like everyone else in Hollywood, under the influence of Marlon Brando's performance in *On the Waterfront,* which had just come out. His modern style of acting, the realistic look of the film, the politics expressed in the plot, all created such a revolution in Hollywood that it had become a cult film. I used to see it several times a week—I bought my ticket with the rest of America, at least twenty times. Yes, I admit it, ridiculous as it may be, my inspiration for Cinderella was . . . Marlon Brando.

By the time the film was completed, I was exhausted. The ballet sequences at the end of shooting, after I had acted in nearly every scene, were particularly taxing. MGM had scheduled two weeks of rest before I started *Daddy Long Legs,* a loan-out to Fox. This lovely film tells the story of a millionaire, Jervis Pendleton III (Fred Astaire), whose limousine breaks down in France near an orphanage. He goes in for help with his assistant/secretary (Fred Clark) and witnesses a young girl, Julie Andre (me), giving an English lesson to the children (the number "C-A-T Spells Cat"). Charmed, he decides to give the girl a chance in life and has her sent to the best American boarding school. Julie, who has never met him, keeps writing her benefactor, who by now has forgotten all about her. She calls him her Daddy Long Legs because all she has seen of him is the elongated shadow he cast on a wall. Finally his secretary (Thelma Ritter) convinces him to meet her for the school dance. He comes incognito; he and Julie dance together, have great fun, and fall for each other. He invites her to join him in New York, and it takes him forever to admit that he is in fact her Daddy Long Legs. Roland Petit once again had asked me if he could be my choreographer in order to work near his idol, Fred Astaire. The producer, Sam Engel, asked Astaire if the entire Ballets de Paris, directed by Petit, could be packaged with me, and Fred had generously agreed. I was again delighted. However, Roland, who had to distribute his dancers' paychecks and was also responsible for their lodgings and daily expenses, convinced me to start the second film right after the first. I agreed to his request, which meant that we finished *The Glass Slipper* on a Saturday and started *Daddy Long Legs* on the following Monday.

I first met Fred Astaire in the rehearsal hall at 20th Century Fox in August 1954—with just a handshake and a few words. The whole ballet company was present, very shy and impressed—with the exception of Liliane Montevecchi, who was her usual bold self. She stepped forward, extending her hand like a duchess, and announced, "You don't know me, but I know you." Fred Astaire burst out laughing, as we all did. Mr. Astaire had a sense of humor. He also had breeding. I must use an expression I don't like, but it fits: He had class. Always pleasant, even when his heart was heavy, he lived his role as the greatest performer in the world with rare modesty and simplicity. Much as he was admirably balanced on his feet, he kept a sense of proportion in all things. He couldn't stand fuss, superlatives, pretension, or arrogance. Awards embarrassed him; he was always pushing his assistants forward to receive them in his place. When other stars were calling their producers at midnight to order them to stop the traffic on Sunset Boulevard because it disturbed their rest (as Mario Lanza did), Astaire kept a discreet profile. Yet he was surprisingly chatty and loved a good gossip. Between the scenes on the set, he would discuss a football game or the races with the grips and the sparks. He loved playing pool, which isn't surprising considering how skillful he was. Unlike Gene Kelly, who preferred directing, he sincerely loved to dance. It amused him. Leave Fred

Astaire for half an hour alone in a room with a coat hanger and when you came back, he'd created a number—with the coat hanger. He was as light on his feet as a cat, and he never ran out of breath. He hardly ever perspired, and attaining perfection was for him the fun part of the game. His sense of rhythm was simply natural. I was once in a men's haberdashery and watched him come in and walk up to the counter. There was such an effortless sway to his walk, I'd say he was swinging to his own tune. He even talked with a natural rhythm. He dressed with casual elegance. I always saw him in light gray flannels, with a necktie for a belt, blue oxford shirts, and leather loafers.

When we started rehearsals, his wife, Phyllis, was very ill with cancer. In fact she had just undergone a serious operation. Fred kept hoping she'd pull through, knowing there was no real hope. From time to time, when his anguish was too great, he would bury his face in his towel and after a minute he would ask, "Did you meet Phyllis? She's such a lovely girl. I don't know if she'll make it. . . ."

Fred took two weeks off after the funeral. The whole company was told not to mention his loss. He came back quite altered—his face was very strained. At first he had difficulty concentrating, and he tended to be tetchy. Again, he would stop from time to time, bury his face in his towel, and cry. There was a respectful silence in the rehearsal hall—no loud talk, no yelling, no giggles—we just tried to behave with tact to show him our concern.

He turned up on time and in good shape for the shooting. When we did the numbers, he couldn't help himself, his love of dancing took over—especially during "Sluefoot," shot at the school dance, when it is quite clear that he is having a great time. That number is also my favorite. We are both bursting with fun while swinging around. The joy we both felt is captured there on the screen forever. As it was agreed that I would design my costume for "Sluefoot," he asked me not to wear ostrich feathers, especially not around the shoulders—he still remembered Ginger Rogers's feathers, which tickled his nostrils and got inside his smiling mouth. He was particularly fussy about rhythm, and most of all he insisted on stopping sharply with the music. He made a few irritated comments about Ginger and rhythm.

We got into a tiff only once—how did I dare? Well, I did. The great Fred Astaire had stepped on my foot. Once. He reprimanded me as if

I'd committed the error. I answered right back, "No, it was you, Fred! *You* stepped on *my* foot!" He thought about it, then grumbled, "Yeah, sorry!"

One morning, around ten o'clock, I was rehearsing the final ballet with Roland Petit and the whole company when the first assistant rushed in and said, "Quick, Miss Caron, you must go to makeup and hairdressing. We scheduled a whole day for the trolley scene, but Mr. Astaire has filmed it in one take—a perfect take—so there's nothing more for him to do alone."

"And what are we supposed to shoot?" I asked.

"Mr. Astaire says you can do the nightclub montage."

"But I've never rehearsed it! I don't know that number."

"He says you don't need to learn it, he'll guide you through it."

In the montage we are seen going from nightclub to nightclub, dancing a different dance in each, from the bossa nova to jitterbug to swing. The set was just one long corridor with different-style furniture in each section. Fred guided me through it indeed—it was as delightful as it was easy. His large hand on my back, I knew just what to do next. He was an amazingly skillful partner.

Years later my third husband, Michael Laughlin, wanted to meet the great Fred Astaire. I called Fred, and he said, "Come on over." He received us in his house on San Isidro Drive, courteous and smiling as always, though I could tell that life had lost its glow since the death of his Phyllis. He kindly said, "Leslie, you and Bing [Crosby] were so clever to move on to straight acting. I wish I'd done that early on." He found time passing slowly, now that he no longer danced. After a while he said, "Hold on, someone you must meet. Let me introduce you to my mother." Astounded, I calculated that since he was around seventy-two, his mother couldn't be less than ninety.

Walking in from the garden came a lady with a large bouquet of flowers in her arms. Straight and only slightly stiff, with a well-contoured face, blue eyes, rosy cheeks, and barely enough wrinkles to be called an old lady, Mrs. Austerlitz was wearing a navy blue dress that reached midcalf. If her waist was a little comfortable, I noticed that her ankles were very fine.

"Oh," said she after the introductions, "you're the little girl who danced with my Fred!" I was by then in my early forties.

Nearly ten years later, at an awards ceremony, I was talking to Fred, both of us standing on a step in the middle of the aisle, between the tables. A waiter holding a tray above his head knocked me off balance, and I started to fall. In a flash Fred's large hand reached my back and steadied me. "Dear Fred," I said laughing. "You haven't lost your touch."

10

Renoir

Very early in my years in Los Angeles—as early as 1951, I think—I enjoyed the rare privilege of meeting Jean Renoir and of becoming a good friend of the family. My first sight of the great filmmaker and of his wife, Dido, was at Victoria Station in London in 1948 when I was seventeen years old. I had been invited by J. Arthur Rank to do a three-day film test at Pinewood Studios (and was turned down, to my great relief—England seemed so dour right after the war) but had to return urgently to Paris to perform the next evening with the Ballets des Champs-Élysées. All flights from London to Paris had been canceled because of dense fog, causing a general stampede to the railway station for the night train, the Golden Arrow. A large crowd was pressuring the poor employee at the ticket counter, screaming or pleading for a seat. My mother ordered me to sit on our valise and look sick. She managed to convince the poor attendant that I was in urgent need of our doctor in Paris, and we got our seats.

Two people attracted my attention: a large, rotund man with a pronounced limp, red hair, and rosy cheeks, vociferating with forceful gestures, accompanied by a tall, dark woman with a look both severe and stoic, as striking as an Indian chief. I was mesmerized by this extremely contrasting couple. Their images were indelibly printed in my memory, but it was only three years later, at a party in the New York apartment of French painter Pierre Sicard, that I discovered their names: Jean and Dido Renoir. They told me that just as I had noticed them, they had commented that I would have been perfect casting for the role of the young girl in *The River*, which Renoir was then preparing in London. Later, we left the cocktail party together and waited on the sidewalk for a taxi. Under the persistent drizzle, by the light of a lamppost, we exchanged our phone numbers and planned to meet again in Los Angeles.

After we became close friends, I started to view all the Renoir films I could find. My children and I have a preference for *Une Partie de Campagne (A Day in the Country)* from a short story by Guy de Maupassant—but there is also *La Chienne,* the delightful *Boudu Sauvé des Eaux (Boudu Saved from Drowning)* with the great Michel Simon, *La Règle du Jeu,* considered his great masterpiece, not to mention *La Grande Illusion.* I feel I'm not doing justice to him if I don't also mention *La Bête Humaine* with Jean Gabin and Simone Simon.

The Beverly Hills home of the Renoirs in Benedict Canyon was a rallying point for French and European artists living in or visiting Los Angeles. Following the Burgundian tradition adopted by Jean's mother, Aline Charigot, and by his Parisian father, the painter Pierre-Auguste Renoir, Sunday afternoon was the time to receive friends and family. A phone call was required to make sure that the afternoon hadn't been reserved for a very special visitor—Charlie Chaplin and his wife, Oona, for instance (as in 1972, when Chaplin was honored with a Life Achievement Award), or François Truffaut, the favorite son, who came regularly to show his latest work. Many film people came often to warm themselves in the sunshine of the Renoir home. Tony Curtis and his wife, Christine Kauffman, and Peter Bogdanovich and Cybill Shepherd were assiduous friends. David Hockney avidly admired the paintings when I brought him with my friends Jack Larson and James Bridges.

The French identity of the house was established immediately at the entrance by the presence of a large provincial armoire. In the little open corridor leading to the living room, shelves exhibited Jean's ceramics, pots and plates, reminders of his first profession—potter. Two grandfather clocks—one in the living room, the other in the dining room—designed by Renoir himself were synchronized to ring the quarter hours, the halves, and the hours.

In the living room, you were offered a large Indian armchair, placed on a colorful Persian carpet. White wine, served in silver goblets, with olives grown in the garden and cured by Dido herself, and later in the afternoon, slices of French saucisson, immediately created a warm atmosphere. Inevitably you looked around the room, amazed.

Even if you came to visit several times a week, as I did, it was always

an immense pleasure to rest your eyes on the surrounding objects, from
the plaster head of Aline Charigot in a straw hat—presented in the corner between the two sliding glass doors—to the full-size painting of Jean
as a young hunter with his dog at his feet. There were always flowers on
the piano, next to the bronze head of Jean's brother, "Coco" (Claude),
and more flowers on every table. The walls, bare bricks painted white,
held many small paintings by Pierre-Auguste, each one with a story. The
little aquarelles always drew my attention. I was told that father Renoir
used to start the fire in his studio stove with similar watercolors, painted,
he would say, "Just to get my hand going in the morning." These had
been saved by his model, Gabrielle, who thought they were much too
charming to let the boss burn them. One aquarelle of similar size was by
Cézanne, of the famous *Bathers*. The two friends, Renoir and Cézanne,
were painting together outside Paris when Renoir felt the need to relieve himself. "Have you got a piece of paper?" he asked Cézanne, who
handed him the sketch. Renoir, in the bushes, having already crumpled
the piece of paper, took a second look at it and decided to spare it and
use leaves instead. The preserved Cézanne sketch now hung on the wall,
ironed out and framed.

Immediately upon entering you felt that all outside agitation had
disappeared and given way to a joyous serenity. There was around that
house, designed by Renoir himself, such a hum of color and such a
feeling of conviviality, perhaps because the open space created a flow
from room to room. Simplicity and harmony best describe the living
room, where large sliding glass doors invited you to gaze outside at the
gnarled olive tree. Renoir expressed particular concern and affection
for this tree when it nearly died after a frost. A magnificent bronze
statue of Aline, breast-feeding one of her three boys, sat under its silver
leaves. On sunny days, when Renoir was still in good health, visitors
were often taken on a walk winding down the hill where Lillian Gish
lived—a model neighbor, said the Renoirs. During the promenade he
would point to the sky and say, "Look at those interesting clouds," and I
thought about how his father had opened his eyes to beauty just as Jean
was opening mine.

The conversation was, at first, simply an expression of contentment
at being together. Eager to entertain his visitors, Jean would soon begin
to talk about events or names in the news but avoided saying anything

disparaging about anyone if he could. He would stress the good qualities in people—unless a person was quite without redemption, in which
case he would remain silent. Example: A name is brought up in conversation, the perfect occasion for character assassination. Renoir engages
in a description of this man's admirable ability to lift a chair just by
holding one leg, and praises his physical strength—obviously the only
positive quality he could find in this man, otherwise quite stupid.

Without ever being pedantic, his talks unfailingly ran on philosoph-
ical topics, history, politics, and human nature. He was a past master in
the art of conversation and would speak on different subjects until he
found the one that interested his listener. It was then developed in broad
strokes, with Cartesian clarity and simplicity. If the conversational partner was not entirely convinced by his argument, Renoir would switch
with the same passionate conviction to an alternative opinion, until he
had obtained complete adherence. I often wondered if he believed his
own arguments, since he seemed so willing to adapt them to his listen-
ers. However, his digressions were always eloquent, brilliant, convincing. His driving concern was to communicate—to exchange. He cared
above all to establish bonds of friendship. Since it was impossible to
perform the act of love with everyone, second best was conversation.
Shyness was such a waste of time, he thought. He once told me, "I wish I
could warm up those little hands." This was at a time when I didn't have
a companion. He thought my heart was frozen, and he was right.

His heavy limp dated from the First World War; a bullet had pierced
the fuselage of his plane (I seem to remember that he was navigator) to
lodge itself in his right thigh. The story of how his mother, already very
sick with diabetes, came to the hospital where he lay wounded waiting
for the surgeon to amputate is infinitely touching. After hearing her
pleading to save the leg, in which gangrene was already starting, the
young surgeon suggested as a last resort a totally unorthodox treatment:
He ran cold water from a rubber tube through the wound until the gangrene disappeared. However, Renoir limped throughout the rest of his
life, and from time to time the infection would reappear.

Jean Renoir had not been raised in a bohemian home, nor had he
known poverty in his childhood; he had been sent to a good school by
a family who lived by sound bourgeois rules. However, father and son
considered themselves craftsmen rather than bourgeois. Much as his fa-

ther had, Renoir adopted workmen's clothes, the kind you could buy on the third floor of the Paris department store La Samaritaine. His shirt was never white, but dark blue or gray. He wore a workman's cap on his head, rarely a hat. If he had to wear a tie, it would be of knitted cotton. In the winter he always wore an English tweed suit, the kind favored by Oxford professors. I never saw him in a tuxedo, although he probably owned one. He was, paradoxically, extremely interested in fashionable women's clothes and could talk about them with pleasure. In his early films, his actresses were dressed by the two greatest couturiers, Paul Poiret and Madeleine Vionnet. He chose Givenchy for my dress when we did a play together.

Following the principles set by his father, according to whom you should not wear out your eyes after sundown, work on weekdays stopped at around five or six, depending on the season. Intimate friends would then pay a visit. This is how I came to meet Gabrielle Renard, the distant cousin from Burgundy, his father's famous model and Jean's nanny. She was by then aged, quite small (whereas she's quite voluptuous in the paintings), and dressed in black turn-of-the-century clothes. After her death, her son, Jeannot Slade, Jean Renoir's *frère de lait* (literally, his milk brother), came every evening until the end of Jean's life. Gabrielle and Jeannot had a house about fifty yards away from the Renoirs'.

If the atmosphere in the house was mainly French, the exchanges between Dido and her Costa Rican maid, Zeneda, later replaced by Zoraïda, were in Spanish. The cat, the only authentic Californian in the household—not always the same animal but always called "Minou"— was a product of the television generation. At five minutes before the news broadcast, she'd perch herself on the back of the armchair, waiting for the TV to be turned on.

If you were lucky enough to be invited for dinner, you had the chance to gaze your fill at the statue of Venus (by Pierre-Auguste) outside the windows of the dining room. Dido and Zeneda would do the cooking, unless chicken was on the menu, roasted on the spit by Renoir himself. He had designed the chimney with its intricate motor-activated spit and took a craftsman's delight in basting and timing the cooking of the bird. On the table, vegetables were plentiful, portions generous—a whole quarter pound of butter sat on a plate, never just a measly slice. Bread was regularly bought at the French bakery. There was cheese and fruit for dessert, the latter preferably from the garden. Their avocado tree provided the first course.

Dido was born Dido Freire, from a rich Brazilian family of landowners and diplomats. It was while finishing her studies in the best Parisian convent (Les Oiseaux) that she was brought to a film set and met Jean Renoir. She quickly became his assistant and never left his side. She was as jealous as a lioness, and her passionate love for him never wavered. She had a strong personality and was feared by all the young people who wanted to approach Renoir for advice or for interviews. Firm but with a wisecracking sense of humor, she often added a sarcastic postscript to his tirades, deflating his oratorical extravagances. She camped something of a caballero when she smoked her little cigars, until she realized that it disturbed her husband and so gave them up. Dido possessed another South American attraction: She could eat the hottest peppers raw, when anyone else would be gasping for air. I used to bring her a handful of those fiery little condiments when I went to the Mexican border for the weekend. For official functions she dressed in severe dark suits embellished with gold Mayan jewels, which suited her dark looks admirably. At home she usually wore trousers. When Renoir became ill, she took care of him with patience and good humor and couldn't wait to leave this world and join him after he died. Life wasn't worth living without him.

It was at first impossible for Renoir to divorce his first wife, Catherine Hessling, because of the war. He nevertheless married Dido in California and was for a while a bigamist. This didn't disturb him personally—he was broad-minded—but it upset him that Dido could not enjoy the respectable position that was hers by right. It also created legal complications. Despite this ambiguity, Jean and Dido Renoir went to Mass every Sunday and took their maid with them. I believe that Renoir lent himself to the practice of Catholic rites with good grace rather than out of profound faith. There is no doubt that he was a spiritual man, but being a Catholic was for him more a matter of birth and tradition than of doctrine. He became interested in Buddhism and Hinduism after his long stay in India to film *The River* and said he could easily have stayed there the rest of his life. The profound respect of Hindus for all living creatures corresponded to his ethos. Renoir held animals, especially dogs, in great esteem because of their undying fidelity. He placed them above humans in this respect. "Faithful as a dog" was his highest form of approval.

His courtesy, especially where women were concerned, was so well known that many articles written about him mention it. He really did get up when a woman entered a room, even a servant. He removed his cap for young girls and gave his chair to anyone of the female gender. And he could not bear rudeness or even tactlessness. Once he told me how, after a driver behind him honked impatiently, he stopped his car, got out, and went to the driver, who lowered his window in a rage. In very courteous terms, Renoir offered his car keys to the boor, suggesting he drive the vehicle, since he obviously thought he could do better.

I realized little by little that Renoir represented paternal authority for me. I listened to him. Having severed all family ties when I left France for Hollywood, there was in me something anarchic. Here was a father figure who respected the words of God, Country, Police, Doctors. Apart from his unavoidable bigamy, everything was meticulously correct in his affairs. Renoir, who had made the most iconoclastic film about a homeless tramp in *Boudu Sauvé des Eaux,* was himself an upstanding citizen. He followed the code of honor of aristocrats as depicted in *La Grande Illusion.*

He claimed that he was against formal education and used to say that young people should be allowed to roam around freely like wild horses in a field! I was respectful of this theory, which relieved me of my feelings of inferiority about my own haphazard schooling. If Renoir wasn't interested in mathematics—he admitted not knowing his multiplication tables—he was brilliant in what mattered to him—literature, philosophy, and history—and he had the work ethic of his father, with a craftsman's patience and modesty.

Even when terminal illness hindered him from moving or speaking clearly, he would still be at work every day with his secretary, who understood his garbled sounds. Tirelessly, with infinite pains, Jean Renoir dictated his last novel, written in clear and concise sentences. He let himself slip into eternity when the novel was finished.

I first tried my hand at writing around 1970, when I reached forty and my career as an actress seemed to be in decline. Early on, when I had succumbed to the weakness of beginners for vengeful endings, he gave me this advice: "Never kill hope." When I complained about the hard work this new craft required, his response delighted me. "One must hit the nail over the head many times before it *consents* to enter."

Quite discouraged about the prospect of years of apprenticeship, I asked him how late in life one could envisage starting to learn this new craft. He thought about the question, then looked at me quizzically and offered, "Eighty?"

When I first met him, because of his exuberance and delight in everything and its contrary, he could, to some, appear to be disorganized, if not muddled. Nothing could be further from the truth. He had a remarkable memory and was as precise as a Swiss watchmaker. He had a great aptitude for everything mechanical and explained to me how he had designed the body works of his first cars. I learned later that he had even taken part in car races. He still drove his finely tuned Jaguar with remarkable precision.

When starting in films, his passion for the mechanics of cameras made history. He developed a steel head (the stand on which a camera is fixed) that allowed the camera to pivot 365 degrees in order to follow a character coming downstairs without ever cutting away. This piece of equipment is still in use today. And the shot for which this camera was first used (in *Le Crime de Monsieur Lange*) is still taught in film schools.

He told me that he later lost interest in the technical side of filming and concentrated on emotions, drama, the frailties and contradictions in human behavior. "The trouble in an argument," he would say, "is that everyone is right." He loved actors more than any director with whom I have ever worked. He often chose the same ones for his films because he had developed a friendship and admiration for them. He rather approved of what we call a ham actor, provided the hamming was good.

His originality naturally frightened many producers. There were no clear heroes or villains for him. His heroes had flaws and his villains charm and redeeming graces, even justification for their actions. Never sentimental, he described harsh realities without affectation. He even encouraged clowning in dramatic scenes, and death was often treated with a sort of careless good humor. I remember a close shot of crowds laughing while watching from a bridge the title character in *Boudu Sauvé des Eaux* start to drown. Technically, too, he had idiosyncrasies that were unacceptable to Hollywood. He preferred the imperfections of direct sound rather than corrected or rerecorded sound. Confident in his convictions, Renoir nevertheless suffered from being marginalized in Hollywood, much as he had been in Paris. He concluded philosophically, "My father suffered from being misunderstood, why shouldn't I?"

In difficult times he needed the reassurance of viewing his own films. A friend, Robert Weymers—a Belgian lighting expert—offered to run the projector, set up against the wall of the living room. After the viewing, Renoir took a childlike delight in compliments. He was particularly pleased when told that he had achieved with his films a greatness comparable to his father's paintings.

I loved his schoolboy jokes. *"Comment vas tu yau d'poile?"* was a favorite—untranslatable but something like "See you later, alligator!" Many will remember his quip when having to mention in public the film studio that was giving him so much trouble: "I want to thank Nineteenth Century Fox. . . ." But while he usually fought stupidity with humor, he could at times burst into force-five tempests. He once blew up when I mentioned that I admired John Huston's film *Moulin Rouge.* He despised the tricks used by the director, who slid colored gelatins in front of the lenses to create the effect of impressionism. He further disapproved of lowering José Ferrer onto a little wheel-driven platform so that he would look as short as the character he was playing, the painter Toulouse-Lautrec. These artifices were an insult to Renoir's principles, and I received fifteen minutes of serious lecture to that effect.

Seeing Hollywood's infatuation with *Moulin Rouge,* he decided to make his own film on the same subject, *French Cancan,* offering the world his accurate version of the time and place. No one knew the life on the hill of Montmartre better than he did, considering he was born there, in the neighborhood called Château des Brouillards (Fog Castle). Incidentally, as he told me, the can-can was a kind of wild shaking of the legs that the rough laundresses, who worked standing up all day, did on Saturday night to let go of fatigue and stress. After a glass of wine or two, out of sheer provocation, one girl who wore no underwear lifted the back of her petticoat with a yell. This pornographic prank was quickly imitated by all the girls. The word got around, and bourgeois gentlemen, lovers of licentious and libertine exploits, heard of it and rushed to the washhouses. The police quickly moved in and forbade bare bottoms. The dance little by little adopted a formal choreography and moved into theaters, and the washerwomen became professional dancers with knickers and extra frills on their petticoats.

After a few years in Hollywood, being a ballet dancer while also acting in dramatic parts created a sort of conflict in me. Somehow I found the contrast between the two disciplines difficult to harmonize within the studio exigencies. I knew that ballet, like piano or violin, demanded total dedication, and at that point I wasn't sure which I preferred, acting or dancing. A dancer who is not improving is slipping technically. I couldn't bear this painful option. After finishing the film *Gaby* for MGM, I went to see Renoir and asked his advice, as I did so often. He answered; "Leslie, I don't know if you are a good dancer—I don't know much about ballet—but I think you are an actress."

Some months later Jean Renoir wrote a play to make a real actress out of me. We went to Paris to work on *Orvet* (Garden Snake) and opened on March 12, 1955, at the Théâtre de la Renaissance. The character I played was inspired by an encounter in Renoir's youth. A young girl, barefoot and in rags, lives in the forest together with her drunken father, a poacher (Raymond Bussière—reminiscent of the Julien Carette character in *La Règle du Jeu*). She makes a few francs selling wild mushrooms and occasionally, with the utmost candor, her charms. She appears at the house of a writer (played by Paul Meurisse). He is intrigued by her provocative bluntness and starts to educate her. He introduces her to his romantic nephew, who lives in jaded Parisian society and has never met such an authentically primitive creature. The two extremes are attracted—the nephew is enchanted with her, while she, of course, falls hard for this "monsieur." He takes her to Paris and starts to introduce her to his world. She is transformed—the rough little savage becomes socially acceptable, at which point the young husband loses interest. Desperate, she goes back to the woods of her childhood to die of a broken heart. The story structure is somewhat parallel to that of "The Little Mermaid" by Hans Christian Andersen, which Jean used to read as a child while his father painted him. It also has echoes of *Pygmalion* by George Bernard Shaw.

The rehearsals were carried out not just at the theater, but also in other ways, spontaneously—at the café, during long, copious meals full of conviviality, or during drives to the countryside. All day I was plunged into the Renoir world, rich in memories, lessons, anecdotes. My gratitude is immense for the generous education he gave me. We opened and played for five months, to wildly conflicting critical response—either unconditional admiration or hostile panning. Renoir's work always aroused extreme reactions. As for me, one critic said, "She is not acting, she is." Renoir explained that far from being negative, this comment paid me the greatest compliment. "They used to say the same about Jean Gabin," he would tell me kindly.

On Easter weekend, German tourists occupied a good part of the orchestra seats. The shock of my life! I was playing in front of the enemy! But as the war was long over, I just had to adapt. François Truffaut—a very young man, not yet a filmmaker—came several times. The poet Jacques Prévert was there quite regularly, as were all of Renoir's friends. Ingrid Bergman came, dressed in a poor little gray coat, looking quite thin, tired, and discouraged. Dido and Jean took her to dinner after the show. The next day Renoir explained that after the meal Ingrid had sat down on the edge of the sidewalk and cried bitterly because all the films she made with Roberto Rossellini were box-office disasters; she was penniless and exhausted with all those children to look after. "So you see, Leslie," added Renoir, "I won't be doing the film I was planning to do with you. Not right away. I promised Ingrid I was going to help her." Renoir made *Elena et les Hommes* (*Paris Does Strange Things*) with Ingrid, which revitalized her career.

Three or four years passed before I saw the Renoirs again, because I had by then married Peter Hall and was living in England. We corresponded, and I received numerous letters with proposed plots for films. For a reason that I cannot quite explain, Renoir always envisioned me as a tramp, a slut, an orphan, a victim, a thief shacking up with a lion tamer/conjurer. . . . Eventually he came up with *Three Rooms in Manhattan* by Georges Simenon, to which I consented with great enthusiasm. The trouble was, no studio would agree to finance a film with Jean Renoir directing and myself as a wanton woman. After seven months of hopeless discussions with agents and producers, we gave up and I accepted the role of *Fanny* under the direction of Joshua Logan.

In 1969 I settled back in Los Angeles and had the great fortune of seeing Jean and Dido quite often. I also met his delightful son, Alain, as lively and brilliant as his father. In the early seventies, Renoir became weaker and for no apparent reason seemed unable to walk. Dido believed or pretended that the doctors couldn't find a reason for this infirmity. François Truffaut, who came twice a year or so and who was his main moral support, believed it was psychological: Since Jean's father had finished his life in a wheelchair, he was convinced that the same fate awaited him. The unhealed wound in his leg seemed to predict the handicap. Ultimately, Parkinson's disease was diagnosed, and Renoir slowly developed motor disorders. But there were still good times; laughter never disappeared from the Renoir home.

In the last decade of Jean's life, my friendship with the Renoirs became more precious with the years. Each time I landed in Los Angeles, my first call was always to their house—sometimes I would drop in on the way from the airport to my hotel, and of course my last call was also to them.

Renoir's second play, *Carola,* was written for his great friend Ingrid Bergman, who wasn't free to do it. In 1973, Channel 13, the Los Angeles public station, was eager to stage it as the play of the month. Although the part demanded a more mature actress, Renoir asked me to play the lead with Mel Ferrer. During the German occupation, a French actress who owns a Paris theater has to choose whether she will run away with the German officer who was her lover before the war or be loyal to her country and to her theater and remain in occupied France. In 1980, François Truffaut was inspired by this plot for his famous film *Le Dernier Métro (The Last Metro).*

However, when the time came to start rehearsals, Renoir wasn't well enough to direct. The director of the program, Norman Lloyd, a very distinguished actor/director who had worked with Renoir, Orson Welles, Chaplin, and Hitchcock, took his place. We did our best to perform the play in the Renoir spirit, but an essential element of gentle chaos was missing. For reasons of running time, one of the comic elements—a Gestapo guard who wanted an autograph from the actress—had to be cut. The story was very romantic and Mel Ferrer is excellent, but I'm not sure I did it justice. I had the pathos for the part, but I don't think I had the authority or the maturity.

Every effort was made to improve Renoir's health. Doctors and specialists were consulted; hospital tests, a series of therapies, treatments, and medications were tried. And finally, with everyone at wit's end, an original idea was attempted. Someone knew a hypnotist who used to perform at the magicians' club in the hills above Hollywood. This artist agreed to convince Renoir that he could still walk. We all sat around Renoir's wheelchair and followed the session attentively. Renoir, entering the game with good grace, had his eyes fixed on the hypnotist's gaze. The man, speaking in a low, convincing voice, exhorted him to submit to his power. This went on for several minutes, but clearly nothing was happening; Jean remained perfectly in control. The conjurer said the trouble was with the light. He switched places so that he was now facing daylight and tried again to control his client's mind. Again Renoir's eyes followed the magician's dutifully, but I could detect a skeptical glint in their depths. Renoir's will and intelligence were blocking any attempt at influencing his mind. When finally the experiment had to be abandoned as a failure, I noticed that while it hadn't been effective with Renoir, it was starting to work on me. A kind of numbness was overtaking me. . . .

Once, when I visited him in his bedroom, he told me, anxious as a child hoping to pass an exam, "Leslie, you must excuse me, the doctor wants a urine specimen for a laboratory test. I must obey him, so I will ask you to wait next door." I went into the living room and was talking with Dido when an imperious call interrupted our conversation. "Dido!" She rushed to Renoir's room, alarmed, but soon came back discouraged. "Jean says he cannot. What shall we do?" Zoraïda, who took care of the garden as well as of the house, had heard the commotion. "Let me take care of this," she said. She went into the garden, turned on the hose, and directed a strong blast at Renoir's windows. We were giggling in the living room waiting for the outcome. Within one minute, Jean's voice shouted, "Dido! Dido! *Ça marche!* It worked!"

In 1974, after several years in Los Angeles, Michael Laughlin, my third husband, decided we should now go and live in Paris. Renoir didn't believe he should influence or persuade anyone, but Dido tried her very best to get me to stay in California. She didn't like to lose her friends. Nevertheless, the decision had been made by Michael. I followed like a dutiful wife, and once again a house I had so lovingly designed was sold. This parting was most poignant—we all knew this might be the last time I would see Jean alive. As usual, I stopped to pay a visit on the way to the airport with a half hour to spare. When I arrived in the driveway, Renoir was waiting in his wheelchair outside his front door. The afternoon was mild, but he wore on his shoulders the little plaid blanket that my daughter Jenny had hand-woven for him.

"Why are you waiting here, Jean?" I asked.

"In case you didn't have time to stop. I wanted to make sure we had time to say good-bye." For the first and last time he addressed me using the familiar *tu.* I was deeply moved.

The last sight of him waiting on his doorstep is imprinted in my mind, bathed in the love and protection he had so generously offered me—a very frail old man hunched in his wheelchair. I thought how appropriate was the title he wanted to give his book of memoirs, *Wait for Me, Gabrielle!* He died on the twelfth of February, 1979, at the age of eighty-four; I still think of him constantly.

11

Gigi

After the thrilling experience of working in Paris with Jean Renoir, I had to return to Los Angeles in 1956 to do a disappointing film, *Gaby,* a remake of *Waterloo Bridge.* During the war a young dancer, Gaby, meets Greg, a soldier on a three-day furlough (John Kerr). The whirlwind romance makes her miss a performance, and she is fired from the ballet company. He wants to marry her before returning to the front, but red tape makes it impossible. After a while his letters stop; she hears rumors that he is killed and finds herself in great financial difficulties. Indifferent to her fate now that she thinks he is dead, she lets herself be convinced by her roommate to resort to prostitution—she haunts Waterloo Bridge Station for clients. But Greg is not dead, just wounded, in a French hospital. Frankly, I can't remember the end of the film, because the naïve Hays censorship bureau was undermining every love story in the fifties, and this was no exception. Also, I couldn't see the point of redoing something so brilliantly done with Vivien Leigh. I vaguely recall a very cloying reunion scene, which I strongly disapproved of. However, my agents convinced me that I must overcome my reticence or face "suspension," which meant no salary and no possibility of working with anyone else for the duration of the filming or the equivalent time.

I didn't get along with the director, Curtis Bernhardt, who flaunted a disturbing German accent and was what I can only call a martinet. It was a frontal clash with someone I perceived as an autocratic personality. Working with my co-star, John Kerr, a really talented but rebellious young man, burdened at the age of twenty with twin daughters, wasn't easy either. He has since quit the acting business to become a successful lawyer. During the film I amused myself as best I could with learning photography and took a whole succession of dramatic shots of heaps of mannequins dressed and made up as bomb victims.

While filming *Gaby,* for the first time I made concessions to my movie-star status and rented a lovely house on the flats of Beverly Hills. Apart from the spacious house and beautiful garden, I really appreciated the early-morning cold swim in the pool before going to the studio. My parents had agreed to come visit me from St. Thomas, in the Virgin Islands, where they were now trying to establish themselves in the luxury trade with a shop offering famous French labels like Limoges, Lalique, Boucheron, Van Cleef & Arpels, and all the French perfumes. My father was also nominated *agent consulaire* for France—a title that entailed a good deal of administrative work but held some prestige for an expatriate. My brother, Aimery, who had joined me in Los Angeles in 1951 before my marriage to Geordie Hormel, and whom I had been able to help a little, had taken up his studies again. After a brief enrollment at friendly little Palos Verdes College, he entered UCLA, where he obtained a B.S. in chemistry, then moved to USC, where he earned an M.S. and a Ph.D., also in chemistry—a great satisfaction for me. He later joined the Northrop aerospace laboratories and was then hired by Amherst College in Massachusetts as an assistant professor. Soon after receiving his UCLA degree, he married his college girlfriend, Susan Farnsworth, who later worked as a probation officer. A very bright and precocious blond child, Chantal, eventually blessed their union.

Inevitably, tension built up between my mother and me. The last ten years' financial difficulties, the family's loss of social status, and wartime privations had embittered her. I had not realized that she had, during the war years, started to rely on alcohol and pills and was by now inextricably dependent.

Her lack of tact toward me wounded me constantly. Her tendency to control had become worse, while I, at twenty-five, wasn't the pliant little girl she once used to manipulate. One day, thinking I was alone in the kitchen with my father, I asked him if he could use his influence to moderate my mother's meddlesome interventions on the movie set—I had enough on my hands with my arrogant director and defiant co-star. Unfortunately, my mother overheard the conversation. An explosive confrontation ensued, with the consequence that my parents left immediately.

After *Gaby* was completed, I did what I had yearned to do for a long
time: I gave away all my toe shoes to the American Ballet School and
felt immensely liberated. I asked MGM's permission to go to Paris while
waiting for the script of *Gigi* to be written. This time there would be
no work involved—I just wanted to have a good time, see if I had any
friends left, go to the theater, live a normal life in the normal world. I
took a small suite in the Hôtel San Régis on the Right Bank and really
enjoyed myself. My darling, brave grandmother was now living in Paris.
Having lost her husband and her vast fortune, she gallantly organized
her life within one room in my Aunt Lucette's flat. There were only two
splendid Louis XIV armchairs left from the grand old days. To occupy
her time, she took bookbinding lessons, read, listened to the radio, and
had a circle of friends whom she received for "fifth o'clock tea." One
such guest was a lady in her fifties, distinctive for having been saved
by her nanny from the sinking of the *Titanic.* "She was just a little girl
of five," whispered my grandmother, adding, "She has suffered from
tuberculosis ever since." My grandmother was still acquainted with interesting people. She had, in my eyes, the immense prestige of dignity.

A distinguished British theater owner and producer, Donald Albery,
came to see me in Paris to offer me the part of Zuleika Dobson in the
play based on Max Beerbohm's novel. We both agreed that it could only
be played by an English actress; yet, still interested in a collaboration,
he asked if there was anything I cared to play on the London stage. The
idea strongly appealed to me, and I suggested that since I was going to
do the film of *Gigi,* it might be appropriate to do the play. He was quite
taken by the idea and asked me to choose a director.

Kay Brown and Audrey Wood were the star MCA agents who took
care of me in New York. Kay, who was also Tennessee Williams's agent,
told me when I asked her advice that Tennessee swore by a young
Englishman of twenty-six, Peter Hall, who had brilliantly directed his
Streetcar Named Desire in London. As luck would have it, Peter Hall
could free himself long enough from his contract with the Arts Theatre
Club to direct *Gigi,* and so we planned to meet soon after I arrived in
London.

The young man I met had an aura of success, a great vital force; he
was also tall, handsome, brilliant, charming, ambitious—I could add

beguiling and persuasive. One of those men who smile while they speak, even when the message is not pleasant. He was a self-made man with a brilliant Cambridge education, which meant everything to me. The attraction was immediate—a magnetic pull. We fought very hard to keep our relationship professional, and we managed until we got together after the opening night in Oxford. I do believe that my son, Christopher, was conceived during that first night in Oxford, which of course explains why he is so very bright. The next morning, when I woke up, I said an urgent prayer: "Please God, make this last forever." I was alive at last. I had found in Peter Hall everything I hadn't even dreamed of.

We opened *Gigi* on May 23, 1956, at the New Theatre, the perfect-size house. Colette's novella, adapted for the theater by Anita Loos, is the story of a young girl of fourteen, Gigi, who is raised in a family of courtesans where women never marry, and is destined to become one herself. Gaston Lachaille (Tony Briton in that production), a rich young man-about-town, likes to come to her house, play cards with Gigi (at which she cheats shamelessly), and drink a cup of chamomile tea with her grandmama—a welcome respite from his furiously fashionable Parisian life. Suddenly he realizes that Gigi is turning into a lovely young lady, but she refuses his offer to become his mistress, preferring to remain his chum and go on with their card games. His only resort is to ask her to marry him, and she finally accepts. The part of Great-Aunt Alicia was played by the extraordinary Estelle Winwood (my fairy godmother in *The Glass Slipper*). Early in rehearsal Estelle ticked me off when she said firmly, "Ducky, please stand still while I speak my lines." Although old-fashioned, the principle had some value. Cary Grant, who came from British vaudeville, made the same demand years later—especially, he said, during a punch line. I remembered the lesson and never transgressed again. After glowing notices and full houses, and when the play's success was firmly established, Estelle engaged me in girl talk. "Now, ducky, you have everything you could wish for. You're young, pretty, and successful. All you need now is a nice young man to carry your luggage at the train station and take you out to dinner." That's what men were for, according to her.

Esmé Percy, who played the butler, was another extravagant character. A contemporary of Cecil Beaton and Noël Coward, he sported embroidered purple waistcoats, colorful silk neckties held down with a diamond pin, and a black velvet hat, which he later gave me. He came to rehearsals with a little black notebook, bound by a rubber band, in which only his scenes were recorded. His partners' lines were written in black, while his own were in red. The rest of the play didn't concern him. Esmé had only one eye, a dog having bitten the other one, which was replaced by a glass eye. During one of the performances, the stagehands who worked the Theatre Royal, Oxford—students, of course—misheard the cue to pull off the set planted on a wheeled platform. Esmé and I tried to hold on while we were being whisked away, but he lost his balance, and his glass eye fell and rolled on the floor. The curtain was brought down while everyone, on all fours, went searching for Esmé's eye.

Esmé went around theatrical circles pretending that he was Sarah Bernhardt's natural son, and on the basis of his uncanny resemblance to the great actress, he used to give lectures in which he shared the secret of "his genes" and took on his "mother's" voice to illustrate the acting lessons she had given him. I kept for a long time the recording of his lecture but lost it in one of my numerous moves. When he died in 1957, soon after our play, his friends and admirers in the British theater pooled together to commission a carved-stone dog's trough in his memory. It still stands in Kensington Park in London, slightly to the right of the Knightsbridge entrance, with a plaque mentioning his name and his love for dogs.

One night the zipper of my costume got caught, and I missed my entrance cue. Esmé was onstage, together with the girl playing the maid, and found himself with nothing more to say. With delightful aplomb he launched into a narrative about his brother Alfred, a mischievous rascal. While in the wings my dresser was pulling and tugging at my zipper, I was entranced by the tale of Alfred's misdeeds. From that moment on, I postponed my entrance every night to hear the latest about Alfred. Finally Peter Hall came to check on the play, and when he discovered this new character who had not been in the original cast list, Alfred was fired.

After that first night in Oxford, Peter and I had to admit we were very much in love. I found out almost immediately that I was pregnant, even though, since my first marriage with Geordie Hormel, I was convinced that I couldn't have children. This was a magnificent, awesome, unexpected event, disrupting my already tenuous sense of security. Uprooting myself from Paris to Hollywood had been hard enough to overcome; now this new situation was destabilizing me again. I had to make a fast decision, one that would, once again, completely change the course of my life. But in fact I had no hesitation—I was ready to accept this immense benediction: a child! I moved into Peter's sparsely furnished little flat, where we slept in his single bed. But who cared? My theater dresser became our housecleaner. She was one of those old chorus girls who can't give up show business and who wear, way past their prime, stage makeup and a flapper's hairdo. She called us "dearie" and mothered us with food taken from the theater bar. She much preferred giving to taking.

Soon enough, rumors of my love affair with Peter Hall reached the ears of Jules Stein, president of MCA, my agents. Their imposing office building in London had a penthouse apartment where the Steins stayed when in the city. I was invited there for a serious talk with Jules and his wife, Doris. They were, of course, hostile to any idea of a marriage away from Hollywood and applied strong pressure, using the hot-and-cold method—the carrot and the stick: ascending career in Hollywood at my fingertips versus the ruin of my prospects if I persisted. "You mustn't let this unknown British theater director interrupt what both MCA and MGM studios are building into a solid international success," they insisted.

For better or worse, just as I had with Mademoiselle Jeanne Schwartz when I left the dance conservatory, I decided to follow my instincts. I was so ill at ease in Hollywood, where I felt in real conflict with the accepted values, that it seemed a matter of survival to have this child and live with this remarkable man. After only six years under contract, I told MGM that I wanted to live in England and marry Peter Hall. What were my expectations? Well, to spend my life with him and bond professionally as strongly as we were going to privately, even if it meant a career reduced from international status to local theatrical proportions. Other film actresses had succeeded—Vivien Leigh most notably. Working with Peter Hall for the rest of my life would satisfy me totally.

Our marriage took place on August 6, 1956, in the registry office at Marylebone (a lovely contraction of Marie-la-Bonne, "Benevolent Mary") in the presence of my grandmother, who had made the trip from Paris, and a small crowd of British theater people. My parents didn't come. I was quite sure the news had hit my mother like a bomb, as it had my agents, the studio, and the Hollywood gossip press. I wanted above all to avoid the three-ring circus to which the press would subject us; I wanted to keep our wedding an intimate occasion, with no publicity, no photographers or journalists to cheapen the day. Peter begged me to allow just one photographer to take the wedding pictures—a beginner named Tony Armstrong-Jones, a friend of his who needed the money. The *Evening Standard* had offered him one hundred pounds for a single photo. I agreed.

I had designed my knee-length dress in champagne-colored organza, with a large crown of leafy silver and blue roses in my hair. Except for the fact that my waistline was a little thick, it looked like the costume for the ballet *La Sylphide*. MGM had, of course, suspended my salary. We were still living in Peter's furnished flat, at five pounds a week. Peter was earning a very modest twenty-three pounds a week.

In the immense whirl of excitement that had overtaken me, just a little note of warning lodged itself in a corner of my brain. As we were driving from Oxford to London, Peter asked me, "Are you planning to continue your career?" To my positive answer, he then asked, "Why? Why . . . so ambitious?" The question surprised me and threw me off momentarily. I replied, "Because I'm a professional actress. I've been trained to work. It's my life." I thought the subject closed and worried no more about it.

This conversation must be situated in context: Peter came from a very modest background (his father was a railway stationmaster, in East Anglia) where the woman's place was clearly defined, at home—to cook, clean house, and raise the children. In the England of the 1950s, which was quite the most misogynist country in Europe to begin with, the working class was almost Middle Eastern in its treatment of women. Women couldn't be seen in pubs. Schools and clubs were segregated and still are, to some extent.

In those days London was still painted battleship gray, and there were many bombed sites around town. I visited countless neglected apartments trying to find a place to live, now that we were going to have a baby. I said with good humor that I'd left Hollywood and its boring sunshine looking for "bad plumbing" and had found it at last. Peter couldn't help with the search, as he directed a different play every six weeks at the Arts Theatre Club and was constantly reading new scripts, casting actors, and rehearsing. Besides, that wasn't a man's problem. Peter was a no-nonsense husband who made it a left-wing political point not to open the car door for a pregnant woman. We went to the theater about three times a week, sometimes driving to the provinces to see a particular actor. I remember very well the night that we discovered a young Peter O'Toole at the Bristol Old Vic, playing a vibrant and provocative Hamlet, blazing a modern trail in the provinces. Peter Hall immediately hired him for the next Stratford-upon-Avon season, where he played Petruchio to Peggy Ashcroft's Katherina in *The Taming of the Shrew,* and the world has admired him ever since.

Peter Hall was the new boy wonder, revolutionizing the crusty, respectable British theater. But his fame came at a cost, as he was systematically brought down in flames by the critics. The most disrupted evening was the first night of Samuel Beckett's controversial *Waiting for Godot.* The public was scandalized. People kept leaving during the play, slamming their seats as they departed. At the end came whistles, insults, patrons stomping out even before the curtain came down. Peter kept smiling. And then on the weekend the wind changed. Harold Hobson wrote in the *Sunday Times* a wildly enthusiastic review, followed by Kenneth Tynan in the *Observer.* That weekend the British theater entered a new age. It slowly dawned on the public that the theater could also talk about ordinary people, even about the working class, in situations of despair. I was an eager spectator, passionately involved in this iconoclastic theater, even though I wasn't a part of it.

Peter became the champion of a young actor-turned-playwright named Harold Pinter—the voice of the everyday man, writing dialogue so bland as to be menacing. Pinter expressed all the unspoken frustration in conventional British behavior, pent up to the brink of implosion. Notwithstanding Harold's elusive nature, our meeting was immediately quite intimate. Peter had an MG sports car then, and when we had to take Harold back to our house, Avoncliffe, where he was spending the night after a Shakespearean evening at the theater, there was nothing to do but to let him sit in the bucket seat and nest myself on his lap. Not

a problem when you are thirty, except . . . you couldn't help wondering
who the real Harold Pinter was. He was so well disguised, you wondered whether he was an irreproachable bank manager, a respectable
mortician, or a member of MI5. Just like his dialogues, he looked so
clean as to be slightly worrying. But overcoming my suspicion, I could
sense a remarkable new talent, and when Peter asked me to help back
the film version of *The Caretaker* together with Lars Schmidt (the Swedish producer who married Ingrid Bergman), I didn't hesitate. I gave all
the money I had put aside in my years at MGM. It didn't amount to
much; I seem to recall something in the region of twenty-five thousand
dollars. (Still, in those years you could buy a house in Beverly Hills for
ninety thousand.) Of course, I never expected the return of this money,
but to my intense surprise, over the years I was reimbursed in dribbles,
and just the other day—forty-some years later—I received from Caretaker Films Ltd a check for £683.25. The small individual voice of Harold Pinter has asserted itself into a loud world clamor.

During January 1957, Peter, overworked and vulnerable as he was,
got into a serious conflict with the director of the Arts Theatre Club.
Sensing the risk of a depression, I suggested a visit to Tennessee Williams, who had asked us to come and see him in Florida. Even though I
was only two months from giving birth to my first child, we flew to New
York. During the night in the hotel, I was awakened by violent pains in
my side, which became so unbearable that an ambulance was called and
I was rushed to the emergency room of a hospital, sirens blaring. Before
I was administered morphine, the front-desk person asked Peter what
religion I belonged to and that he write down what his decision was in
case of a turn for the worse: Were they to save the mother or the child?
In terrible distress, Peter chose the mother. It turned out that the flight
had dislodged some kidney stones, which were dissolved within twenty-
four hours. So relieved to have lost neither the mother nor the offspring,
Peter went to the hospital gift shop and bought a stuffed elephant in a
blue tutu, which I kept for many years.

Restored and happy to be out of the depressing hospital atmosphere,
we continued on the last leg of the journey, a flight to Key West, where
Tennessee lived. The house was a simple bungalow, comfortable but not
ostentatious. His companion, Frank Merlo, and his two pugs greeted us
warmly and seemed to communicate a feeling of easy living. Immedi-

ately after setting down our suitcases, we joined Tennessee for drinks on the patio. When meeting a giant such as he was then, you expected a certain pomposity or at least an awareness of superior rank. With Tennessee there was none of that. He announced that he had just received a letter from his mother and proceeded to read it aloud. It shared news of Tom's (Tennessee's real name) sister, Rose, who had just been committed to an asylum, and the trouble his mother was having with Tennessee's brother, Paul. His candor and simplicity amazed me—I could even say they shocked me, at a time when family secrets were carefully hidden and even buried, as they were in my family. I understood why he was such a great playwright—to him, every human experience held potential drama that should be shared.

Soon after this trip, luck—or, rather, the famous theater director Glen Byam Shaw—offered Peter the direction of the Shakespeare Memorial Theatre in Stratford-upon-Avon. Shocked by the daring idea of this controversial young director being given the keys to this venerable institution, the press was out waiting for him at every one of his opening nights. Nevertheless, the advancement in his career was spectacular—here was the possibility to give full expression to his talent. He threw himself into plans for the following season and lost no time in writing to the queen, asking Her Gracious Majesty for permission to rename the theater from Memorial to Royal. He received an affirmative answer, and the Royal Shakespeare Theatre soon gained in glamour and renown. We were given a beautiful grace and favor mansion to live in, Avoncliffe, five kilometers from Stratford. The house turned out to have been built by a member of the Hamilton family (of Lady Hamilton and Lord Nelson fame) after returning from India, where the lord was viceroy. Erected in the early part of the nineteenth century, Avoncliffe had a very pleasant glass gallery running alongside two of its façades. I turned this into a hothouse, grew potted plants, and started to paint there. Inspired by its elegance, I threw myself into the study of botany and designed an elegant garden, unaware that I was creating bitter feelings with the theater management, who thought I was spending too much money on the project. I am sorry to say that after my departure, the garden was destroyed and the mansion torn down to be replaced by ordinary little brick bungalows.

My son, Christopher, was born on March 30, 1957, between the last run-through and the dress rehearsal of *Camino Real* by Tennessee Williams at the Phoenix Theatre—in other words, between six and eight o'clock. The cast congratulated me on being so professional that I didn't disturb the schedule. I was present at the premiere, released for two hours by the hospital, where I returned soon after curtain-down. Three months later I boarded the plane for Paris to start on the filming of *Gigi,* the nanny and I holding the handles of Christopher's straw bassinet.

Five years had passed since I'd first suggested *Gigi* to Arthur Freed on the set of *Lili.* It had taken all this time to secure the movie rights and for Alan Jay Lerner to write, first, a straight comedy, which probably met with censorship difficulties, and then the definitive script, in which the immorality of the premise is toned down behind the musical notes.

I think this may be the right time to clear up the gossip that went around that I had "stolen" Audrey Hepburn's part as Gigi. I'll relate the story as Arthur Freed himself told it to me. When the press published the news that MGM and the Freed Unit were planning to film *Gigi,* Audrey, who had done the straight play in New York, and her husband, Mel Ferrer, came to see Arthur to ask if Audrey could play the film part. Arthur answered that the part had been written for me, but if Audrey was keen to do a musical, there was something that he could do to help. He picked up the phone and called Paramount Pictures and asked for Fred Astaire. "Hello, Fred? Listen, you're looking for a partner for your next film, *Funny Face,* I've got her right here with me, Audrey Hepburn!" The rest is history.

MGM was now ready to put into motion the immense apparatus of a studio on location. Shooting a musical in its natural setting, Paris, was a first for MGM and for Arthur Freed. The hazards of weather, traffic, sound pollution, and television antennas, added to the difficulty of obtaining police permits, were nearly insurmountable. It is only thanks to the blessed month of August, when every Frenchman is away on holiday and all restaurants and shops are closed as soon as the summer school term finishes, that we could film in such locations as Maxim's, the Palais de Glace skating rink, place de la Concorde, the Tuileries gardens, and the Bois de Boulogne, not to mention the Museum Jacquemart-André (Chevalier's house) and the Place Furstenberg (Gigi's home).

I was given a large suite on the second floor of the Hôtel Raphael, on avenue Kléber near the Champs-Élysées, the HQ of the film. Wardrobe, makeup, dressing rooms, and the secretarial offices were on the top floor. The Raphael made a point of welcoming film people. I remember meeting Rossellini and Ingrid Bergman there. At the same time as us, Marlon Brando, Monty Clift, and my good friend Liliane Montevecchi were also staying in the hotel while filming *The Young Lions*. It was amusing to meet them again so far from Hollywood.

The story of *Gigi* the film is much the same as that of the play—the education of a young girl destined to become a courtesan rather than a wife, in a line of unwed but successful professional women. Maurice Chevalier (Honoré Lachaille) is the older roué who tells the story. Louis Jourdan (Gaston Lachaille) is the spoiled, rich young man who finds social life such a bore and discovers that his heart beats for that little kid Gigi, who is growing up fast. Hermione Gingold plays my very warm-hearted grandmama, while Isabel Jeans is Great-Aunt Alicia, who gives Gigi professional lessons in the art of ensnaring men.

We were not lucky with the weather, as 1957 had the most rotten summer anyone could remember. In the scene when I arrive at Aunt Alicia's house for my lesson, Joe Ruttenberg, the director of photography, was watching the clouds with his little dark monocle, timing a hoped-for sun ray between two clouds: "Ten seconds . . . five seconds . . . three . . . two . . . one—roll 'em!" We had just one minute of sunshine! To make the moment more natural, I looked up at the second story, where Aunt Alicia's salon was, and—oh, horror! I felt my hat leaving my head! I turned around to pick it up—it wasn't there! Like a puppy trying to catch its tail, I made a full turn. No hat! It was being held by my hatpin on the back of my head! Furious, I plunked it down to my eyes, ready to cry, convinced I'd ruined the only shot we could get that morning. The shot remained in the film, and it looks convincingly like juvenile frustration.

At the start of the fittings, the legendary designer Cecil Beaton, who won the Oscar for the costumes and the sets, had left me in the hands of Madame Karinska, the famous theatrical dressmaker in Paris, while going off on a trip with his friend Greta Garbo. Upon his return, he saw my finished tartan outfit and exclaimed that the braiding on the bolero wasn't on his design! I had to explain that, having just weaned my three-month-old baby, I needed to contain my feminine shape, particularly

since I was playing a fourteen-year-old in that costume. In a slight state
of shock, he acquiesced.

Cecil Beaton was at the wardrobe department every morning before
eight, to supervise the looks of the costumed crowd. The same twenty
hat frames were handed around to the ladies, lovingly redressed by
Cecil every morning with a different garnish for each scene—cherries,
flowers, bows, or feathers. I can still hear the second assistant trying to
round up those undisciplined ladies: "All the *cocottes* this way, please!"
A dandy satyr in a large-brimmed panama, Beaton dragged the young
ladies into the bushes to take imperishable photographs that were later
printed in *Vogue*. He was also extremely concerned with makeup and
hair and made sure that all the ladies, the *cocottes* as well as the respectable ones, had pale skins and very discreet pink lips. On this occasion
he mentioned pointedly that Garbo didn't need false lashes. "Her own
are long and beautiful, you know." He also was the only photographer
who asked me not to smile for the camera. He used to say, "Leave your
face in repose, please," a leftover from the Victorian era, when camera
shutters were slow, I guess, and of course it is much easier to read people's personalities from a blank look. I welcomed this novelty, as I had
become very tired of the Hollywood mania for smiling at the camera.

We started filming, in the Bois de Boulogne, with the very last scene
of the film, where I am wearing a sumptuous lilac lace dress and a tall
feathered hat. This dress was constructed like a work of art—no seams,
with the lace entirely appliquéd on a transparent base. Here Maurice
Chevalier again picks up the refrain "Thank heaven for little girls"
while I step into a carriage, radiant with happiness, Louis Jourdan at
my arm. In reality, the scenes in the Bois de Boulogne were hellishly
difficult to film; there was so much traffic—carriages, promenading
crowds, everything coming and going in complex motion. We had to
repeat the shots many, many times. Chevalier was getting grumpy being
asked to wait between scenes; I have a vision of him sitting in his chair
with his secretary kneeling at his feet to tie his shoelaces. Then the playback started again, and that debonair smile lifted up the hard corners
of his mouth, his eyes twinkled, and the professional Maurice Chevalier
crooned charmingly about little girls "who grow up in the most delightful way." I finally went and changed into the little girl's outfit, and we
moved on to the beginning of the number "Thank Heaven for Little

Girls," good for catching a heavy cold after running around with real children the rest of the day, when I was, in fact, twenty-six and a very new mother.

Vincente Minnelli was a driven man. In a trance for the duration of the film, he heard and saw nothing around him. Since we had begun shooting, my grandmother had become extremely ill in Biarritz. If I wanted to see her one last time, I was told by Aunt Lucette, it was imperative that I take the train down to the Pays Basque. I was given two days off. On the way south with my baby, the heat was such that I kept dousing Christopher with cold water in the toilet's washbasin. When I told this to Mamy, she whispered with her dying breath, "Careful . . . Wrap the tap with a handkerchief. . . . It can be hot and burn his tender skin." She discreetly left this world after I kissed her for the last time. Strangely enough, while the pain of losing her was not insurmountable then, it lingered on for the rest of my life. In fact, I believe I miss her more now than ever.

Back in Paris, I visited the set at place de la Concorde. Vincent barely glanced at me, totally wrapped up in his work. "How are you, angel?" he asked, distractedly but nonetheless kindly. I sighed, hoping for sympathy. "I'm sad, Vincent. My grandmother has just died." Vincent smiled wanly, his eye roving on the traffic in rehearsal. "Oh, that's nice, angel, that's nice." I didn't bear him a grudge.

Maxim's was a nightmare! Vincent was really sick with the worst cold, caught coming from the frosty Palais de Glace skating rink into the overheated salons of Maxim's during the heat wave. From the sidewalk entrance to the dining area, the space was crowded like an anthill, full of technicians trying to set up the lamps, the black flags, the cables and sound equipment—a constant flow of ladies in evening dresses with hats bigger than the waiters' trays, makeup artists wiping the sweat off the gentlemen's brows, the blaring playback music drowning all else, adding to the confusion. Vincent was on edge, making Louis and me repeat the entrance again and again. The action was quite simple: The maître d' had to lead the way, weaving between the tables, until he sat us down at a round table and offered the menus. No one could understand why Vincent was so dissatisfied and getting more irritated by the minute. He finally shouted in a rage, "Can't somebody show that man how to hold a menu?" There was an embarrassed silence until the first assistant rushed over and whispered in his ear, "Mr. Minnelli, this is the real maître d' from Maxim's."

Later, we were filming the first scene with Gigi and Gaston sitting at the table. I went to see Vincent and put a Stanislavski question to him. "I understand that after we sit, you are going to track slowly toward us until you have us in a waist shot. Do you want me to be talking intimately with Louis and raise my voice as you get nearer? Or do you want me to be speaking louder when you are far, to get more intimate when you come in for the close-up?" There was a moment of silence, when Vincent just stared at me. His mouth twitched for a few unformed words, and he finally said, "You cook it up in your clever little head."

Notwithstanding the weather problems, everyone was enjoying filming in Paris. Alan Jay Lerner was happy with his new wife, trying all the fine restaurants that were still open. Fritz (Frederick) Lowe, our lovely composer, was resident at the very elegant Casino d'Enghien, where he couldn't wait to lose his handsome salary. Peter came briefly to visit and enjoyed meeting Maurice Chevalier, who invited the cast to a delicious dinner at the restaurant of the Eiffel Tower. Arthur Freed, not to be left out, invited us to an unforgettable supper on one of the Bateaux-Mouches, the tourist boats on the Seine.

I thought to myself, *This is dangerously perfect. The actors are so remarkable. Joe Ruttenberg's camera work is so beautiful. The script, music, and lyrics are so fine. The costumes so elegant. Careful! the mayonnaise could curdle! We mustn't become complacent or arrogant.*

The interiors, shot in Hollywood, were equally pleasant, except for one sequence, the "ortolans (buntings) scene." Poor Isabel Jeans, knowing that I had to eat the real birds, bones and all, whereas she had fake pastry ones, kept forgetting her lines. We had to redo the scene at least six times, with reverse shots on me; I must have eaten three or four of them (in the film you can see the bones poking through my cheeks). It felt like I had a stomach full of nails—I feared a case of peritonitis and asked to go to the hospital to rid myself of the darling birds.

Louis Jourdan, one of the handsomest men in Hollywood, was not comfortable with his image, yet his wit and self-deprecating humor were rare and unique. (I think they stand comparison with Marcello Mastroianni's.) He tended to express his angst with constant negative comments about Minnelli's staging, but instead of having it out with

Vincent, he poured his grudges out on me. I was quite exhausted to hear, every time the camera stopped, his litany of grievances. Alan Jay Lerner confessed that he had tailored the song "It's a Bore" to Louis's personality. That being said, fifty years later I now stand in admiration of his charm and his melodious voice.

Would it be fun to know that for the card-game scene where I cheat on Gaston, I took my inspiration from a film by Vittorio De Sica, *The Gold of Naples,* where the janitor's son—a shrewd little ten-year-old swindler—cheats at cards against the grand old aristocrat who owns the mansion (played by De Sica himself)? You get inspiration wherever you can!

Hermione Gingold was nothing like her stern character in the film. Irreverent, naughty, and fun, she had a great appetite for life, like a cat lapping up a bowl of milk. During the long waits while Joe Ruttenberg was adjusting the lights, she would pull up her skirts and start kicking up her legs like a can-can girl.

Isabel Jeans was sweet and very disciplined—she never undid her corset at lunchtime like we all did, and she kept the straight back of a real pro from morning to night.

A lot of the film was cut by the time we left Paris. My number "I Don't Understand the Parisians" was short of close-ups on me— especially short of a sparkling finale. When we got to Hollywood, a set was built on Lot 3 to look like a corner of the Luxembourg Gardens, with a pond and a bench. A pond calls for swans, of course. There were at least two swans. Vincent made me redo the end of the number three times, five times, ten times. . . . I couldn't for the life of me think what I was doing wrong. When asked, Vincent just formed unspoken words with his mouth and invariably said, "Do it again, angel." I was getting quite desperate and feeling nauseated (I was already pregnant with my daughter, Jennifer). Finally, around take nineteen Vincent shouted, "Cut! Print! Great!" He turned to me with a victorious smile. "The swans were great!" I hadn't realized that I was in competition with the blessed birds. (It wasn't until the opening night of the film that I noticed I had stolen my last pose in "I Don't Understand the Parisians" from Rex Harrison's at the end of his number "Why Can't a Woman Be More Like a Man?" from *My Fair Lady.* Innocent plagiarism!)

During the filming of the interiors of *Gigi* in Hollywood, I kept going to my favorite cinema, the Los Feliz, where I discovered a new Swedish filmmaker, Ingmar Bergman. I was extremely struck by his *Wild Strawberries,* so much so that I talked Vincent into using a Bergman-inspired camera movement for my number "Say a Prayer for Me Tonight." "Look, Vincent, the camera is outside the window—the wind blows the white curtains, allowing the camera to come into the room—we track slowly from the window, lingering in front of the bed where the magnificent white evening dress is laid—we continue the pan to discover me in front of the mirror with my cat, while the music starts the introduction music. In front of the mirror, I start singing, 'Say a Prayer for Me Tonight.'" The only false note in this idyllic scene was the cat, who didn't fancy being in films and had to be heavily sedated to remain on the set. When I picked him up, his head lolled to the side and his little pink tongue hung out. He had passed out in a near coma. I had to prop up his head with a finger under his chin throughout the song. I was assured that he would recover after a long siesta.

At some point Vincent and I became close friends—his wife had left him, and he was quite lonely. I used to drop by his house of an evening, to talk. His daughter, Liza, was by now an adolescent, unsure of herself. She didn't have the supervision of a mother that she so needed. I remember a dramatic Sunday afternoon when her German shepherd was wounded by a car, and she was devastated. Another day I combed her hair and applied a very light makeup for her first date, but she only had thoughts for Hollywood's heartthrob, George Hamilton. She had, even then, the openheartedness that later made her into a huge star.

Cecil Beaton was thrilled beyond words when the doors to MGM's furniture warehouse were opened. A three-story building full of priceless antiques from medieval to art deco to choose from, to furnish the interiors of Gigi's and Aunt Alicia's houses! He couldn't believe the treasures the studio had accumulated over the years. We still had a new costume to try out, the Deauville dress, which was going to be filmed on the Santa Monica beach. Here I have to applaud the Hollywood custom of testing the clothes in front of the camera at the same time as makeup and hairdos. Unexpected details come to light. The beach costume was in white piqué (which I think I had asked for). When we viewed the rushes, the dress turned out to look stiff and to swallow light like blotting paper, making me appear twenty pounds heavier. I learned my lesson about materials that absorb light against others that reflect it; similarly, about materials that move well against materials that remain stiff. Cecil had the dress redone in thin white cotton broderie anglaise, and it moves very well throughout the tennis and the donkey beach scenes.

In my long career, Beaton is the only set designer I met with so high a degree of professionalism. I discovered during the film a strangely sweet and vulnerable person, incapable of defending himself when it came to coarseness or vulgarity; he felt equally threatened by very assertive people. In London once, he begged me with panic in his eyes to show him the service entrance of my house so he could sneak away, because Peter Brook was ringing the front doorbell. And God knows that Peter Brook is a very nice man. Again in Hollywood, Cecil didn't know how to escape the invitations of Quike Jourdan (Louis's wife). His excuse was that the wall-to-wall carpet in their house was more than he could bear.

I was called back from England to do a few retakes—the swans number, among others. And here a factual error perpetuated in several accounts on the film must be put right. To the best of my recollection, Charles Walters (ex-dancer/choreographer and my director in *Lili* and *The Glass Slipper*) did only a day's "choreography" on "The Night They Invented Champagne," and that is all. History has now inflated his participation beyond the truth. Much as I loved Chuck Walters, I have to insist that the rumor is wildly exaggerated.

As I was walking the streets of MGM, I met André Previn (composer of background music, musical supervisor, and conductor on the film), who stopped me in my tracks. "I think perhaps you haven't been told . . . your voice has been dubbed?" "What?!" I was dumbfounded. "No! Of course I wasn't told. Are you sure?" "Alan Jay Lerner and Arthur Freed want to release the record before the film opens. They feel your voice isn't professional enough. You've been dubbed by Betty Wand, who imitates your French accent." I was destroyed by this piece of news. It is true that I didn't have a trained voice, but my pitch was very true, and I had worked hard at improving my control in "Say a Prayer for Me Tonight." My straightforward boyish harshness in "I Don't Understand the Parisians" and "The Night They Invented Champagne" was intended to show a girl in adolescence—a little tomboy. To her, Gaston is just a buddy, just as he hasn't realized yet that Gigi is

becoming a young woman. This lack of sexuality in the voice is essential
to the believability of the film. To this day, the childish cuteness of Ms.
Wand and her artificial French accent hurt my ears. The filming of the
musical numbers (always done on prerecordings) had been done on my
voice, and it didn't occur to me that Freed might dub me. (Now, fifty
years later, MGM has inserted my voice on the DVD—wicked, is what
I say!)

In shock, I went straight to Arthur Freed's office and asked to see
him. His faithful secretary let me in. "Arthur!" I started, rather worked
up. Arthur said, "Sit down." I sat and started again, full throttle. "I've
just met André. He tells me that I've been dubbed. That's not true, is
it? You can't have done that without telling me . . . without giving me a
second chance!"

Arthur stood up, lifted his finger, and said, "Just a minute." He
walked around his desk and out the door. After about ten minutes
alone in the room, I got up from my chair and walked to his secretary's
office.

"Margie? Where is Arthur?"

"Oh, Miss Caron," she said, very surprised, "didn't he tell you? He
went home about ten minutes ago." There was no catching him in a
confrontation.

When I want to be angry with Arthur, I remind myself that he is the
one who invited me to Hollywood and also that he is the genius who
came up with the title *My Fair Lady* for a musical version of a play by
George Bernard Shaw that wouldn't have done half so well had it still
been called *Pygmalion*.

It was during the shooting of *Gigi*'s interiors that I met Christopher
Isherwood and his much younger companion, the painter Don Bachardy. Cecil Beaton, who enjoyed the financial and prestigious position that Arthur Freed's contract offered him, gave extremely pleasant
dinners at the Beverly Hills Hotel, just as he always did in his London
house. It was during one of those evenings that I had the privilege of
meeting Isherwood, which dates our friendship to 1957. With time he
became my second mentor, right up there with Jean Renoir. I fancied
his company so much that I waited for him to be gone before I started to
read his books. I think that I didn't want to be in awe of him—I didn't

want the legend to come between us. He was my friend Chris before becoming the renowned literary figure. Don Bachardy was exactly my age; we had met several years before I met Chris, at the premiere of *An American in Paris*. He had asked for my autograph while his brother snapped the picture, which now stands on my mantelpiece.

Chris himself was rather short, slim, and fit—I later learned that he and Don both ran on the beach every morning, no matter how excessive the night before had been. Chris wore beige cotton trousers, oxford shirts, no tie but a T-shirt visible under the first undone button, a rather tightly strapped leather belt, and, to perfect the California-student look, brown leather loafers. His aristocratic English good looks were evident; the dull blond hair framing the fine features was always savagely clipped in military style.

On first meeting him, one could make the wrong judgment. His voice was very British and affected. How could someone so exceptional be, at times, so outrageously cynical? Just for the fun of it, I guess. Chris was full of contrasts. In a very British way, he was the most irreverent person I'd ever met. He liked to take you aback, shock and amuse you. I remember well the dinner at his house when he revealed that he had been published at first by Leonard and Virginia Woolf's Hogarth Press. I had in mind the vision of Virginia herself turning the wheel of the press in the evenings, after a day's writing. I became quite excited.

"What was she like?" I asked, extremely curious.

"Very vivacious, witty, worldly, and sometimes cutting. I didn't stay with them very long."

"Oh, dear . . . Why, Christopher?"

"She was the high priestess of this very distinguished group, the Bloomsbury set, with amusing, modern friends, Duncan Grant, Lytton Strachey, Vanessa Bell—her sister—Clive Bell, and others. She and Leonard didn't invite me to their parties. [Burst of laughter!] Frankly, she was a snob."

So much for Virginia Woolf . . .

If he could at times be dismissed as frivolous, one had to remember that he put his reputation on the line when he involved himself in moral issues, such as the Vietnam War. He was a staunch pacifist. Under no circumstances was he ready to hold a gun and kill a human being. He also walked the line with a picket sign to brave the Hollywood monopoly on salaries and residuals. Chris was deeply religious, or, rather, spiritual—you couldn't invite him for dinner on Wednesday nights, I think it was, because that was his evening with his guru.

Excessively tolerant, he corrected me once—only once. We were sitting around my dining table one night when I made an arbitrary statement about Montgomery Clift. I said I couldn't understand why he couldn't behave himself, considering the incredible gifts he had received from life. Chris's voice rose, chagrined rather than reprimanding. "Leslie, you can't make a categorical judgment like that!" That is all he said; he didn't elaborate or develop the argument. Chris was someone who walked away rather than argued.

Following the British tradition, he had a large collection of friends. He enjoyed diversity in people—originality, even eccentricity, amused him. He loved receiving at home. Don's painter friends, usually at least twenty years younger, were often present, as well as visiting British film people and writers. At first Don and he would do the cooking, but eventually it became too time-consuming, so a cook named Natalie was called in. The prototype of Austrian motherliness, Natalie knew all the guests and would cook generous dinners with a touch of homeland flavor in the potatoes. When she was nearly ready to serve, she would rush through the living room brandishing a carving knife with determination, like the murderess in a German expressionist film. After a minute she would rush back in, victoriously waving the weapon she had sharpened on the stone edge of the sidewalk.

During the meal, white wine flowed generously—always California wine; Chris and Don were no snobs—voices rose to a pitch, and every film or film project was thrown into the arena to be discussed, admired, or panned, with a relish for insider details. If a newcomer was present, Don would discreetly make an appointment for a sitting. And during the whole evening, the eyes feasted on the modern paintings lining the walls, gifts from Don's friends. The famous David Hockney painting of the room you sat in, with its two residents in bamboo armchairs, was always a joy to see.

Chris and Don were having dinner at my house on the day W. H. Auden died. This dates the occasion to September 29, 1973. Christopher and Auden had met when they were schoolboys, at St. Edmund's prep school, in Canterbury—they had worked, lived, and traveled together and had both settled in California. Auden, in his will, had named Chris executor of his estate. During the evening not a word was spoken of this dramatic loss. Chris behaved in a perfectly normal way, laughing and talking and even gossiping. I discovered the news of Auden's death only the next day and was immensely surprised at his discretion. He was equally discreet about his erudition. A mine of information, Chris possessed a remarkable number of dictionaries. Out-of-print dictionaries dating from the nineteenth century, American dictionaries, an English encyclopedia, plus synonym, polyglot, slang dictionaries as well as technical reference books lined a whole shelf. I was amazed to discover that, long before Google appeared, Chris could come up with the nom de plume of each of the Brontë sisters.

Around the autumn of 1984, when I was in Paris, my friend Jack Larson called me from Los Angeles with alarming news.

"Leslie, I'm awfully sorry to tell you this, but if you want to see Chris again, you must come as soon as you can. He is very ill."

"Oh, my God! What is the matter?"

The words fell like the blade of the guillotine. "Cancer of the prostate. Try to come if you can."

It was some three or four months later that I finally had the opportunity to fly from Paris to Los Angeles. I was in time; Christopher was still with us. It had been arranged that I would drop my luggage at the hotel where Jack Larson and Jim Bridges would come and pick me up; we were to go straight to a Japanese restaurant, on Third Avenue, where Chris and Don would join us, together with John Travolta, who was a close friend since the film *Urban Cowboy,* made with Larson and Bridges.

They had arrived a little before we did. I immediately searched for Chris, expecting a pale, emaciated, wan-looking specter of his usual self. To my utter surprise, I found him plump, rosy, and vivacious.

After the opening chitchat, the satisfaction of old friends reunited settling on our smiling faces, I asked the burning question: "Chris . . . please . . . I was told by Jack that you were extremely ill and that I must come urgently. But I have never seen you looking so well. Please tell me. What is this mystery? How is it that you look so well?"

"Oh," replied Christopher, matter-of-factly, "I didn't think it was the right time."

"What do you mean?" I asked hesitantly. "You haven't finished the book you are writing?"

"Oh, no." Chris turned his face toward Don, who was sitting opposite him. "No, I just thought *he* wasn't ready to see me go."

A silence followed this amazing declaration. It occurred to me that they formed the most harmonious couple I knew. The respect and affection they showed for each other was a lesson for any couple, heterosexual or gay. I never heard a sharp word or saw a sign of irritation between them. In their harmony there was also the freedom for each to express his individuality.

In the summer of 1985, I was offered an American tour of the French play *One for the Tango* (*Apprends-Moi Celine*) by Maria Pacôme. Hard and lonely work in an America where, since the Watts riots in 1965, the middle class had deserted city centers for the suburbs. If a restaurant was open after theater hours, the front door onto the street was usually boarded up—you could enter only through the parking lot, guarded by a security man. I am describing Denver, Colorado, in the burning heat of summer. This is where Chris, accompanied by Don, decided to come to say his final adieu. After the two-hour flight from L.A., he did not look too altered—a little thinner, perhaps. The show over, we took two taxis. Why two? There must have been other people with us. I found myself in the first taxi with Chris, separated from Don. Chris panicked. He kept looking back at the other car, where Don was seated. I told him we would soon be together, as it was just a one-minute ride.

During dinner the subject of conversation, led by Chris himself, settled on his impending death. Amazing though the discussion was, I realized it was much friendlier to broach the subject rather than adopt the hypocritical "you're looking so much better" to someone who knows he is dying. There was evident comfort for him in talking about it—no embarrassment about the subject, and no sadness either.

"I'm ready now," he said, and looked at Don, who returned his gaze with shared tenderness. "And I'm very relieved," he added with a giggle. "I found a wonderful doctor who swore to me that she wouldn't let me die in the hospital and wouldn't keep me on life-sustaining machines."

After the dinner we kissed good-bye with deep affection, knowing that we would never see each other again in this life.

Chris died soon after—Don kept sketching him until the hospital came to claim his body, which he had bequeathed to science. During those last days when Chris wandered in and out of consciousness, he suddenly said to Don—mischievous, as always, "I like the one where he's dying."

The next time I saw Don, I asked him for the supreme gift of one of the many paintings that he had done of Chris. I knew that he'd never sold or given any away. He very generously parted with one of his most precious possessions. The painting is now on my wall, and I consult it frequently when I need advice. Chris's face, extremely vibrant, looks back at me kindly and always answers my prayers.

12

Family Life

*P*regnant again during the additional shooting on *Gigi,* I still managed to slip in another film before the birth of my second child, my daughter, Jennifer. *The Doctor's Dilemma* was taken from the play by George Bernard Shaw. (My daughter is named after the character I played, Jennifer Dubedat.) In the spring of 1958, when I was five months pregnant and looking forward to a serene few months of gestation, the British producer Anatole de Grunwald offered to interrupt my lazy days to film *The Doctor's Dilemma,* under the direction of Anthony Asquith. I said there wasn't time, but Mr. de Grunwald insisted, arguing that they were ready to start the following week. I finally accepted but warned everyone involved that I could be photographed in a full shot only until the sixth month. That left us four or five weeks of disciplined work. The pace had to be kept up, but, alas, none of the people involved were familiar with or recalled the inevitable change in appearance of a pregnant woman. De Grunwald was by now a grandfather and did not remember, Anthony Asquith was homosexual, and so was Dirk Bogarde. I need not mention Cecil Beaton, who nevertheless understood the principle of pregnancy and designed dresses that didn't need a corset. I kept begging, "Quick, quick! Let's move on, baby is going to pop up!" I became very fond of the distinguished Anthony Asquith, son of the first liberal prime minister, who had declared war on Germany in 1914 and forced through Parliament the first notions of national insurance and pensions. Quite the most erudite as well as eccentric person I had yet met, Anthony was the proverbial "absentminded professor." I saw him literally beg forgiveness of cables when he tripped over them on the movie set and stand up to shake hands with the maître d' at a restaurant. "How are you?" he would question with concern. His sister,

Lady Violet Bonham Carter, interrogated me and must have found me incredibly ignorant politically. At least I was deferential. When meeting any member of that family, you knew you were sitting in front of history in the making.

Dirk Bogarde was a very subtle actor, attentive to every intangible signal—a real pleasure to ping-pong with. His downfall—and we all have one or more—was his vanity. Convinced that his right side was not equal to his left one, he wouldn't look toward me during his death scene (his bed was set against a wall with a window throwing side lighting on his "bad" side). I settled the "dilemma": "Don't let that worry you," I told Anthony (Puffin) Asquith. "I'll play the scene with my back to the camera."

Dirk became a good friend whom Peter and I visited in his successive houses—each more charming than the last. He had a decorator's talent; no sooner was a house finished than he would put it on the market and start doing up another one.

After our experience on *Gigi,* I had asked for Cecil Beaton as my costume designer. This was once again a very harmonious collaboration. My concept of the character was that as an artist's model and wife to Dirk's character Louis Dubedat, a painter, Jennifer ought to dress as models do, with a sort of manly cheekiness. Beaton agreed and added his own idea, an element of Pre-Raphaelite style. The result was a set of amusing costumes with a masculine hat, an exotic Japanese kimono, a Greek tunic, and other imaginative ideas. Trying to breathe a little sensuality into one scene (to be honest, Shaw is quite cerebral) where husband and wife are together, I tried to explain to Cecil that the couple had just been making love—hoping that he would design something more *déshabillé* than a dress. He listened to me attentively and then exclaimed: "Yes, I see! We can roll up her sleeves!"

Cecil Beaton's house in South Kensington was always decorated at the height of elegance. In the fifties his salon was boldly Edwardian—red flocked wallpaper and papier-mâché furniture with mother-of-pearl inserts. Later, after a trip to Japan, he adopted a stark, modern simplicity—black velvet walls, with colorful Japanese silk pillows made from obis on all the couches. And flowers—a profusion of flowers on every table. He admitted that on receiving days he would go to Covent Garden early in the morning and buy crates of flowers. Royalty was invited to his parties, and royalty came. During the introductions Cecil pronounced very clearly the names of his guests—I learned that technique from him—introducing the younger to the elder, while of course never introducing any member of the royal family. You just had to know. I was first introduced to Lady Diana Cooper, who was extremely gracious, and again to an elderly lady, to whom every woman present made a small curtsy. I did the same, of course. The lady firmly said, "Sit here beside me," and proceeded to ask a few questions. I knew my protocol— you are not supposed to question or suggest topics to royalty—so I just answered, wondering all the while who the charming lady was. I only later learned that she was Marina, Duchess of Kent, sister-in-law to King George VI and Queen Elizabeth, the queen mother. I was also told that the royal family adored musicals and that *Gigi* was a favorite.

A house had to be bought for the new baby, and I found one in Knightsbridge on sale for the extravagant price of fourteen thousand pounds! I signed the papers despite the horrified cries of my friends and accountant. "You're mad!" they all exclaimed. Throughout the war the house had become almost a slum dwelling—one family to a floor, with excessive partitioning but no bathrooms, each floor painted in garish greens, blues, and hot Indian pinks. The restoration included raising the roof for the comfort of the staff on the top floor. I had the whole façade wired to give support to a climbing wisteria. In the spring during the exuberant blossoming, American film units never failed to use the house as a background in commercials. I took the initiative of buying a swing for the enclosed gardens and was at first reprimanded for not consulting the rest of the proprietors. I noticed with a certain glee that, fifty years on, this swing is regularly renewed and included on the annual expenses of the key owners.

Found through an ad in the *Figaro,* a young governess arrived from France, who turned out to be a distant cousin of mine, Marie-Hélène Chalumeau de Verneuil—Lilène, to the family. She stayed ten years, looking after everyone's happiness and sanity.

The spring after Jennifer's birth, my darling nanny Greta, with the cornflower blue eyes, came to oversee the London house while Peter and I left for a motor trip through France and Italy, stopping wherever fancy took us. A Michelin guidebook in hand, we loitered our way south

My grandmother Mamy in a Greek costume.

At my First Communion in Paris with my grandparents.

My grandparents loved to host themed parties. Here they are at a Venetian ball at their estate in Vaux-sur-Seine.

My mother wearing a Degas costume.

My father, Claude Caron.

Wearing
Cecil Beaton's
sensational
costumes for
*Devoirs de
Vacances* at
Les Ballets des
Champs-Élysées
in 1949.

With Jean Babilée in *La Rencontre* at
Les Ballets des Champs-Élysées. Gene
Kelly saw me on the opening night and
invited me for a film test.

This was the Hollywood publicity shot to
present me to the world press. The costume
I was given to wear was Vera-Ellen's and was
too long in the waist.

Opening night of the film
An American in Paris in
1951—the shyest star ever . . .

The Douanier Rousseau scene with Gene Kelly in
An American in Paris. Each sequence in the ballet had
a set inspired by a different Impressionist painter.

With the incredible Gene Kelly again in
An American in Paris.

Dancing with a chair caused censorship
problems and had to be shot a second
time!

In the film *Lili* with Mel Ferrer and puppets Carrot Top and Renaldo, 1953.

In 1955, MGM let me go to Paris to appear in the play *Orvet*, which Jean Renoir wrote for me.

With Jean Renoir in his home some years later. The large portrait of him in the background, *The Hunter*, is by his father, Pierre-Auguste Renoir.

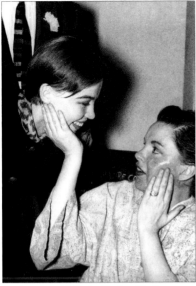

Backstage with Judy Garland in her dressing room during the tour of her one-woman show.

The Glass Slipper, with Michael Wilding as Prince Charming, 1955.

The kitchen scene from *The Glass Slipper* with the Roland Petit Ballet Company.

Just after Peter Hall and I married, he was appointed director of the Royal Shakespeare Theatre. Here we are in the garden of Avoncliffe (the grace and favor mansion that went with the job).

Rehearsing with Fred Astaire (without his toupée) for *Daddy Long Legs*.

Performing the "Something's Got to Give" number in *Daddy Long Legs* with Fred Astaire.

Tony Armstrong Jones (Lord Snowdon) took this photo of me in the London stage production of *Gigi*, which was directed by Peter Hall in 1956. I treasure the signed copy he gave me.

Arriving in Paris with Peter Hall and our son, Christopher.

Cecil Beaton's photo of me in *Gigi*, which he was kind enough to give to me.

Gigi again, with Maurice Chevalier and my son, Christopher.

In my flat, in front of Don Bachardy's portrait of Christopher Isherwood. It is dated August 14, 1977. I first met Christopher at a dinner given by Cecil Beaton in Beverly Hills.

Stills from the 1958 film adaptation of George Bernard Shaw's play *The Doctor's Dilemma*. The lovely costumes are by Cecil Beaton, as are these photos.

Family portrait with Peter Hall, son Christopher, and baby Jennifer.

With Peter and the children on the beach in Majorca.

With Henry Fonda
in *The Man Who
Understood Women*, 1959.

The "proposal" in *Fanny*
with Maurice Chevalier,
1961.

With George Peppard
and Roddy McDowell in
The Subterraneans, 1960.

With the marvelous Tom Bell in
The L-Shaped Room, 1962.

Receiving a BAFTA award for *The
L-Shaped Room* from Prince Philip.

With Charles Aznavour in the film
segment "Les Deux Pigeons," directed
by René Clair, 1962.

With Orson Welles in *Is Paris Burning?*,
a blockbuster film based on the bestselling
novel by Larry Collins and Dominique
Lapierre, 1966.

Shooting *Father Goose* in exotic Jamaica with Cary Grant, 1964.

With Warren Beatty in the 1966 sex comedy *Promise Her Anything*.

In 1966, at a Royal Command Performance of the film *Born Free* with Julie Christie, Warren Beatty, and Catherine Deneuve.

My two children, Jennifer and Christopher, in Rome, where I was filming *The Head of the Family*, a picture dealing with the place of women in Italian society.

During a pause in the shooting of the 1977 film *Valentino*, comparing my dancer's feet with Rudolf Nureyev's! This film was directed by Ken Russell.

The "Camille" kiss in *Valentino* with Nureyev.

In 1969 with Michael Laughlin, my third husband. We lived in London before returning to Hollywood.

In London in 1974 for the premiere of *That's Entertainment!*, with Cyd Charisse, Fred Astaire, and Gene Kelly.

Playing the great Coco Chanel in the TV film *The Man Who Lived at the Ritz*, 1988.

Going to the first César Awards in France in 1975 with François Truffaut.

In the TV film *Lenin: The Train* with Dominique Sanda and Ben Kingsley.

In Venice for the festival for *Le Divorce*, with Ismail Merchant, James Ivory, and Thierry Lhermitte.

Le Divorce, with Naomi Watts, Sam Waterston, and James Ivory.

Fierce-looking writer Petrolacci, who taught me to write . . .

Beside the river that flows past La Lucarne aux Chouettes, the stone warehouse that I converted into an auberge and continue to run today.

Reading a bedtime story to my two grandsons, Freddie and Benjamin.

In Hollywood, where I received an Emmy for *Law & Order: SVU* in 2007.

around a few châteaux, then followed the trail of the famous Italian towns Peter had visited in a broken-down jalopy as an impoverished student. Lake Como fulfilled my romantic expectations—in La Spezia I learned to love the trompe l'oeil decors that enrich even the poorest façade. In Siena the flag wavers' spectacle in medieval costumes sent my heart soaring. We saw Pisa and wondered how long the tower could stand. Peter's knowledge of the classics enriched these days of beauty, harmony, and marital bliss. My heart was content, I had made the right decision; it looked as if breaking my contract with MGM was a brilliant move.

As Stratford-upon-Avon's first lady, I played my part as best I could in welcoming prestigious guests. One of the first to be invited for lunch in our flamboyant Victorian dining hall was Benjamin Britten and his collaborator and companion, the tenor Peter Pears. Peter Hall had a solid musical education, and he was a Suffolk boy, like Britten. I suspect he would have liked to ask Britten to compose music for Shakespeare's plays; Stratford always had excellent music played by its own little brass band. For Britten's visit I was quite nervous about fulfilling my function of hostess and asked the theater restaurateur to advise me on the dishes and wines. I chose sole in béchamel sauce—I felt up to advising our bad-tempered Austrian cook on the sauce—but found myself quite ignorant when it came to the wine. The maître d' mischievously let me point to the only name on the white wine list that I seemed to recognize, the very famous sauternes, Château Yquem—a sweet dessert wine, served at Christmastime with foie gras but most often with dessert, and certainly never with fish. Benjamin Britten was talking animatedly when he was served; he brought the wineglass to his lips, stopped in midsentence, shocked, and blurted out, "It's sweet wine!" He looked at the bottle and smiled in my direction as one does to a small child, "Château Yquem!" He shook his head and added, "You should never serve that wine with fish." I stuttered lame excuses about having made a mistake and never recovered my composure. It took me years to learn. Sometime later Peter and I went to the Aldeburgh Festival to hear Britten's *Turn of the Screw,* an inspired opera, but I kept remembering my faux pas.

John Gielgud came to Stratford for a season to take on a few of the parts he hadn't played yet. Invited for lunch at Avoncliffe, he arrived late, rushed into the dining hall, where we were already seated, waving

triumphantly a charming nineteenth-century chamber pot, of a sugges-
tive brown color. "Leslie! Look what I found! A French chamber pot!"
A fit of laughter started that lasted for fifteen minutes before we could
all calm down. Whenever I give a large party, I never fail to serve it
filled with chocolate mousse in tender memory of that delightful man.

Peter and I gave a grand reception for Franco Zeffirelli, whom I
knew well from my friend Lila de Nobili, the set and costume designer.
Both Franco and Lila had been assistants to Luchino Visconti, but I
knew Lila earlier, from my ballet days with Roland Petit. I am proud
to have introduced Lila to Peter Hall, who did his most memorable
Shakespearean comedies with her. The party was on the opening night
of Franco's *Othello* with Gielgud—not a successful production, I must
admit, as the passionate Moor was not a part for Gielgud, but I didn't
care, I only had eyes for Ingrid Bergman, who had made the trip from
Paris, where she lived, to be present at Franco's premiere. The event was
highly publicized, very fashionable, but a disaster with the critics.

Franco and I were good friends, too. He tried to set up, with me
in the lead, a film of *La Dame aux Camélias* from the novel by Alexandre Dumas *fils* (the basis for the American film *Camille* and the opera
La Traviata). Franco's angle was that the lady who inspired Dumas—
Alphonsine Plessis was her real name—had died of tuberculosis at
twenty-three. Although the role had always been played by mature
actresses, from Sarah Bernhardt to Garbo, he wanted to do a version
where she was played by a young woman. Unfortunately, the project
never left the ground.

I think it might be interesting here to relate my contribution to one
of the world's greatest stage and film successes: *Becket,* by Jean Anouilh.
When news hit England in 1959 that the best playwright of the day had
written a play about Thomas à Becket and King Henry II of England,
Peter immediately set out with me for Paris, even though Anouilh's
business lawyer had been quite adamant: Anouilh did not want the
piece to be done outside of France because of the disastrous notices it
had received. We went to see it and understood soon enough why the
press had been so hostile. Anouilh himself had done the staging, and
it was pathetically nonexistent! There *was* no staging. The actors, lined
up on the front of the boards, spoke directly to the public, without the
least effort of contact with one another. No interaction! I knew Jean

Anouilh from my days with Roland Petit, for whom he had written several ballet scenarios. While Peter had to go back to England, I called Anouilh, who was kind enough to agree to an appointment. We met in his suite in what was then the Hôtel France et Choiseul (now the Hôtel Costes). Anouilh was polite but firm: Under no circumstances would he allow the play to be done outside of France—he had been brutally slain by the press and didn't want to be exposed to more outrage. I took a deep breath and told him bluntly that the reason the press had found fault with his marvelous play was the staging, or rather the lack thereof. He was a writer, not a director. Anouilh stopped breathing for a second, then recovered his composure. I continued. I told him with fervor that under Peter's staging the play would be a hit. I swore to him that it would—the material was so great. I pressed on further, reminding him what a success Peter had had with his *Waltz of the Toreadors* and said that Peter felt *Becket* would be an even bigger hit. I finally convinced him. He agreed to let Peter direct it in London, where it became the play of the year before reaching New York with the same success. Hollywood continued its triumphant trajectory. *Becket* the film won the Oscar for Best Screenplay and received some ten other nominations.

In 1959 Hollywood called me again, to start *The Man Who Understood Women* for 20th Century Fox, from an idea by Romain Gary, with the great Henry Fonda, Cesare Danova, and Marcel Dalio in a small part. The character played by Fonda was loosely based on Orson Welles in his relationships with women—more precisely, with Rita Hayworth. Romain Gary was a charming man, delightfully narcissistic and sentimental like a Russian, obsessed with women to his sad end. I met him and his wife, Lesley Blanch, on this film, and they became close friends. Their home, the French consulate on Outpost Drive in Hollywood, was the place to meet for exotic dinners (their cook was a grumpy old Russian woman) and smart conversation, perhaps the only place in Hollywood where politics was an accepted topic of conversation.

This film would have been a real pleasure if Nunnally Johnson, the renowned scriptwriter, had not decided that he wanted to direct as well. Brilliant as he was at the typewriter, he was hopeless behind a camera. His daughter Margie, the film's editor, was called in every half hour to tell him where to place the camera. His rhythm of work reflected all the

charm and shortcomings of the South—namely, a snail's pace. Hank
Fonda, who could tell from years of experience that the film was getting
bogged down, simply retreated in aloof irritability, every once in a while
blowing up in exasperation. Most of the time we sat on the set while
waiting for our scene to be lit, and I could think of nothing to say to this
long and lean figure, brooding over his anger. He was the great Henry
Fonda, but his shyness and uncommunicativeness equaled my own. I
couldn't have been more surprised when, years later, his daughter Jane
told me that he had been in love with me during the film.

Socially, life was quite enjoyable, though. The children, Lilène, and
I were staying at the Chateau Marmont. I socialized with the Fondas.
If Hank was undemonstrative, his wife, Afdera, was extravagant and
amusing like the Italian socialite that she was. She bid at a Beverly Hills
auction sale for a bed supposed to have belonged to Marie Antoinette.
"Only its price can attest to its authenticity," remarked Fonda with a
sigh.

Later we met in New York, where my memory situates us in Edith
Piaf's dressing room. I had seen the Piaf phenomenon operate several
times in Los Angeles. A few notes into her song, the noisy audience
would fall under her spell, in awed silence. At Carnegie Hall, riding a
wave of adoration, she didn't let her public down. In her dressing room,
finding herself in close contact with one of her idols, Edith Piaf—all
five feet of her—looked up with ravishment at the six-foot-tall Henry
Fonda as if she were seeing an archangel—I think I noticed him blush
under his tan. She kindly showed concern at my single state. "On your
own, really? How do you manage? I couldn't live a day without my
man." True, I was on my own. Peter had come to Los Angeles for a visit,
but a very brief one. I missed him badly.

I think it must be during that short visit on that film that Peter and
I went to see Aldous Huxley, who lived in the Hollywood hills. Peter
wanted to commission his friend the writer John Whiting to write a play
on Huxley's historical book *The Devils of Loudun,* a horrendous account
of a rejected woman's fanatical revenge. The fact that the woman was
a nun (Sister Jeanne-des-Anges) and the man a priest (Father Urbain
Grandier) makes the story all the more provocative.

We were invited to lunch at the Huxley house, in old Hollywood.
Huxley looked ill and weak and wore extremely thick glasses. His wife

was there, and I looked upon her with great curiosity, as I had read his novel *The Genius and the Goddess*. There were already three guests when we arrived. Two were father and daughter; the third was a doctor. During our entire stay, the conversation ran on the subject of the ascendance of mind over matter. The topic, which was obviously of urgent interest to Huxley, began when the doctor in question explained how he had been diagnosed by colleagues with an aggressive lung cancer and was given barely three months to live. At that point he had abandoned all professional activity to concentrate solely on curing himself. Within six months his colleagues were mystified to observe that not only was he still alive but there was no trace left of the disease. We were all hanging on the words of this man, who then described his therapy. Every hour (or perhaps every two hours; I don't remember precisely) he drank a different juice—red peppers, extracted with a juice extractor, raw liver juice (ugh!), and so on—during the course of the day. One detail seemed especially mysterious to me: This doctor kept his body below normal temperature in order to slow down the progress of the disease. There was later extensive talk about psychedelic drugs and their effects.

Then the father and daughter told of their experience, which was even more astonishing. They insisted that human beings had faculties of vision that were neither discovered nor used. Humans could see from other parts of their body than with their eyes—their skin, for instance. Peter and I came out of this luncheon not only pleased to have obtained the rights to Huxley's book—which in 1960 became a very successful play, *The Devils*—but quite disoriented about basic laws of mortality we'd never questioned before. Perhaps, with enough concentration, one need never die, and perhaps, with the proper training, even blind men could be taught to see? Aldous Huxley himself died the twenty-second of November, 1963—incidentally, the same day JFK was killed.

Later in 1959, Arthur Freed decided to do a film about the Beat Generation from a novel by Jack Kerouac, *The Subterraneans,* in which I had to play a very neurotic girl (part Cherokee in the book), given to wrist-slashing and self-destructive behavior, who flips for good when Leo, her lover, dumps her. We filmed the exteriors in the heart of San Francisco, a very wise move, considering the uninspiring, lethargic nightlife of Beverly Hills in the 1950s, where the movie community worked from 6:00 A.M. to 6:00 P.M. and turned their lights off by 9:00. Nothing, however, could shake the quiescent placidity of a cast and crew who—at that time—knew little of the drug scene of San Francisco. (I was just as ignorant as the others.) The film should have been done with real violence and despair, black-and-white photography, and handheld camera—preferably by John Cassavetes. But even then I don't think that a small minority of the public would have seen the movie, as Cassavetes's work gained real recognition in the United States only after Europe discovered him. Still, I had to perform one of the most daunting scenes in my career—running naked in a crowded San Francisco street. The camera was hidden in a truck under a tarpaulin, and the side streets had been blocked off so that nothing could stop my hysterical flight, but for weeks afterward I could hear the yells of women in my ears—"Look at her! She's naked! Stop that girl!"—and their extended arms trying to control me. After it was over, I trembled with shock for quite a while, as one does after an accident.

An unpleasant atmosphere developed on the set. The cast, including George Peppard and Janice Rule, who up to then had been my best friend, banded together against me. The script was written by Robert Thom, Janice's husband—who might have thought she should play the lead. At a dinner before the film started, George Peppard put it to me straight, with no emotions or frills: "Since we are going to play lovers, we should go through the experience." I turned down his offer but never quite recovered from the unease that set in. I thought then, and still do now, that he was a wooden actor. The director, Ranald MacDougall, spelled it out to him: "George, you have only two expressions, the front and the profile." Only the genial Roddy McDowall would talk to me, and remained a very dear friend. I'm sorry this film didn't turn out better, as there were some great musicians among us: Gerry Mulligan and André Previn, accompanied by Shelly Manne and Red Mitchell, not forgetting the great Carmen McRae.

Peter didn't come to visit during this production; in fact, he came less and less to my film locations and even disputed my right to go and work abroad. My loneliness was extremely painful for the six to eight weeks that the filming lasted; long-distance telephoning was no consolation for an empty bed. Retrospectively, I think his absence was somewhat deliberate, to discourage me from pursuing my film career. Temptations to have affairs were sometimes avoided, sometimes not—for both of us. Why couldn't we manage our lives more harmoniously? All I wanted was just to work with him and have a place in his life.

The moments when we were together were rich and fulfilling. The smell of pine trees by the salty beach still fills my nostrils when I think of the perfect September holiday we spent in Formentor, Majorca, when my darling Jenny had her second birthday. With blond curls framing her rosy face, she strutted into our bedroom at eight in the morning and opened the conversation with, "Anyway, I've got pretty hair. . . ." That day she showed her mettle by refusing to be carried when we came back from the beach for lunch. Bare feet on the hot sandy path, she wasn't going to have the baby treatment anymore. I only wished I hadn't been chosen as the background of every snapshot on the beach. A husband would say to his wife, "Move a little to the left," and that meant right in front of me. I decided, we really must buy a summerhouse. . . .

Since my contract settlement with MGM, I was free to accept European offers. An attractive one came in 1960 for a part in an international film by Abel Gance, who in 1927 had revolutionized the technique of cinema with his film *Napoleon,* which played on three screens. He now proposed a new film on Napoleon, featuring the coronation and the Battle of Austerlitz, and had enough male and female parts for nearly all the European actors—Elvire Popesco would play Napoleon's mother; Claudia Cardinale and Anna-Maria Ferrero had been requested; and among the men, Vittorio De Sica, Orson Welles, Jean Marais, Jack Palance, Jean-Louis Trintignant, Michel Simon, and the least famous among them all, Pierre Mondy, playing the great man himself.

Peter wouldn't allow me to go to Paris; his fear was that I wouldn't come back. I had all the trouble in the world convincing him that I'd be gone less than a week. My part was that of Mademoiselle de Vaudey, a spirited young lady, ravished between the sheets by a hasty Napoleon. I was quite apprehensive about acting in my mother tongue, French, after nine years in American films. My worries were unfounded; in fact, the experience was extremely gratifying. I was at ease in my native language. After we finished our scene, Abel Gance wished there were more of it. "Let's make up another scene," he declared, delighted with the first one. "But, monsieur, I don't have a second costume!" He brushed the problem aside: "Get wardrobe to fit you with something." The improvised scene was fun. Unfortunately, the film was already too long, and the scene ended up on the cutting-room floor. At seventy, Abel Gance was younger in spirit than most directors in their youth. Some journalists asked me what the difference was between working in France and in Hollywood, and all I could think of was that in contrast to Hollywood, where everything was so very controlled, in Paris the press was allowed on the set. During the rehearsals so many photographers stood between Pierre Mondy and myself that I could hardly see him!

After refusing the offer for seven months because of a project with Jean Renoir that ultimately couldn't get off the ground (*Three Rooms in Manhattan,* by Georges Simenon), I finally accepted in 1960 *Fanny,* from the plays by Marcel Pagnol, to be directed by Josh Logan. Marcel Pagnol was amenable to an American production of his work but recommended that Logan cast the part of Fanny with an actress eminently "faukable." (I saw the letter in which that term was written—Pagnol was an Old English scholar.) The musical version had been a success on Broadway, but apart from the theme music ours was going to be a straight romantic drama, compressed from the Pagnol trilogy into one romance.

In the film, César (Charles Boyer) owns a bar in the port of Marseilles, and his nineteen-year-old server/son (Horst Buchholz), after seeing ships and sailors all his young life, dreams of going to sea. His only hesitation stems from his love for Fanny (me), who sells fish at a waterfront stall. After they spend a night together, Fanny encourages him to go, convinced that he must fulfill his longing for the sea if he is to be happy in life—only what she didn't expect happens: She becomes pregnant. With Marius gone off on a long voyage and seeming to have forgotten about her, she is urged by her mother to marry the older but rich widower, Panisse (Maurice Chevalier), to give her child a name. After three years Marius comes back disenchanted from a trip around the world to discover that Fanny is married, but he is unaware that she has a child. With maturity he realizes that only Fanny matters to him, and he comes to tell her so, hoping to get her away from Panisse. He hears a child cry and realizes what has happened. Only a few years later, when Panisse dies of a heart attack, can he be reunited with Fanny and his own son.

Josh Logan (nominated for an Oscar for *Fanny*) was a giant in size and in spirit. He had such grand visions and emotions that I called him "Jupiter." Filmed in the south of France with a magnificent cast, *Fanny* turned out to be a rich, colorful production. The flirtatious scene between Maurice Chevalier and myself stands in my memory as one of the most enjoyable of my career. Maurice relished his part and brought nuance to every line of his script—I think we played a fine duet together. (Maurice was nominated for a Golden Globe.) Charles Boyer, a consummate actor, showed that he was capable of playing a far wider range of roles than was usually offered to him. He dropped his suave French-lover persona and played with great humor the southern excesses of his character César. (He, too, was nominated for an Oscar.) Horst Buchholz was the most delightful accomplice, tender and sensitive, with a romantic flow that made love scenes easy and memorable. Fanny is probably the most romantic part I was given to play; I allowed myself to reveal emotions that enriched me—that role was such a treat. I was also nominated for a Golden Globe, but my time hadn't come yet.

We all stayed in a charming hotel in Cassis, where Charles and Maurice remained for dinner every night, while we, the younger crowd, went down to the port for grilled fish and lots of laughs. Maurice had the reputation of being parsimonious. Understandably, his very modest beginnings had left scars. One night, coming back from dinner at the port, I dropped in at the table where Maurice and Charles were finishing their dinner. Maurice whipped out a platinum pencil that was tucked into his breast pocket with its twin, the platinum pen, and marked his wine bottle with his name—and then, with careful concentration, did the same on his bottle of water. A faint grin on his lips, Charles remarked on the beautiful pencil. "Right you are to notice," purred Maurice with pride. "I have the same in gold, and I decide every morning whether I will use my gold set or my platinum one." Maurice was obviously pleased with the immense success of his career.

It would have been utter bliss if Peter had come for even a short while. Other wives and husbands visited, attracted by the irresistible Mediterranean climate—couples formed among the singles in the crew and cast, as always on location. But I was alone—too much alone. True, the children were with me—Christopher even played a short scene as my three-year-old child—but I needed my man, as Edith Piaf said. In the evenings, when the first assistant shouted, "It's a wrap!" my heart had nothing to contemplate but woeful solitude. In need of fulfillment, my longing heart turned to Jack Cardiff, our remarkable cameraman. Just a passing infatuation, but what became very clear was the difficulty of reconciling marriage and a movie career.

When I went back to England, the days dragged on, as Peter was always busy—too busy even to be on hand when his parents came to visit. The children were starting school, and I turned to primitive painting and gardening but watched wistfully the rehearsals and performances directed by Peter at the Royal Shakespeare Theatre in Stratford—wishing I were part of the company. Even the acting classes given by Michel St. Denis were off-limits for me. Peter explained that my participation would be construed as favoritism, since I didn't belong to the company. I knew I had a long way to go if I were going to share in Peter's professional life. According to him, my French accent was a drawback, and I needed to learn my way on the stage. I desperately wanted to.

At that point Peter Langham, the director of the rival Shakespeare company in Stratford, Ontario, in Canada, where Sir Tyrone Guthrie had mounted such magnificent productions, made an amazing offer— two great Shakespearean parts for the summer season: Cleopatra and Rosalind. Exactly what I longed to try. If Peter didn't think I was ready for his theater, I could develop my skills in Ontario, where director and public were not so doctrinaire. On the other hand, I was aware that it would mean another painful separation of three months. Peter's reaction was unambiguous: I was embarrassing him. His wife was not to play Shakespeare with a rival company. Brokenhearted but conscious of my duties to my family, I complied and backed out from a contract I had already agreed to verbally.

Peter finally became aware that my distress was real and that our marriage was heading straight into a brick wall if he continued to ignore me as an actress. In 1961 he decided to stage *Ondine* by Jean Giraudoux at the Aldwych Theatre—the London home of the Royal Shakespeare Company. Ondine, niece of the king of the Waterworld, is a water nymph with magical powers. A roving knight, Hans von Wittenstein zu Wittenstein (Richard Johnson), enters one stormy night the fisherman's hut where she lives with her foster parents. He falls in love with this enchanting, whimsical girl and decides to take her to his castle, although he is engaged to Countess Bertha (Sîan Phillips). Before they go, the king of the Waterworld warns her of the pact that binds her should she fall in love with a human: Her betrothed will die if he is unfaithful to her. But Ondine, as sure of him as she is of herself, follows Hans. Of course, within six months he is unfaithful and announces that he wants to marry Countess Bertha after all. The king of the Waterworld tells Ondine that Hans must die. She pleads that he be spared, but the king is relentless. As soon as Hans passes away, she also loses her human memory. Looking down at Hans, lifeless at her feet, Ondine murmurs, "How sad! I would have liked to meet him. I think I could have loved him!"

The production was magical and romantic—the sets with green fluid lighting were pure enchantment. Right from the start, however, I was "the boss's wife" and wasn't treated kindly by the company. Every "movie princess" who thinks she can measure her skills against those of the old British stage warriors is in for a rude awakening. Because I was not armed to defend myself, I got the rookie treatment: My native shyness gave a free hand to the disgruntled actors who played every stage trick on me. Unfortunately, Peter had other worries and didn't have time to give me the training and support I needed. My fault. Serves me right for trying to invade his world.

Here I can perhaps recall our last holiday en famille—in Maratea, south of Naples. On our first day, a visit to Naples was planned, where all the seductions and historical splendors of the jaded Mediterranean town assault you with a pervasive odor of rot. Later we also visited Capri, but without the children—a short day visit. Capri had been too renowned for too many centuries to appeal to my taste; nothing to discover there.

But the inaccessible village of Maratea itself was not yet fashionable. The road to Locanda delle Donne Monache Hotel, which had been nearly washed away by recent rains, was easily some four hours' drive from Naples to what seemed like the world's end. In those days poverty and, more specifically, tuberculosis colored the cheekbones of every villager with pink fever spots. The contrast between the primitive conditions in the village and the white-glove service in the hotel would have been shocking were it not for the general conviction that the success of this hotel was going to encourage tourism and bring work to this arid village in Calabria. Every morning a minibus with the elegant hotel crest painted on its doors drove us to the pebbled beach, where I remember teaching my children the basic swimming motions on a beach towel.

13

The Prediction

*D*irector Peter Brook, who is Russian and therefore superstitious, believed in occult forces; he recommended to me a fortune-teller with genuine talents of divination. I went to see her, intrigued and apprehensive. The lady announced with authority that she could see three films in my immediate future. I corrected her, "No, two. I have *two* films planned." She became adamant. "Why do you contradict me? I know, I can see. You will do three pieces of work very close to one another, and the second one will bring you great recognition." I stopped disagreeing and thanked her, thinking that I should not antagonize a lady who might have some influence on events. She soon proved right.

The first film was a mediocre adventure, *Act of Mercy,* retitled *Guns of Darkness,* directed by dear Puffin Asquith, who was far too sophisticated and sensitive for action films. His intimate knowledge of ancient Greek and Latin didn't prepare him for outdoor adventures. He dressed in blue overalls like a mechanic and wore workman's boots, but braving the wilderness was still not his cup of tea. David Niven was my partner—no love lost between us. He and David Opatoshu competed like schoolboys for the dressing room closest to the set. To settle the dispute, I asked to have my trailer outside. The story of the film relates the escape, across dangerous insurgent territory in South America, of an ambassador and his wife, with every deathly danger lurking. I learned how not to touch or eat cactus flowers, even when starving—the little prickly hairs stay in your mouth for several days. The film doesn't reveal anything new about human behavior, any more than my colleagues' childishness did. Having nothing particularly nice to say about David Niven, I'll clam up—only this: He had the largest hands of any partner of mine. It seems that during my young years the scripts often included a scene in which I am slapped—I'm glad to say that striking women is not politically correct anymore, but in the fifties and sixties leading men had a field day smacking women.

The only redeeming grace of that film was the east coast of Spain, where we shot the exteriors in a beautiful arid landscape with a quaint village hanging on the edge of an impressive cliff. At mealtimes the production served two different meals—bland English fare for the Brits and, for the local crew, hot, colorful, and tasty Spanish food, my favorite.

Next, against Peter's vehement wishes, I accepted a role in one of four sketches in a French film directed by René Clair, with a delightful Charles Aznavour as leading man, under the overall title *Les Quatre Vérités*. The story is loosely based on a fable by Jean de La Fontaine, "Les Deux Pigeons." The moral of the story is this: No need to travel far to find happiness, look right in your own backyard. A young model finds herself locked in her apartment just as she is ready to leave for the most fashionable weekend of the year, *le 15 août*, when Paris is totally deserted. She calls an SOS locksmith (Aznavour), who inadvertently locks them both inside with no way of contacting help. (This film was made before portable phones.) They find each other's presence very pleasant and spend a delightful weekend spread out on a beach towel, way up on the roof of the six-floor apartment building, culminating in a candlelit dinner—the rest is happily predictable.

Charles Aznavour was thrilled to be in films and honored to be cast by the great René Clair. He told me that he'd accepted the part without even reading the script. He had a sweet, naïve side to his personality. He idolized Frank Sinatra. Having seen a movie still of Sinatra lounging about on a chaise longue surrounded by his cronies, he did the same and received his pals all the livelong day. I've never met a more relaxed actor—perfect instincts, never gave a false note, in acting as well as in singing.

I very much enjoyed the experience of working with René Clair, who had been directing legendary comedies since the silent days. He had a unique way of working. The picture was timed and edited even before being filmed. René would first stage each scene, playing the leading part—man or woman—with swiftness and wit. His script girl read the other characters while she timed the scene with a chronometer. He would then ask her, "How long?" She'd give the timing, accurate to the second. "Too long!" and he would play the scene again, finding ways to make it tighter. Only when the timing was as sharp as he had planned on his drawing board did he give the actors the green light to copy him, again controlled by the chronometer. This method quickly became very frustrating, as I like to participate in my work. He gave this excuse: "Most actors"—I think he said actresses—"don't know how to act, and I don't have time to teach them. The only actor I could ever trust was Gérard Philipe. He knew what he was doing." I told him that I wished he would let me show him what I'd prepared. I surprised him with little inventions, and from that moment on he let me participate in the creation of my character. The key words were "sharpness," "rhythm," "color." I followed those precepts perfectly. He was remarkably thrifty with the film negative, doing a second take just to cover, in case of a mishap in the printing process. He said there hardly were rejects on the cutting-room floor, as his films could only be edited the way he had planned them. This method seems to reflect a great deal of self-confidence—which I suppose he had—but he was also remarkably modest. He thought his career in Hollywood had been a failure, because it had been so short. He'd forgotten that nearly every one of his Hollywood films was a masterpiece: *The Ghost Goes West, I Married a Witch, It Happened Tomorrow,* and *And Then There Were None.* He was friendly and chatty and spoke with affection of Veronica Lake: "The trouble with her is she didn't have confidence in herself. Nothing could convince her that she was beautiful. It was a fight every morning to get her to face the camera."

During a dull moment on the set, René started to berate a member of the crew—the scene was turning ugly, but no one seemed to come to the defense of the poor victim. Shocked at first, I asked someone, "What's going on? How dare he talk like this to a subordinate." Then I saw the wide grins on the faces of the crew and the guy himself, who didn't seem affected in the least. Someone finally explained, "It's just an act. René never does a film without this guy. They go through this routine when things get a little slow." René Clair had another memorable talent that impressed me: He could taste a glass of wine—good wine—and tell you whether the vineyard was on the flat or on a slope. He was a *chevalier du tastevin.*

*   *   *

Then, suddenly, in the winter of 1961–62, the important project predicted by the fortune-teller turned up: *The L-Shaped Room,* from the British bestseller by Lynne Reid Banks. Producer James Woolf of Romulus Films (*The African Queen* [uncredited] and *Room at the Top*) proposed I play the part written in the novel for a British girl. I was flattered, but the press demanded to know: Why a French actress? Jimmy Woolf didn't bother to answer. My performance was my answer: I won the BAFTA (British Academy Award) and the Golden Globe. I was also nominated for an Oscar but didn't win.

At the height of the so-called kitchen-sink movement (realistic dramatic films about the struggling classes), the director of our film was going to be Academy Award winner Jack Clayton; the scriptwriter, Bryan Forbes; and director of black-and-white photography (incidentally, this was my last black-and-white film) Douglas Slocombe, with editing by Anthony Harvey (who was later the director of *The Lion in Winter* with Katharine Hepburn). This was the most prestigious British project of the year.

The first good thing that happened was meeting Jimmy Woolf, a British producer in the grand old style. Kind and generous, he insisted on starting everything with a dinner—and in the best restaurant, at that. He lived in Grosvenor House on Park Lane and quite obviously loved luxury—he simply respected and promoted everything expensive. He always thought that I was far too reasonable, and just like Aunt Alicia in *Gigi,* he gave me lessons on how to sharpen my taste. Example: the grand actress Martita Hunt, who, looking at a wine list, kept her eyes at the price column on the right rather than on the label column on the left and, running her finger down, invariably stopped at the bottom of the page on the highest three-digit figure. "This one!" she would command. He also gave as an example Paulette Goddard, who demurely asked her paramours for a painting when love was on the horizon. The clever girl had assembled quite a collection, he told me, adding wisely, "Jewels are far too obvious, and they can lose their value." His best pupil was Laurence Harvey, whose exploits he proudly listed: "His private 'charms' got him everything." There was such a sharp contrast between Jimmy's message and the sad situation of Jane Fosset, my character in *The L-Shaped Room,* that he may have wined and dined me royally to compensate for the heavy acting I had to do. He was a prince, and I loved him.

Early in the project, Jack Clayton called me to say that private circumstances made it impossible for him to direct the film. During dinner Jimmy Woolf courteously asked me to name another director. I immediately mentioned Bryan Forbes, whose enchanting *Whistle Down the Wind* had just come out and who'd done beautiful work on our script. He had written a grand melodrama, with plenty of colorful characters, rich intrigue, and a semi-happy ending that was realistic rather than sentimental. I was thrilled when he agreed to direct. I did, however, find a serious weakness in the script regarding my character. Jane Fosset was too passive on the whole, and especially in the main scene. "Have it out with Bryan," was Jimmy Woolf's suggestion.

So there I was, developing my argument to Bryan Forbes, who seemed to be doodling with a pen, hardly looking at me, to the effect that I expanded and repeated my point several times, with more and more conviction. I finally stopped, thinking *Well, isn't he rude? He doesn't even listen to me.* At that point Bryan handed over the pages he was writing on and said, "Is this what you mean?" He had rewritten the scene while I was speaking. It was perfect, and we played it word for word as it had been set down then. Bryan was a very rapid wit with an ear for popular vernacular. If I found his directing a little controlling at times, I am immensely grateful for his help in peeling away the onion skins until I reached the right level of emotion.

This was my greatest challenge yet as an actress. In my heart of hearts, it was the kind of dramatic part I had longed to play. My experience during the harsh days of the war and later in shabby digs on the road with the ballet company came rushing back to feed my imagination. Jane Fosset is a French girl from a middle-class family who becomes pregnant and, against everyone's advice, decides to have her child. Rejected by her family, penniless, she courageously takes on a job as a waitress but can only afford a shabby room in the slums of London, where she finds friendship and even love with a penniless young writer. This was so enormous and demanding a part, with such long hours of work, that I found it difficult to keep my emotional balance during the film. After a dramatic scene, I usually needed to sleep. I would ask Dougie Slocombe how long would the next lighting job take. "How

long do you need?" he would ask. "Give me forty minutes," I would
answer. "You've got it," he'd say, and I would curl up right there on the
set with the electricians and the grips calling orders to one another.
Workmen's voices were as comforting as a lullaby to me.

My parents came for a visit and stayed at our house in London—a
delicate situation, not to say stressful. My mother, who had gained a good
deal of weight, admitted for the first time that she had a problem with
alcohol. The revelation surprised me, as I hadn't noticed anything out
of the ordinary, other than that her mood continued to deteriorate—she
had become very touchy and carried on long, bitter harangues. Everyone had to walk on eggshells around her. I felt very sorry for her evident
unhappiness, yet I didn't know how to react to her revelation. I hadn't
been in close contact with people who drank heavily. I didn't even know
there was a disease called alcoholism. Peter would have a beer once in
a while, and personally I didn't like alcohol. I hardly ever drank anything except water or milk at the table. I hoped that my father could
deal with her. A cowardly reaction, I'm sure, but I feared my mother,
and was quite incapable of giving her advice or reprimanding her. I just
concerned myself with the film and my children.

To be as authentic as possible in the scene just prior to the baby's
delivery, I wore my old blue nylon dressing gown, stretched out of
shape on a realistic nine-month belly, when the American columnist
Sheilah Graham walked onto the set. I heard her lungs empty with an
"Ohhhhh!" of shock. No Hollywood star had ever shown herself on
the screen, with the bulky shape of a woman near delivery, especially
wearing as unflattering a garment as I was. This simply wasn't done. I
also believe I was the first movie actress who played with veracity the
tearing pains of giving birth. Male actors had always expressed pain
with crude honesty, in westerns and other action films, but a discreet
euphemism was all Hollywood good taste would allow to women. Now
such scenes are quite familiar, but as it was then, I broke the rules. It
took some courage; I was aware of the risk.

I cannot praise enough my generous partner Tom Bell. Destined
by his talent and good looks for a great future—he had the profile of
Gérard Philipe and the talent, too—but due to his weakness for alcohol, he ruined his chances. His acting was modern and strong, but I
had the overriding leading part. On the night of the BAFTA Awards,

Tom heckled Prince Philip, who was on the stage presenting: "Give us a joke, Philip!" he called out, over the prince's voice. The prince, pretending not to hear, just carried on. Tom repeated, louder, "I said, give us a joke, Philip!" Interrupting his speech, Prince Philip turned toward our table and said with great *à propos,* "If you wanted jokes, you should have hired a comedian!" A thunder of applause followed, but on that very night Tom Bell's film career was over—he never got a leading part again.

Peter wasn't with me on the evening I won my Best Actress award. No doubt a dress rehearsal or a premiere kept him in Stratford-upon-Avon. The next morning I rushed home by train, to find Peter holding a meeting with the management of the theater. Several times during the day, he asked me to prepare coffee and sandwiches for the group. There was hardly a thank-you thrown in my direction, and how could he forget to mention my achievement to his colleagues? Of course, I should have spoken up for myself; in fact, I should have shouted, "Hey, I won the BAFTA for Best Actress last night!" But I didn't, and I felt hurt.

After the BAFTAs came the nominations in Hollywood for the Golden Globes and the Oscars. The fortune-teller was right—this film was bringing me honors and recognition as an actress. Unfortunately, it didn't alter Peter's attitude toward my work. He was about to do *A Midsummer Night's Dream* with Charles Laughton as Bottom. Charlie spoke up for me. "She would be a fine Titania. Her French accent doesn't matter in this fairy tale." Peter asked me to read the part on three different occasions, then turned me down in favor of Mary Ure—who had a Cockney accent and no more stage experience than I. My dream of creating a theatrical team with Peter was fast vanishing. He didn't see it that way. Perhaps I didn't have the necessary talent or enough experience, though Peter confessed later that his behavior was dictated by professional jealousy.

At this point, I was earning large salaries, and Peter suggested that I fire my agent—he wanted to negotiate my contracts and get the remuneration. But I think that what he wanted most was to stop me from working altogether. In those years not just Peter but the whole of England pointed the finger at a working mother. Depression started to gain ground with me during the long inactive periods between films, and I felt once again caught in a quagmire. *Where is my life going? I've*

taken the wrong road—so stupid to insist on teaming up with a man who
only wants me as a housekeeper. I used to wake up in the morning and
think, *What shall I do with myself today? Tomorrow? With the rest of my*
life? I was only thirty-one years old, and the future with Peter stretched
with stultifying monotony between the kitchen, the nursery, and the
garden. His secretary shared more of his life than I did. In order to
take his dictation, she sat in the passenger seat of the Aston Martin
when we traveled from Stratford to London, while I had to perch on
the back plank. In London again, this young lady would inform me that
I must eat in the kitchen on such and such a day, because Peter would
be hosting his colleagues in the dining room. We'd go out in theatrical circles where I heard nothing but contempt expressed toward film
people, until I felt like screaming, "What about the cars, the London
house, the lifestyle that my work allows us?" But I said nothing and let
resentment build up. . . .

My heart soared sky-high when my Hollywood agent called to announce
that Cary Grant had seen *The L-Shaped Room* and wanted me to be his
partner in his next film, *Father Goose,* a comedy written by Peter Stone.
I was amazed! I was thrilled! Cary Grant! The name ringing in my
heart made me dizzy.

In April 1963 I escaped to the sunny skies of Hollywood for the
Golden Globes, where I won, and the Oscars, where I didn't. During
a party given in my honor by my agents, the inevitable happened: I
was seated facing the most talked-about young player in Hollywood—
Warren Beatty. Irresistibly handsome and intelligent, flirtatious banter
flying back and forth; lots of fun. The dinner over, Warren offered to
take me back to the Beverly Hills Hotel and . . . swept me off my feet. I
never arrived at my hotel room. The break I could see coming was happening. I lingered another week in Beverly Hills and had what they call
a "good time."

Back in Stratford I told Peter about Warren. I told him that I wanted
a separation. He tried to salvage our marriage with a trip to Marrakech.
Disastrous. Much too late in the day. We sat across the restaurant table
at mealtimes like two strangers trying to find a subject of conversation.
Unable to communicate, we came back sooner than planned and contacted our friend the playwright and lawyer John Mortimer. For me this

relationship was over; our worlds were too far apart. I had finally come to admit that our careers were irreconcilable. To this day I reproach myself for my immaturity, my lack of strength to overcome our difficulties. I had never been able to fight for my rights. Pain and an immense guilt about the children overcame me. Depression settled in my heart, the beginning of a long, intimate relationship.

There was a short respite when I was invited to the eleventh San Sebastián Film Festival, where for three days I was feted for my performance in *The L-Shaped Room*. People were warm and friendly, and I was in the Basque country, close to my beloved Goyetchéa.

It was in this state of turmoil that I flew to Hollywood to do *Father Goose*. Perhaps this is the moment to recall my first meeting with Cary Grant—in 1951, I think. He was married at the time to the very charming Betsy Drake. For some reason I was invited to dinner and to a performance of Mae West in *Diamond Lil* as part of a foursome with the Grants and young Mr. Loew as my escort. The show was fun, a caricature of sexy double entendre, not too subtle and, I'll admit, utterly foreign to anything I'd seen or known in my convent days. After the show Cary said we must go backstage to congratulate Mae West, who'd given him his first chance in films. He knocked on the door of her dressing room. A black maid opened and asked us to wait in a little salon while Miss West was getting herself ready. I remember wondering if the maid was called Beulah, as in "Peel me a grape, Beulah" (a very famous line in Mae West's play). Ten minutes went by before the door opened. Miss Mae West, no more than five feet tall but propped up on platform shoes, was standing on a little twelve-inch-high stage with two pink spotlights directed toward her. We stood in a straight line in front of her. Nothing would make her move her face right or left, out of the perfect position of the spots. She opened her arms and exclaimed, "Cary!" Whereupon he stepped forward like a little boy to be embraced by the pink-corseted lady. A friendly conversation ensued. The legend wished me good luck in friendly terms, as *An American in Paris* hadn't been released yet. I was surprised by the simplicity and warmth of her voice in contrast to the femme fatale pose, which she kept up resolutely—the businesswoman never dropped her guard.

The plot of *Father Goose* is quite classical. At the onset of World War II, a grumpy, whiskey-drinking dropout, Walter Eckland (Cary

Grant) is forced to run a radio station on a small island in the Pacific, to spot and report on enemy movement. Father Goose (his nom de guerre) discovers unwelcome neighbors, in the persons of a stern schoolteacher (me, playing Catherine Freneau), stranded after a shipwreck with seven schoolgirls, dressed in the best British school uniforms. Miss Freneau forces him to polish his act in front of her charges, which he doesn't like, but after many adventures he discovers that she is just the female he needs in his life. He even goes as far as shaving his beard for the hut-in-the-jungle-over-the-radio marriage ceremony.

Filming the exteriors of *Father Goose* in Jamaica was a brief season in heaven. The film company rented a lovely villa for me near the beach, with a cook in formal starched apron and a butler in livery—George—who took his shoes off every morning (he wore a black bow tie but no socks) and, with his cutlass between his teeth, climbed the nearest coconut tree to strike down a fresh one for breakfast. My friend Jack Larson came down to write the libretto of *Lord Byron* for Virgil Thomson. Later Warren paid a discreet visit. It was hot and sunny, with sudden evening winds swaying the palm trees like Balinese dancers. Nights sparkled with stars while frogs and exotic birds took over loud possession of the surrounding garden. One night George the butler heard footsteps in the bushes surrounding the house. He rushed in to grab a gun. I screamed at him, "Not the gun, George!" The prowler turned out to be a private detective sent by Peter's lawyer to gather evidence for the divorce.

What was Cary Grant like? Certainly not the relaxed, easygoing individual he seemed on the screen, but a very complex man, full of contradictions. There were the blessed moments when Archie Leach (his real name) would take over from Cary Grant and the acrobat/variety artist was back in the music halls of his youth—his eyes would twinkle, the mischievous adolescent would reappear to sing one of the nineteenth-century ditties of his repertoire, in the purest Cockney accent. On good days we would hear the story of his arrival in New York, when he sold neckties out of a suitcase, opened right there on Times Square's sidewalks, while he furtively checked right and left for "the heat." In case of trouble, he'd slam the valise shut and run.

But charming Cary had another, less appealing side to his personality; he could swiftly become the tyrannical producer who tormented the first assistant because the kid actors were straggling behind. Constantly complaining about money—"This film is ruining me!"—he postponed the start of shooting for several weeks suppposedly to refine a script that was already quite delightful, but blamed everyone else for the delay. He had mercurial mood swings. One day he gave me a wise lecture about raising children to be ambidextrous (left-handed at birth, he had taught himself to use both hands), but he flew at the prop man for placing a whiskey bottle near his right hand. After a moment during which everyone kept out of his reach, he would crack a joke, and his good humor would return. He kept us on our toes, all right. Cary was protective—I almost want to say paternal. It was evident that a child was what he wanted most in his life at that point. He was then going with Dyan Cannon, and his future daughter, Jennifer, must have been in his thoughts. His need for a family also included his own mother, whom he planned to visit at the end of shooting, as he did after every film.

He liked women who had a certain distinction and a natural look. He had a phobia about makeup and was quite right about that. In the 1960s movie makeup was thickly pasted on, with bold eyeliner, false lashes, and heavy lipstick. His own solution to makeup was simple: Every day at lunchtime, he would sit in his patio with a reflector to boost up his tan. The sun smoothed any blemishes on his dark skin. Of course, on the day when he shaved his beard for our marriage scene he had to cover his white chin with makeup. I pointed out mischievously that this is exactly what we ladies do when we wear makeup—smooth out the imperfections.

He had the same principles as Garbo did about the press. Seeing that I was pursued by the paparazzi because of my affair with Warren, he strongly advised me to remain totally aloof. "Don't talk, don't reveal, don't give away anything."

His way of learning his lines and testing the jokes came straight from his early variety days. He, too, had a black book—his was a fat black book containing all the jokes in the repertory. When we started on a new scene, he would gather us in his trailer, run the scene as written by Peter Stone, then consult his book for a similar situation. He would then come up with a lengthened version, usually lacking in finesse. An assistant would run off to have it printed while we tried it out in the trailer. The new pages would be distributed, and of course after a while Cary would recognize that Peter's version was the more concise and effective, and we would return to the original script. Peter Stone lent himself with good grace to this familiar routine, knowing that Cary needed this charade to learn his lines and feel comfortable with the material. Next, Cary had to convince himself that the scene worked with the public. Our public was the crew. Cary was never so happy as when a scene was ruined because someone had giggled during a rehearsal. On one of my close-ups, Cary was clowning so much that after the third take I had to beg him to turn his back to me. He taught me to keep a blank space after a punch line, like comics do on the stage. "Don't move during my punch line or after! Give 'em time to laugh."

I'm really quite pleased with myself in this part (except for the color of my suit—why on earth did I choose that weird mustard shade?). I have authority, a good sense of timing; I hold my own very well in the drunk scene. Except for the fact that I used to crack up a lot, I loved to do comedy, and Cary Grant was . . . well, simply the grandest partner one could dream of, and very sweet when in a good mood.

An amusing detail: In the scene where all the girls and I rob his boat during his sleep—napkins and linen are being looted away by seven little sprites while Mr. Eckland sleeps off his whiskey—Cary had actually gone to sleep during the take and had to be woken up when the director said "Cut!"

I was amazed at his exceptional physical fitness. Cary was sixty when we made *Father Goose.* In one scene he had to run in the jungle to avoid being spotted by a plane. I watched with admiration the incredibly graceful way this middle-aged man covered the ground as fast as the camera could follow him—with the agility and suppleness of a tiger in the forest.

On his sixtieth birthday, a telegram came from *Time* magazine to the desk of Universal Studios' press office. HOW OLD CARY GRANT? Not knowing how to handle the matter, the office sent the telegram to Cary's office. Cary read it and dictated the answer: OLD CARY GRANT FINE— HOW YOU?

Back in Hollywood after *Father Goose,* Warren wanted me to be his co-star in his next project, *What's New, Pussycat?,* which he was preparing with his close friend and surrogate father, the powerful producer

Charlie Feldman. Trouble! A matter of male pride had them both flexing their muscles. Warren insisted that his girl—me—play the female lead, while Charlie was adamant that his own girl, Capucine, be cast. I protested that I had another film to do with Rock Hudson, but Warren had to have his way. A tug-of-war took place, which Warren lost, because Charlie Feldman carried infinitely more weight in Hollywood. He controlled the money. Peter O'Toole was cast in Warren's part, with Capucine and Peter Sellers. Warren was extremely upset to have lost out on this modern comedy and blamed me! Meanwhile we went to Manhattan to see the nightclub show of a young comedian whom Warren had suggested write the script. His name was Woody Allen. Fresh and cheeky, he had a very different style from anyone else. He was like an impertinent student on the campus. Backstage after the show, Warren asked him, "How's the script coming on?" Woody was sort of self-deprecating, but Warren encouraged him. "Come on, it'll be great. And while you're at it, don't hesitate to write yourself a small part. . . ."

Universal, which after *Father Goose* thought one good thing should be followed up by another, had sent me a new script: *A Very Special Favor,* with Rock Hudson and Charles Boyer, directly in the vein of *Pillow Talk, Strange Bedfellows,* and *Lover Come Back,* all huge box-office winners. This time I'd take the part of a rigid and pathetically inefficient psychologist. Although I privately disliked the misogynistic, broad bedroom farce written by Stanley Shapiro, my agents thought it was foolish to refuse. "Just look at it as a career move," they said to convince me.

I have recently taken the trouble to view the film again and laughed for an hour and a half at the outrageous plot and over-the-top dialogue: Michel Boullard, a French father who lives in New York (Charles Boyer), is desperate because his daughter Lauren (me), whom he hasn't seen since she was three, is now thirty and still unmarried. He then discovers that the starched old maid is engaged to a namby-pamby nerd (Dick Shawn) who doesn't even know where her bedroom is. Boullard begs the jet-setting businessman/playboy Paul Chadwick (Rock Hudson), who owes him a favor, to save Lauren from the horrible fate of wearing the pants in her marriage. One or another character is forever engaged in deception and counterdeception, until Paul Chadwick pretends to be gay to appeal to Lauren's savior complex. But as this film was made in 1965, when sexual deviance was taboo, the homosexual interest is a woman in drag (Nita Talbot)! The film ends at the hospital, where Paul and Lauren are the happy parents of what appears to be an entire day-care center.

I am particularly proud of the scene where I am desperately trying to call Paul's room while carried on the shoulders of a demented herd of "Bisons" (an order of Shriners)—quite funny—and also the scene where I dance a wild flamenco after my love therapy with "El Magnifico."

The most attractive part of the film was that, at my request, I was sent to Paris to have my wardrobe designed by Yves Saint Laurent, whom I always considered the greatest designer of all. In the script breakdown, he had to design four business suits, two day dresses, two house dishabilles, and several elegant dinner outfits. Universal did things in a grand way. With a friend as chaperone, I stayed for two weeks at the Hôtel de Crillon. I was given the royal suite with a balcony over the place de la Concorde and its fountains. At night I would gaze endlessly at the original of the set I'd danced through with Gene Kelly. The only false note: Peter Hall's lawyer served me the divorce papers as I walked out of the plane, right in front of the press flashing their cameras. I don't think the photographers understood what was going on, but I went into shock. I was also served with an injunction against taking the children out of England for the holidays. While talking over the events of the day, my chaperone and I had a whiskey every night after dinner. She sipped and savored hers, while I downed mine in one swig to knock myself out. And I really hate whiskey.

And so I met Rock Hudson. I think we worked well together. Of course, everyone knew that he was gay, but the film community wasn't about to expose its most popular leading man and smash the golden egg. The description that fit him best was "a really nice guy," almost too nice to be true. He offered a totally smooth surface, so that his sexual inclination couldn't be detected. The fact that he chain-smoked was indicative of the incredible stress caused by his dissimulation—as was this nervous tic: He rubbed his thumbnails constantly, so that they were completely deformed, as if smashed by a hammer. He felt embarrassed, as if these nails could reveal his true leanings. He was grateful when I suggested that he glue on false ones for filming. So many actors have a minute defect that reaches major proportions in their own minds. I remember that Natalie Wood's left wrist bone was a little prominent—the result of a riding accident, I think. She concentrated all her anxieties on this wrist, as if anyone would notice the difference when no one ever looked at anything but those eyes of hers.

In February 1965 my divorce with Peter Hall was granted. The judge decreed that the children must go to a boarding school by the following September. Bedales was selected, and it was a good choice. Laurence Olivier's children with his third wife, the actress Joan Plowright, were there, as well as Daniel Day-Lewis and his sister Tamasin, the children of poet laureate Sir Cecil Day-Lewis, who became friends of my daughter's. A while after my children arrived, Princess Margaret and Tony Snowdon's children also enrolled at Bedales. It wasn't run on rigid military rules but had a liberal, artistic tone, and most important, it was coeducational. The children learned to play musical instruments—for Christopher the piano and the French horn, for Jenny the piano and the flute; they made all sorts of handmade crafts and worked on farming the grounds in each different season. From then on, my children came home to me one weekend, to Peter the next. They seemed to take to the new situation well—still, they were so young, so very young. . . . Parting on the train platform on Sunday evenings was always desperately wrenching for me. At least Peter and I didn't use the children as pawns on a bloody battlefield. I don't think Peter ever knew that his lawyer had forgotten to request custody. I had what is called "care and control." I never tried to take advantage of this.

Universal offered a third film that year, with Gregory Peck—*Mirage*. They must have been pleased with me. Warren, who now controlled my life, made me refuse it, to the chagrin of my agents. In retrospect, I'm sorry I declined the part, too. I would have loved to make a film with the great actor and star. We became friends later on, but I lost an important opportunity. At this point it is hard to explain my complete submission to my companion. Warren was very controlling, and I can only add that I had been so well conditioned by my mother that it took me many years to rebel against men's domination. And, with hindsight, it is also hard to say whether I used Warren to break up with Peter or whether Warren used me to further his career. Equal responsibility, I'd say.

14

Life with Warren

Warren and I were the flavor of the year, and we lived on the scale expected of us. We moved to a penthouse suite at the Beverly Wilshire Hotel. Warren drove a black convertible Lincoln Continental, and we ate at Frascatti's three times a week with other loose luminaries, when we didn't go to a party or a premiere. Basically Warren was a very sensitive, private person and not really comfortable in a crowd, but he played the part of a playboy movie star conscientiously, as if it were an acting job. He was totally absorbed by our new relationship. His all-enveloping tenderness—or almost motherly concern—was very flattering after a husband who'd had no time for me. An enormous telephone bill arrived each month when we were separated, even for a day. Warren would explain to his business manager that it was infinitely preferable to liquor or drug bills.

Because he believed that his girl should look like a top model, he took me to Jax (Jack Hanson's shop), where they made the best-fitting slacks in town. (Christian Dior was simply not suitable in the Beverly Hills of the sixties.) He told me what to wear, how to make up, and how to comb my hair, and he suggested his analyst to redress my imperfect personality. Warren was generous. When he thought he ought to give me a sizable piece of jewelry, he asked, "What do you want?" "Nothing," I answered, laughing, "I'm not interested"—until the day I suggested "A diamond ring?" like the one Arthur Loew had given Natalie Wood. Now he was the one who laughed it off. He longed for the approval of his sister, Shirley MacLaine, and admitted that we had a certain resemblance. "Neither of you is beautiful, but . . . you're both dancers, after all."

First thing in the morning, Warren wants to know what's going on today in Beverly Hills, but also in New York and Rome—and London and Chicago as well. Phone calls all around. "What's new, pussycat?" really was his opening line—to girls, at least.

Midmorning there's a phone call from the front desk. "Mr. Beatty, a messenger with an envelope for you?" Warren says, "Send it up." Scripts pile up, Warren can't make up his mind. He's deeply suspicious of anything commercial and rejects most offers. And yet he wants to work with the really great, the kind of filmmakers the Hollywood studios call "arty"—those who have difficulties setting up a project. He urges me to introduce him to Jean Renoir and suggests a new version of Gorky's *Lower Depths,* which Renoir had filmed years earlier as *Les Bas-Fonds* with the great French actor Louis Jouvet. Renoir plays along until he understands that Warren wants to play the lead; then he backs away like a cat from water. Renoir cannot stand any form of control.

By midafternoon, friends are talking about the evening's plans. "Tonight? Well, tonight we're going to So-and-So's house for spaghetti. Want to come, you and Leslie?" or, "Larry is having a projection of . . . Want to come?" Warren is elusive. "Maybe. I'll let you know later." We end up at Frascatti's, where we see Natalie Wood and Arthur Loew. Elliott Kastner comes along, and William Peter Blatty, escaped from the Valley, where his family lived on a very tight income. He keeps us in stitches with the spoof he played on Hollywood snobs, posing as the son of a sheik.

When things become a little quieter, Warren decides it's time to go to Europe. So off we go to spend Christmas in Rome. Once there, Warren refuses to leave his hotel bed and be a tourist. I'm so disappointed I roam the streets alone, stop to buy myself an expensive gold-and-diamond bracelet that I never wear and, farther down the same street, a carved stone fountain for my London home. Warren finally gets out of bed to go see Rex Harrison on the set of *Volpone* with Maggie Smith. Paparazzi follow us—that's the idea, isn't it? And why not spend New Year's in London, where we end up fighting in the streets like stray dogs, right in front of the Connaught Hotel, where we are staying. The cause of this fight? We can't get a table because we didn't make a reservation. We'll just have to order room service. It's so sad to be on the loose on New Year's Eve with no children, no party, no home, nothing convivial organized. We make so much noise yelling in the street that from a third-floor window an exasperated voice shouts down at us, "Shut uuuup!"

True, Warren was the most concerned lover one could hope for. Too much so, sometimes. One morning at 5:00 A.M. he shakes me awake. "What . . . ? What's the matter?" I ask. He answers with a frown, "You're sleeping. You're not thinking of me."

Two years of this. I'm not sure I can last at this pace. I suffer a bout of anorexia, like when I was a child. The stress is such that I suddenly get a very clear signal that I might start to drink or take drugs, anything to escape. Not good.

The fanfare continues with the premiere of *Father Goose* in New York and the endless lineups with the press, TV, newspapers, radio interviews, as well as photo shoots, followed by the opening in Chicago, where I find myself in the Christmas parade—I'm hopeless on a parade float. The whole extravaganza leaves me feeling even more stressed and desperately lonely. I cancel the rest of the tour and run back to Warren—crazy as he is, he's my only available pair of comforting arms. In London the premiere at the Odeon Leicester Square is a nice evening. I'm close to my children, and I'm at least home.

Warren has found a script for us to do together: *Promise Her Anything,* written by our friend William Peter Blatty, to be directed by Arthur Hiller. He manages to set it up with Warner Bros., then it falls through, then it's on again. To every day its own drama! Everyone loves Warren, but he can't do anything the easy way. To go from one point to another, mistrustful of the straight line, he's got to take complicated zigzags, lose himself, find the road again, until, after fighting all the windmills, he arrives out of breath and blames you for the delays. Everyone is too exhausted or exasperated to fight anymore, and he gets what he wants! He's manipulated me into accepting second billing—anything to stop the raging arguments! For tax reasons, Warren decides to do the film at Shepperton Studios, outside London. New York City at Shepperton! I'm not sure it's economically sound, but I suspect he wants me to be close to my children. He does have a heart, and he loves my kids. The film is the closest thing to a 1960s version of the Marx Brothers. Warren is a very good actor, he teaches me a lot, but what a hassle! He wants me to marry him. "No way!"

For the summer of 1965, Warren rents a mansion, which we call

"The White Elephant," in Holmby Hills, where the really big mansions are, on the edge of Beverly Hills. There are two swimming pools—his and hers—and the master bedroom is so large you need roller skates to reach one of the bathrooms. The owner, a poor bleached-blond lady in pink Jax slacks, is already so drunk at nine in the morning that she bumps into the walls while she shows us the house. The children come for the holidays (I pay a heavy security deposit—Peter has insisted that the children must never meet Warren, as if he were a pedophile or a dangerous criminal). They enjoy the sun, the swimming pools, and the tennis lessons, Disneyland, Marineland, cinemas, the beach, and so on. My brother Aimery and his daughter Chantal come for an afternoon party with the Gregory Peck children. Nice family fun. Too rare.

In September 1965 I have to fly to Paris to be in the great international film *Is Paris Burning?* directed by René Clément, written by Gore Vidal and Francis Ford Coppola from the book by Larry Collins and Dominique Lapierre. The film narrates the events of the summer of 1944, after the Allies have landed in Normandy and are coming close to Paris. The Germans are still sending Jews to the gas chambers and trying to clean up the horrors. The Resistance movement comes out in the open to start liberating Paris, while every day Hitler yells down the phone to General Dietrich von Choltitz, head of the collapsing occupying forces, "Is Paris burning?" He wants every bridge and monument in Paris blown up.

The film has the most stellar international cast ever put together. Every leading actor in Europe and America plays a part in it. I believe that only Jeanne Moreau was missing from the long list, because I played the French Resistance character, Françoise Labé, originally meant for her.

Amazing coincidence: The taxi that transports me to the producer's home for a first meeting takes me straight to 35 boulevard de la Seine, Neuilly—the house where I was born, built by my grandparents! The large glass dining-room table designed by the architect is still in place. I'm very moved.

Warren hasn't let me go ahead to Paris in time to get over the jet lag I always suffer from. René Clément is not pleased, and he's right. Working with the great Orson Welles, who plays the Swedish consul Raoul Nordling, is fascinating. I never thought I would find him a timid man.

Did he pose as timid just for me? Probably. He certainly is a seducer. A smooth talker, he takes endless trouble to charm everyone. During the day we spend in a taxi for our scene, he tells me that he sat by the phone in a Copenhagen hotel room for two days, unable to pluck up the courage to call Karen Blixen (Isak Dinesen) to tell her how much he admired her writing. He eventually did make a film from one of her *Seven Gothic Tales.*

René Clément is highly irritated when Orson Welles suggests—very politely—a simple camera move to film the whole scene in one easy take. Clément takes his revenge. In the hot sun, he makes Welles climb the steps again and again. I'm afraid the portly man will get a heart attack, so I buy him a small bottle of champagne. Orson can't help but give me directions conflicting with the ones from Clément. I'd love to do a whole film with him. My other partner is Alain Delon—dead smooth, a dark archangel with velvet eyes. He, too, is an irresistible charmer. "Anytime! Anywhere! Just call me . . ." were his parting words. We have to kiss in one scene to fool the Gestapo into believing we're just a normal couple. Sweet lips . . .

The Duke of Windsor comes for a visit to the set, brought by the press agent. No duchess around, not even an equerry. Everyone seems to steer clear of him. Did everyone but me know that he had Nazi leanings? I learned only much later of the reprehensible financial speculation he carried out during the war. I suppose René Clément knew. In any case, the duke sits there quite alone, abandoned by all. I think it's sort of rude, so when I'm introduced by the press agent, I stand by him for a minute to chitchat about the scene being filmed. His visit coincides with filming at the Hôtel Meurice, rue de Rivoli, the HQ of the German top brass. Is the duke trying to buy himself a new respectability with the international and the French press? I find him a frozen, wizened little man, with only the most banal things to say. I think he felt very uncomfortable.

For my grand scene by the Drancy cattle station, Clément doesn't give me any instructions. Instead he comes over, kisses me on the cheek, looks into my eyes with a world of unspoken compassion, and nods silently. He shouts, "Action!" and the whole horror of the scene unravels to its tragic end: crowded livestock train going off to deportation camp with real survivors, their numbers tattooed on their arms, hanging on the little airholes; SS guards shouting, shoving more people into the wagons with their gun butts; police dogs barking. I see my husband and shout that he's saved, "I've got the papers, you're free!" He turns, sees me, and takes a step toward me. A soldier shoots! . . . My husband falls, crumpled like a rag before my eyes. I play it only once, but it takes me a week to recover from the emotional shock of this scene.

It seems that a decade had flown by, but newspaper clippings establish my next trip away from home, to the Soviet Union, as taking place in October 1965. In those years Russia was still the vast, unknown country under the totalitarian regime governed by Brezhnev and his party. In a timid overture to the West, I was officially invited to Moscow for a premiere of *The L-Shaped Room.* The Russian public had never been allowed to see an American musical or comedy (*An American in Paris* was not screened for the public until 2004, thanks to the Alliance Française), but this black-and-white film showing a lost pregnant girl going through gritty times in the East London slums presented an image of the West that was acceptable to the authorities.

Moscow was drab and gray, its buildings run-down; passersby had a look of bitter determination to survive. I was eager to see everything, but I think I sometimes lacked the right sensibility. One day, dressed in a shocking pink suit and fashionable high heels by Christian Dior, as I was walking with my interpreter through a crowded avenue, I realized with surprise that no one even threw me a glance! It was as if I didn't exist. People were looking past me with shut faces and disapproving expressions. Liena, my interpreter, explained, "It's not considered right to show interest in foreigners." One afternoon when our car was late turning up for the opening ceremony, Liena just flagged a passing auto and ordered its owner to drive us to the theater. "Official state guest," she announced with authority. Intimidated, the man took us in and drove without protest through the empty avenues, barely acknowledging me.

Life in Russia was so repressed it was as if fear had stopped most brains from functioning. In the grand old Metropole Hotel, the simple board on which room keys are usually hung from a hook, each one under its appropriate number, hadn't been invented yet; the keys were kept in several rustic wooden boxes. All the boxes had to be emptied on the counter and the right key searched for through the whole pile. Wait-

ing without showing any signs of impatience was the required quality
if you wanted to survive. One marveled at the amazing ineptitude—for
instance, the bath taps barely reaching the inside of the tub, too short by
five inches. My interpreter warned me never to say anything significant
when there was a third person present, in an enclosed space like a car
or the hotel room, where she admitted there were microphones. She and
I could speak openly only while walking rather quickly in the streets.
When I left, I gave her all my creams, and she also asked for the empty
plastic bottle of shampoo. "It's pink and it smells good," she said. Liena
took me to visit GUM, the famous department store. I was wearing a
very nice fur coat made of otter with a fox collar. Nothing extravagant,
but still . . . A rather pretty, slim young woman rushed alongside me
and without stopping begged me with furtive words to sell it to her,
"at any price. . . ." I was slightly shocked; Liena disapproved of her behavior. We walked on past the coat department. I mentioned that there
seemed to be only one model of raincoat. Liena said yes, it was so. "The
authorities didn't think it's necessary to have more than one style."

I asked, "What would happen if someone inventive designed a second raincoat?"

"He would be in trouble or sent to the asylum. People know better
than to design a second style of raincoat." I returned to London from
what seemed another century, relieved to have survived the ordeal but
with a severe case of constipation. For the first course, at every meal,
there was a choice between cucumber and caviar—and good caviar at
that. No other vegetable was ever served, and no fruit either.

In contrast, back in London at The Albany, the exclusive apartment
house near Piccadilly Circus, Fleur Cowles, the famous hostess (creator
and editor of *Flair* magazine and divorced from Mike Cowles, owner of
Look magazine), threw one of her glamorous dinner parties for Greek royalty. Princess Sofia, now queen of Spain, not pretty but so very charming,
and her brother, young King Constantine, were there with their mother,
Queen Frederica. The young king told me, "You and I are in much the
same profession—representation! I watch a lot of films at the palace."
He'd grown since I'd met him in Greece as a little boy, with the Ballets
des Champs-Élysées, when his mother nudged him to offer me his hand.

It was around this time that Warren heard that François Truffaut
planned to film *Fahrenheit 451*. He wanted to meet Truffaut in Paris. I

was intimidated but still made an appointment with the great director, to whom I'd been introduced in Beverly Hills through the Renoirs. We had lunch at the Berkeley restaurant, just off the Champs-Élysées. Warren, who didn't speak French, would only come for coffee. After sitting down with us, Warren expressed his sincere admiration for the filmmaker, but Truffaut guessed the ulterior motive behind this encounter. His response was categorical.

"Sorry, *Fahrenheit* is for Oskar Werner, with whom I've already done *Jules et Jim*. But if you and Leslie want to do a film together, there is a very good script that I cannot do because I'm busy—a sort of gangster story, just right for the two of you, *Bonnie and Clyde,* by two young writers, Robert Benton and David Newman."

I flew back to London while Warren left for New York to meet Benton and Newman. He sent me the script to read and asked for my advice. He was far from convinced about the project, although he thought the script was very good. I strongly urged him to buy it. We argued on the phone.

"Westerns are not popular at all at the moment. They're considered B movies," he protested.

"This is not a western, Warren. It's a gangster film. There hasn't been a good gangster film in a very long time, and it's a great script."

"Also there's *In Cold Blood* about to be done—the two stories will be in competition."

"I think *In Cold Blood* is very different—contemporary, for one thing. Bonnie and Clyde are part of the legends of the West. I really wouldn't worry about the comparison. *In Cold Blood* will be forgotten by the time *Bonnie and Clyde* is done."

So Warren bought the script. From the start he wanted Arthur Penn to direct, despite my urging him to choose someone who had made more box-office movies. Warren had done *Mickey One* with Penn—a very interesting art film, quite obviously influenced by Truffaut. My advice was wrong, of course, and thank God Warren didn't listen to me.

A while later I flew to Los Angeles, and immediately Warren told me that he didn't think I was right for Bonnie. "You're a foreigner. Bonnie must be played by an American actress." He also felt that there was a problem of age. (I was five and a half years older than he.) He expressed himself with straightforward bluntness.

"Let's face it, you're too old for me. I've offered the part to Natalie."
Natalie Wood was his girlfriend before me. That hurt. However, as everyone knows, she turned him down.

Bonnie and Clyde was a magnificent film. Now that forty-plus years have passed, the pain has worn off, and I can smile at his raw ambition and ruthlessness. At the time it knocked me dizzy. Inevitably, we drifted apart. Warren stayed in Hollywood, making the film. I stayed in London, close to my children. Good luck, Warren! We have stayed friends all these years, in a loose sort of way.

Learning Independence

*B*y the late 1960s, actors and actresses had begun timidly asserting themselves as promoters of their own careers, trying to become producers, as Warren had successfully done. I, too, had ambitions to expand my field of work. The Italian cinema was buoyant still, and I had been extremely moved by a historical novel, *The Nun of Monza,* the rights to which I had bought. The drama is the story of a young girl of noble family in love with a young man, forced to enter a convent, where she continues to meet him, but is then punished by a slow, cruel death—walled alive. Hardly the expected vehicle for a musical-comedy star. After scanning the European horizon, I decided that I wanted to work with Nanni Loy, the director of *The Four Days of Naples.* I made an appointment with his office and came to Rome, where I met a tall, charming Sarde aristocrat. While sipping cups of espresso, I developed my proposal with conviction, but I could see that his thoughts were elsewhere. My pitch barely finished, he answered with an appreciative nod, "Yes, yes, I'd love to do it, but not right now. . . . First I am filming my autobiography, or, rather, that of my wife. I would like to ask you, would you play my wife?" The bluntness of the proposition threw me and left me speechless. I was also immensely flattered—after reading the script, I said yes enthusiastically.

In fact this was just the kind of film I longed to do, and we started work in Rome during the spring of 1967. The experience of working on *The Head of the Family* with Nino Manfredi and the great comedian Toto, who died of a heart attack after two or three days of filming and had to be replaced by Ugo Tognazzi, was one of the most rewarding of my career. Nanni Loy was an important figure in Italian film. Head of the Experimental School of Cinema, he was also an excellent comedian and later brought *Candid Camera* to Italy. No one went out on the night it was on television.

The children came with Lilène. We all adored Rome—the antique monuments, the sunny weather, the pasta, the open-air markets, the fake-antique workshops, right there on the sidewalks. We had a roof-top flat with two terraces overlooking Rome and the Trastevere. When asked what she thought of it after a visit to the Colosseum, little Jenny replied, "Oh, I loved it, it's full of cats!"

Il Padre di Famiglia, alias *The Head of the Family,* dealt with an important social and political subject: the place of women in Italian society, where girls often receive an education equivalent to that of boys but are, after marriage, relegated to home slavery and traditionally forced to give up all professional ambition. The background of the story was important, too: land speculation around Rome. The town is choked by a forest of apartment buildings with no city planning of any kind, under the criminal indifference of the authorities, if not their active participation. My part was magnificent; it spanned the life of a brilliant and ambitious young student in architecture all the way to middle age—a woman who, as a consequence of her self-abnegation, ends up in the hospital with a nervous breakdown.

With this film I was initiated into Italian neorealism, a freer form of filming with fewer technical constraints. The first novelty was in the authenticity of the set. Nanni Loy reproduced the exact topography of his own home in the studio. He even used his own front doors, too solid to be reproduced accurately. With sweeping ease he staged scenes in a succession of rooms where several cameras were strategically positioned, recording all the comings and goings. There were no set marks to hit, as one of the cameras was sure to catch the moment. Husband and children were doing their thing in each room, and I interacted with them when I entered and passed through to the next. The soft lighting came from the ceiling, so that no poles or flags stopped my progress throughout the house. This gave us all the remarkable freedom to concentrate on acting almost as if we were on the stage. As everyone knows, Italian filmmakers sacrifice the sound to the image. My English text was roughly correct, while the other actors spoke Italian, but my mistakes and moments of frustration often suited the director, who incorporated them in the scenes when he later dubbed in the Italian text. I couldn't believe how quickly and successfully Nanni had filmed some four or five pages of script, in one single take and only one morning of work. My difficulty in understanding the language almost worked in my favor. I had to pay such close attention to what my partners said that my concentration was acute.

One of the scenes concerned an argument between husband and wife, while they walked down a flight of outdoor stairs, in the quarter called Pincio. When the scene was done, everyone broke into exclamations: "How incredible!" "Can we keep it?" "Is it all right?" "He didn't look at the camera, did he?" I asked what were they talking about. "The man." "What man?" "The man who walked through the scene. Didn't you see him?" No, I hadn't noticed, I was too concentrated on following Nino's lips. The shot was kept in.

In another scene in which we had to almost overlap our lines, an assistant was lying on the floor between us, waving a white handkerchief to give each of us our cue. When we came to film the funeral of the aristocratic old father, which took place in the crowded city center, I still don't know if the incredible confusion between the traditional black-plumed, horse-driven hearse and the scattering cortege of black-attired family and friends, vainly trying to keep together through the honking cars, was part of the film plan or simply the usual Italian street pandemonium. I suspect that Nanni, with the blessings of the police, threw the hearse and the funeral cortege forward with instructions for everyone to fend for himself through this ferocious traffic. The effect is successfully comic.

Toto died a day or two after filming this scene, on the fifteenth of April, 1967, which makes one wonder if the traffic stress wasn't responsible for his sudden collapse. All Italy went into mourning. After the church service in Rome, the train that carried his body to Naples, his place of birth, was dressed in black and crawling at walking pace. For the whole length of the railroad tracks, thousands of people stood silently, crying and throwing flowers at the steam train. I was surprised to find out his real name and titles, so extensive that they take a whole paragraph:

Antonio Griffo Focas Flavio Dicas Comneno Porfirogenito Gagliardi di Curtis di Bisanzio, Altezza Imperiale, Conte Palatino, Cavaliere del Sacro Romano Imperio escarcadi Ravenna, Duca di Macedonia, del Peleponneso, Conte di Cipro e di Epiro, Conte e Duca di Drivasto e Durazzo . . . On the movie set, the crew simply called him "Principe."

As I was playing a mother with four children, I always had a baby in my arms. In a scene where we were visiting a Montessori school, the infant was recalcitrant and he kept howling. After a few minutes, Nanni said to an assistant, "Go out in the street and stop the first woman with a baby." It took less than a minute to get this new cherub, who placidly contemplated his movie debut in my arms. His mother was very pleased with his good fortune.

All those children in the cast also meant the presence of their parents. Each child was accompanied by mother, auntie, mother's best friend, sometimes mother's lover or a grandfather and little brothers or sisters—everyone thrilled to be on a movie set. It became impossible to obtain perfect silence. I loved the first rough cut of the film, when all those lively people carried on their running conversations in barely muted voices. Unfortunately, this impressionist sound was not kept.

Nanni had an unusual way of directing me. He would often give me, on the second take, instructions opposite from those he'd given on the first. When I pointed out these contradictions, he replied that he was trying to get a surge of emotion and that any technique was good to break down my inhibitions—even if it provoked my anger. Whatever its intention, the method worked. I am rather proud of this performance. I felt I had accomplished the kind of work I knew I was capable of doing. I went back to Paris, hoping that more parts like this one would come along.

When the phone rang while I was at home in London in the summer of 1967—on the evening of Sunday, August 13, to be precise—the faraway voice was not that of my agent but of my brother calling from the Virgin Islands. It took me a few seconds to understand what he said. "What? . . . Oh, no! . . . When? . . . How did she do it? . . . Did she mean to? . . . A note? What does it say? . . . You tore it up? . . . Yes, of course I'll come right away. Tomorrow." I was in shock, but somehow I didn't cry. My mother had committed suicide! My cat, lying on my lap, licked my hand for the first and only time ever.

A plane to New York, another plane to San Juan, Puerto Rico, then an island hop to St. Thomas, where my father and mother had developed a very successful luxury shop, La Belle France. I asked Amy, my mother's maid, endless questions. She loved my mother and kept repeating, "Mrs. Caron, she always made herself pretty for your father when he came home from work."

My father explained, "She couldn't stand the new house, the wind whistling through the glass louvers . . . the black marble floors—that depressed her." I heard stories of her deranged behavior, insulting clients at the shop. A bottle of vodka stashed away and a whole bottle of pills—pink froth foaming at her mouth, that's how Amy found her, although she had been watching over her. Amy first called my father at the shop, who called an ambulance. In the hospital they tried to pump her stomach, but her heart failed. The papers said "heart failure," but all the people in St. Thomas knew the truth. My father was grief-stricken. The funeral was unreal—this sinister, improbable ceremony under the bleaching sun. I felt absolutely nothing. My poor mother in this lilac plastic box? I wonder what she looked like. Horrible thought. She was only sixty-seven. When I think of her, I think of a shattered mirror. When we talked about her, Warren and I used to call her Blanche DuBois, after Tennessee Williams's character in *A Streetcar Named Desire*.

Aimery and I looked through her papers and found out that she was reworking the French dictionary, trying to put her confused brain into some kind of order. We burned her demented pages and gave away her clothes; Papa distributed her jewels. The diamond-and-emerald engagement ring went to my brother for his wife, the diamond spray of flowers was for me. Somehow, within a couple of years, I managed to lose that brooch. I left St. Thomas after a few days. "I'll come back for Christmas with the children, Papa."

My father was better by Christmastime. A nice lady, Monique O., helped him find a boat to charter for a weekend cruise with the children. My father was strangely enthusiastic. "Monique is so nice, refined. She works at the store but doesn't want a salary. Just a watch from Van Cleef and Arpels." Excuse me?

Ten years later, after my father's death—more or less from natural causes—my brother and I started to retrieve what "the nice lady" and her husband had swindled from him. Apart from the St. Thomas house was a luxurious apartment on the water near Nice. For that reason there were two court cases—one in France, one in the Virgin Islands—lasting thirteen long years. Aimery and I, after countless appeals from the con artists, won in both countries on the grounds of undue influence. Now Aimery is protected from want for the rest of his life. In St. Thomas, Virgin Islands, overlooking the busy harbor of Charlotte Amalie, he owns a beautiful Colonial stone house, resistant to heat and hurricanes. From its terrace he can enjoy the nightly steel-band concert the locals hold spontaneously down in the town's colorful center. In the mornings, when you open the solid wood shutters, light flows in so violently you get a glimpse of God in His splendor. My father and mother are vindicated.

That same year, 1967, marked the fiftieth anniversary of the Russian Revolution, an event the Soviets wanted to proclaim throughout the world. Among the festivities was the Moscow International Film Festival, where party orders were given to crown the Soviet entry with the Grand Prix. After the premiere of *The L-Shaped Room* two years earlier, it seemed a good idea to ask me to be the member of the jury to represent Western/American cinema. So I was invited.

I found the experience daunting. There were films from all the satellite countries—Hungary, Czechoslovakia, Poland—as well as from less sophisticated ones under the totalitarian regime. The Hollywood entry was a black-and-white film critical of the school system in the United States, *Up the Down Staircase* by Robert Mulligan—fair enough. But unacceptable was a USSR demagogic documentary on U.S. involvement in the Vietnam War. In fact, at that time I was still unconcerned with politics and had no opinion about the war, but I was shocked to be subjected to such manipulation. This film was cheap propaganda; it reminded me of the despicable Nazi propaganda films against the Jews, shown by the Germans in occupied Paris. I felt I should have been previously warned about its inclusion in the official movie list. I am not a courageous person, and yet after its public performance I sprang to my feet in the crowded Palace of Congress and shouted, "I protest!" Not a head turned my way, not even that of my interpreter, who was sitting next to me. I sat down and broke into a heavy sweat. Nevertheless, at the end of the evening, I asked to talk to the president of the festival. I told him that I could not tolerate being used as a political pawn. I had been invited to take part in an international film festival, not to serve a political platform. This documentary had no business being in the program. He assured me that the film would be removed from the official list if I agreed to remain on the jury. I did, and the film was indeed removed. (I noticed with a certain glee that it was later given the USSR agricultural gold medal!) But I would later pay for this act of defiance.

The official Russian entry was a stodgy melodrama espousing the ideology of the party—*The Journalist,* by Sergei Gerasimov. When time came to discuss the merits of each film, instead of letting the apparatchiks have their way, I felt I must fight for my convictions, and my convictions were that a small black-and-white Hungarian film by a young director I had never heard of, István Szabó, should win. *Father* was all finesse, intelligence, and youthful conviction. Against all twelve members of the jury ordered by the party to give the prize to the Russian film—I was the only member of the jury from the West except for Dimitri Tiomkin, the composer, who was making his return to the land of his ancestors—I defended Szabó's film, and it seems that my voice was heard. *Father* won the Grand Prix jointly with the Russian *Journalist.*

Retribution came the following year, at the 1968 Venice Film Festival. After I was voted Best Actress by the jury members for my performance in *Il Padre di Famiglia,* the Russian delegate threatened to resign if I was given the prize. The president of Venice's Mostra—Luigi Chiarini (I think)—was a dedicated Communist. I did not win.

16

Marriage Again

*I*n 1968, in London, I met and got involved with a young American producer, Michael S. Laughlin, who was part of the American New Wave—those bright kids who thought they could make films for under a million dollars and hope for a killing. In those days when studios were making huge-budget films to compete with the serious threat of television, this original idea was very seductive. At the same time, England's chancellor of the exchequer—Roy Jenkins—had the brilliant initiative to give subsidies to foreign films made in Britain, so much so that there was a rash of American producer/directors helming good or indifferent projects and living very pleasantly in London. They all met on Sunday mornings in Hyde Park to play football. Some adopted the British lord and lady manner. Wicked gossip had it that after seeing the changing of the guards at Buckingham Palace you had to see the changing of the staff at the house of director Stanley Donen, better known for his popular musicals *On the Town* and *Singin' in the Rain.*

Michael Laughlin was the son of a very bright woman who had been adopted and raised by a rich, eccentric lady who made her an heiress. He had drawn a lot of attention by producing a little black-and-white suspense film, *The Whisperers,* written and directed by my good friend Bryan Forbes; the film won a few international awards, including Best Actress for Dame Edith Evans, who played the lead role.

Michael was a talent scout at heart. He had a flair for discovering new faces and for predicting the coming fashion. In his next film, he brought to the screen that unique Canadian actor Donald Sutherland, in a frothy comedy called *Joanna,* starring Geneviève Waite, whose baby voice could have dubbed the cartoon character Betty Boop.

By 1968 politics had begun descending from elitist spheres as people rallied around Harold Wilson and his Labour government. Society was adopting its own brand of populism, and suddenly it was fashionable to invite your tailor and your hairdresser into your salon—a strong Cockney accent secured an invitation to the best parties. On the stage, regional accents were the rage; the Beatles had changed the social order.

Under the influence of Twiggy and Jean Shrimpton, all the girls dressed in pinafores, wore flat shoes with a buckle, long, long hair and short, short dresses, bought on Carnaby Street. Why on earth did we all try to look so innocent? Is it because women's liberation had started, and we didn't want the males to feel threatened? "Swinging London" now became the furiously fashionable capital of the world. Because I was alone, I gave parties when my children had to go to Peter's for the weekend. I was on the *Time* magazine map for the best parties in London. In Montpelier Square I gave free-for-all evenings where guests spread out over two floors of the house. Everyone brought a friend or two. Present at some time or other were John Ford, the car magnate; John Huston, the director; Edna O'Brien; Jay Kanter; Alan Ladd Jr. and all the Universal top brass; the composer John Barry and his wife, lovely Jane Birkin; Dudley Moore—easy prey for long-legged girls; Roman Polanski, who was about to marry beautiful, sweet Sharon Tate; Larry Gelbart—something funny always happened on his way to the party—and his wife, Barbara, who was just as witty. Ken Adam and his wife, Letizia—he was the smart production designer of this amusing new spoof based on Ian Fleming's novel called *Dr. No,* which everyone went to see because it was so unreal and so much fun. (The producers, Harry Saltzman and Cubby Broccoli, were shocked at first when the public laughed at the suave spy played by the almost unknown Sean Connery.) Maurice Binder came; he was the first to make a minifilm for the James Bond film credits. Catherine Deneuve was there, the very silent bride of David Bailey, London's hottest photographer. Tessa Kennedy, trying to get started in interior decoration, where she quickly became top guru. She was the gamest of them all and still in great form with Marlon Brando at six in the morning when we cooked breakfast in the basement kitchen. We went dancing in groups to Annabelle's on Berkeley Square and to dinner at Trader Vic's, where Tessa was politely told that she couldn't come in wearing a pantsuit. "Oh, fine," said she, coolly taking off her trousers, with just the jacket to cover . . . the essentials. With a straight face, she handed her pants over to the cloakroom girl, leaving the maître d' speechless.

I also gave sit-down dinners with Lee and Stash Radziwill; Gregory and Veronique Peck; Ken Tynan and his new wife, the intriguing Kathleen Halton; Claire Bloom and Rod Steiger, who wouldn't stay for coffee because Marlon was coming (old feud since *On the Waterfront*). Maria St. Just was recently back from a trip with Tennessee Williams. Robert Bolt, who met Sarah Miles across the dining-room table one night and went off with her for a ten-year-long rocky adventure. And Margot Fonteyn, elegant and refined, whose parting wave was so graceful that I wish I had immortalized it with a photograph.

I hosted a glamorous party for Barbra Streisand on the opening night of her fantastically successful show *Funny Girl*—and everyone flocked to meet her. There was, on the buffet table that night, a dish strangely resembling a whole stuffed pork. Barbra asked in the negative, "You're not serving pork, are you?" I lied boldly, "No, of course not." She knew I was lying. I don't think she was all that religious—she was just mindful of her prerogatives. Right she was; a hostess should be more thoughtful.

I also gave an important open house for Montgomery Clift, inviting every British director, young and old, to meet the great actor, in order to open up his opportunities in Europe. A few years earlier, I had met Monty at a dinner with Jack Larson at the Plaza Hotel in New York. During the meal, Monty, whom I admired a lot, had been provocative and rude—frankly, he was drunk—and I had been shocked and hurt. This event had been the reason for the only split in my relationship with Jack Larson, whom I didn't see for at least a year afterward. But years had passed, and Monty, as I had heard through Jack, had been a broken man since his car accident during the filming of *Raintree County*. Monty had an addictive personality at the best of times, but after his accident, in which his jaw was broken, MGM resumed filming while he was still in great pain, and he continued to use the heavy drugs prescribed by the hospital.

Because of drugs and alcohol, the studios wouldn't touch him anymore; he hadn't worked in four years, not since *Freud* in 1962. Raoul Lévy, the French writer/producer/director, offered him a script—*The*

Defector in 1966—which was actually no more than a first draft. A reckless go-ahead was nevertheless granted, and I was asked to play the female lead. I said, "Yes, but . . ." and we started to meet at my house every afternoon in order to work on the script. These meetings became torture. In the middle of a sentence, Monty would stop speaking to stare with intensity at the carpet until I, too, would search in the red and blue Persian whorls for the point he was trying to develop. Lost in a haze, he was oblivious to the passing minutes. I resigned from the project with a terrible sense of guilt.

It is at this point that I gave the party as a compensation for my "defection." Eager to meet him were Tony Richardson, John Schlesinger, Lindsay Anderson, Arnold Wesker, David Story, Bryan Forbes, Richard Attenborough, Karel Reisz, Richard Lester, and a few others I am forgetting. Bryan Forbes said that if a bomb was set off in my living room, the British film industry would be wiped out.

There were gorgeous photographs of my daughter and me in *Vogue* and *Harper's Bazaar*; there were charity galas at which the queen, in sparkling diamonds, offered her hand and said a few gracious words. I opened the first photo exhibit of Tony Armstrong-Jones (Lord Snowdon) and gave books to students on graduation day. And there was the gala where I read a few pages from the memoirs of that great dancer, Tamara Karsavina, partner of Nijinsky. She was sitting in the front row, and I could feel her vivacious mind following the text while I stood in front of the mike. She came to my dressing room afterward and said those unforgettable words: *"J'ai vu la petite lueur qu'on ne voit que de près"* (I saw the glimmer you can only see close by). The gossip columns mentioned me often. My house decoration covered several pages of *House & Garden*. I was a celebrity. I had at least a dozen hats in my wardrobe and a pair of shoes for every Dior outfit—two drawers were barely enough for my rainbow collection of suede gloves.

I thought I was having fun. Was I? Well, yes, in a way I was, but I started to wake up in the mornings around six or seven, no matter how late I'd gone to bed—a little swig of port would send me back to sleep. The children with Lilène would tiptoe past my door on the way to school, and I felt a pinch of guilt. This new man in my bed, Michael Laughlin, was younger than me by eight years—was this wise? His great quality: He was a fun-loving young man who knew how to amuse my children—I was so afraid that my melancholy would be catching.

I thought I had a handle on my profession. Bound for Hollywood on an airplane and seated next to Charlie Bluhdorn (head of Paramount), I tried to convince him that there was a fortune to be made in the re-release of vintage films—new publics were eager to see the movies their parents had adored. Charlie told me I was crazy. "Let me tell you, a film is dead after a year!" Not long afterward Ted Turner bought the entire MGM film library and made the fortune I predicted. I should have been an executive! An offer came to my agent for a little Canadian film, *Beginners Three.* The plot surprised me: A mature woman (I was thirty-seven but thought I looked twenty-five) agrees to introduce three young boys of fourteen/fifteen to the joys of love. I flew to Toronto and discovered that the actors were in fact around twenty. I smelled a rat and took the first flight back to London. I seriously started to doubt myself. Why did my agent pass along such a mediocre offer? Why did I even consider it? Where were the great Hollywood scripts? Why didn't the studios call?

After a few months, Michael insisted on marrying me. I was less than enthusiastic; a little voice told me that we had very different tastes and temperaments. He had, if truth be told, a fierce temper, at home as well as on the tennis court. I was far from acquiescent. How do you woo a recalcitrant movie star? On a yacht, of course, at the Cannes Film Festival in May 1968 (which was canceled midway—the cause: a student revolution that brought France to a standstill), where Michael was going to present *Joanna.* He chartered a superb boat that swung languorously in front of the festival lights. The first evening held all the expected glamour with candles and soft music. After the essential champagne, the chef served crabmeat salad and other delicacies. By midnight Michael Sarne (director of *Joanna*) and a few other guests left to go ashore, and we weighed anchor. The rest of the trip was less glamorous. Even though the captain told us there was a heavy-seas warning, Michael gave orders to sail for Corsica. It didn't take ten minutes for us both to regret our dinner. Michael went from the dining chair to the couch in the lower deck, and I went up on the top deck, where I breathed deeply until I found my sea legs. At six in the morning, our torment stopped when we finally berthed in the port of Île Rousse in Corsica. The captain comforted Michael by telling him that two of the crew members had been sick as well. That night we slept in a very modest little hotel, overlooking . . . the yacht. Michael wouldn't sail off until the captain reassured him that, out there, the sea was as mild as milk and would stay that way. We then headed for Sardinia, where we berthed for the remaining five days—in the port.

There is no doubt, Michael was an original. Interested only in non-conformist, not to say marginal, projects, he nonetheless liked to live like a millionaire. His favorite fictional character was the Great Gatsby, and his dream was to have a walk-in closet with a range of tailor-made shirts to choose from every morning.

The plan was to get married in the most expensive hotel in the world, in Kingston, Jamaica, where the Frenchman's Cove charged a thousand dollars a day to satisfy all your desires. A wedding? Yes, sir, right away. An altercation did erupt a few days before the marriage, when I guess I said I didn't want to go through with it. Still, I let myself be swayed.

Come December 30, 1968, we went through a pastoral wedding ceremony under a baobab tree; I remember that I was dressed in a beige silk miniskirt and that during the ceremony I was overcome with a fit of coughing. Was it psychosomatic? The children and Lilène had flown in with us from Miami on a little taxi plane. The pilot was a lady who instructed us severely, "Don't talk to me while I fly," but she never shut up. We looked at one another, slightly pale, while the little monoplane bumped around the clouds. My brother had flown in from St. Thomas. My friend Blanche Blackwell, who lived in Jamaica, acted as my witness. My father couldn't be bothered to come, as this was my third marriage. Besides, "Monique" was on his mind. I lost his present at the airport—a ridiculous crystal contraption for serving caviar on ice.

While we were in Jamaica, we went to visit Noël Coward. After he'd shown us his colorful paintings and talked with friendly simplicity about lots of things, the time came to leave. The two chatty young men who shared his life were sent down to their own lodgings—the guardian's house. He insisted on spending the evenings and nights alone—a matter of dignity, I would say. Like a father sending his turbulent children off to sleep in the nursery.

Blanche Blackwell, who had the keys to Ian Fleming's house since his death—and long before that, too—drove us there for the night. It was a simple, masculine place—natural wood and bare walls—nothing to distract his eyes from the sheet of paper in the typewriter. The maid recommended, "When you wake up in the morning, just squeeze the ringer!"

Now that we were married, we were going to live in Hollywood—better than London right now, wasn't it? The Beverly Hills Hotel welcomed us for a month or two, of course, until I put my foot down and decided to buy a house. I would sell my beautiful London house in Montpelier Square and buy one in L.A. Everything was fine, this was a new start— Hollywood was where we belonged, or so I told myself. The children, especially Christopher, would always miss their first London home, a symbol for them—and for me, too—of the days when life was stable, despite the conflicting agendas of their parents.

But first, while still in the Beverly Hills Hotel, we looked around for a quick rental as we searched for the perfect house. Michael remembered a lovely cottage at 10050 Cielo Drive, above Benedict Canyon—a house that Terry Melcher (Doris Day's son) used to rent. We drove up the isolated, rustic road and found Roman Polanski on the threshold. He received us warmly. "Too bad, you're a day late. Sharon and I just moved in yesterday," he said. Disappointed, we rented a little place with a pool down on the flats of Beverly Hills, on Chevy Chase Drive. The house had a memorable aura: Orson Welles had rented it for the duration of his last film, and—the owner revealed in a whisper—he'd had his bed moved to the double living room and walked about naked! The children came for the summer holidays. We had a cocktail party to announce our return to L.A. My daughter, Jenny, still remembers the extravagant length of Barbra Streisand's beige-polished nails.

On the morning of August 9, 1969, when the gory news of the Sharon Tate massacre hit the press, stupor and terror gripped the Hollywood movie community. The phones never stopped ringing. Tears of grief and horror for poor Sharon, eight months pregnant, and Jay Sebring, whom we all knew, and Abigail Folger, and the others. . . . The shock, magnitude ten! What on earth could have provoked that bloodbath? And again the next morning when the bodies of the LaBianca couple were discovered, farther out of town in the Los Feliz district, murdered in much the same savage way by girls who had hitchhiked a ride. I don't think the police or the community immediately linked the two sets of killings, but Los Angeles had become a zone of evil. Within twenty-four hours there were no more German shepherd dogs for sale in Los Angeles; people bought guns and ordered private guards; electric fences were erected, and anything that could offer protection was organized. We didn't feel safe, knowing that we had very nearly rented the house where the murders occurred. Like a lot of movie people, we went to the Beverly Hills Hotel for a few days. The long months of speculation started and continued until one of the girls, Susan Atkins, spoke to a cellmate while she was in jail on some other offense. Charles Manson was arrested during a raid, found hiding in a small cupboard under a sink at a desert ranch. Since those days, forty years ago, I have never given a ride to a young woman hitchhiker.

From the moment we returned to Hollywood, Michael started to put together several projects. All of them contemporary, they dealt with the urgent problems of youth—drugs, speed, car obsession. The first, a semidocumentary titled *Dusty and Sweets McGee,* was written by the young Floyd Mutrux. For the director Michael got in touch with an intriguing young man of twenty-three named Steven Spielberg, who had done a little black-and-white TV film, gripping and suspenseful, called *Duel,* about a killer truck pursuing a car—or how to make a horror film with nothing but talent. François Truffaut had seen and recommended it. Unfortunately, Spielberg was under contract to Universal, who refused to let him go. In the end Floyd Mutrux himself directed the film; *Time* magazine dispatched a writer to the set to cover its realistic treatment of the drug scene. Several of the actors had passed away by the time the film was released. *The Christian Licorice Store,* also written by Floyd Mutrux, was directed by James Frawley and started at almost the same time. This film introduced to the screen the beautiful Maud Adams (later the Bond girl in *Octopussy*) and the elder of the Bridges boys, Beau. The surprise guest was an actor from silent films, Gilbert Roland, in a charming, serene performance.

Two-Lane Blacktop was the third film, and one that could have hit it big, like *Easy Rider,* but somehow didn't at the time. Starring James Taylor, Warren Oates, Laurie Bird, and Dennis Wilson, it was directed by Monte Hellman, the most underrated cult filmmaker of those days.

Michael sometimes dreamed up other projects, only to see other people exploit them successfully. *Cotton Comes to Harlem* by Chester Himes was one; Metro-Goldwyn-Mayer took the idea and did it without him. Michael also took an option on the comic strip *Dick Tracy* long before anyone believed there could be a public for that kind of film. Warren Beatty bought out the rights from him much later. And I know that the idea of doing film clips to sell songs came to Michael before anyone else thought of it. He contacted Randy Newman to propose the idea. Randy said, "I get it," and went off to write the song of "Sail Away." Jerry Jeff Walker was also part of that project, with "Mr. Bojangles." But in Hollywood you have to get up very early to catch the worm. The clips were never made.

Michael treated the children to great summer vacations. He rented the Santa Monica beach house built by Louis B. Mayer's daughter, Edie Goetz, which belonged then to Peter Lawford and his wife, Pat Kennedy. Pictures of the late president and family were everywhere. The Lawfords' cook came with the house. One weekend, when what I used to call "the volleyball team" (James B. Harris, James Caan, Laurence Gordon, and Merritt Blake) were at the house, we found ourselves out of mayonnaise for sandwiches. I told the maid, "Let's make some." When she said, "I don't know how to cook it," I was speechless. "You don't *cook* a mayonnaise. You beat it—raw egg yolk, olive oil with a little lemon juice." "Oooohhh!" she exclaimed. Larry Gordon, future president of Fox and producer of *Dillinger, Predator, Die Hard,* and *Lara Croft,* didn't like that funny homemade taste. But what can you expect from a boy born in Yazoo, Mississippi?

John Milius, anointed as the important scriptwriter of the day (he'd written the great classics *Jeremiah Johnson, The Life and Times of Judge Roy Bean,* and *Apocalypse Now*), came for dinner with his Mexican wife. He told the story of how his agent and mine, Mike Medavoy, went to visit him at his country ranch, way out in the desert, and offered him a bottle of aftershave lotion for Christmas. John opened the fancy wrapping, exclaimed, "What is this s—!" pulled out his gun, threw the bottle in midair, and shot it as if it were a clay pigeon.

On a more civilized note, we also saw a lot of Larry and Susan Turman, Hollywood's royal couple and five-star socialites since he'd made a huge hit of *The Graduate.* Sunday invitations to their Brentwood tennis-court parties were very desirable. Jack (Jax slacks) and Sally Hanson, now living in Pola Negri's mansion, were the other Sunday-afternoon must. An appetizing spread of food was laid out in the kitchen, with all the soft drinks or white wine you wanted; you had to go play a couple of sets of tennis or swim one or two lengths with the girls if you wanted to be allowed in their very select disco, The Daisy. There is no doubt that, ever since Charlie Chaplin, a Hollywood producer has to be a good tennis player if he wants to be in pole position. At that time Lincoln convertibles were being replaced by Silver Cloud Rolls-Royces as the car of choice. Used or new, no matter, but imperatively with Gucci loafers to press the pedals.

We drove all the way to Zuma Beach or Trancas to listen to Joan Didion and John Gregory Dunne, the new voice of California literature, both involved in another drug-scene film, the famous *Panic in Needle Park,* in which a young, undiscovered Al Pacino played the lead. The Dunnes' young daughter Quintana Roo (I never heard them use the "Roo" in referring to her) was a remarkably precocious baby, but already a health worry.

Among my favorite friends were the scriptwriter Terrence Malick (later director of *Badlands, Days of Heaven,* and *The Thin Red Line*) and the woman who was sharing his life then, Jill Jakes. How he came to do *Badlands* is quite an amusing story. Jill Jakes was director Arthur Penn's script girl on *Bonnie and Clyde.* Now, Arthur Penn was born in Philadelphia and raised in New York, New Hampshire, and Philadelphia, whereas Terry was a homegrown Texas boy. I think he thought that Arthur Penn's view of Texas was slightly artificial and acquired, whereas he knew intimately the poetry of the vast, flat expanse of land—corn- or wheat fields—and of its rich cattle-raising people. He was conscious of their eccentricities and sexual deviancies and knew what long days of solitude and heat can do to the human spirit. He did *Badlands* to show Jill, and Arthur Penn and the film community, what Texas was really like. I tell this anecdote not to find flaws with the remarkable *Bonnie and Clyde* but rather to underscore the different message of *Badlands.*

Terry was the gentlest person I knew, even though he looked like an ogre with burning dark eyes, thanks to his Armenian ancestors. He had a gut reaction to Texas—love and hate—and all his films deal with the violence he so abhorred, while his dislike of Hollywood was a response to its brutal opportunism, the lack of sensibility, of those in power. These two worlds he found himself confronted with bruised his tender soul. It's no surprise that he came to live in France, until the pull of home roots got him back to Texas.

While working on the interiors of *Badlands,* he once came for dinner to our Bel Air house, ensconced himself in his favorite chair (a French grandfather's wood-and-sisal seat with a tall back), and told us about his first day of shooting. He had been a scriptwriter up to that day and was so new to the job that he didn't even know the technical terms. After finishing the first overall shot, his cameraman asked him if he wanted a "clean close-up" or an "over-the-shoulder." Terry fixed him with his ardent black eyes for a few seconds, then answered, "When I want an over-the-shoulder, I'll let you know." He then rushed to a telephone and called long-distance to someone in Hollywood who could enlighten him about the term "over-the-shoulder." (The camera frames the edges of the back of the actor who is closest to the camera, thus underlining his presence.) Malick learned very fast; his films are both paintings and poems.

I loved him enough to paint a picture of a quaint Texan scene of which he'd given me an old photograph. Four cowboys in bowler hats—guns stacked up in a circle, bivouac style—sat around a card table in a wheat field stretching as far as the eye could see, with only a small shack on the side to sleep in. The horses are standing a little off, grazing peacefully. The oddity is that each player looks at the photographer and displays his cards without the trace of a smile; I would even say with a certain solemnity. Those guys seldom talked and never smiled. Terry would have liked me to paint similar scenes for the background of his credits, but I told him that it had already taken me two weeks to do just this one.

Jill Jakes, his wife, had the fearless American pioneer spirit. In her thirties, after coproducing Terry's *Badlands* and *Days of Heaven,* she decided she wanted to go into law. Following several years of intense studies, she got her law degree and defended top cases—including defending the child presumed molested by Roman Polanski. She became counsel for the American Civil Liberties Union, and then a Beverly Hills municipal court judge.

Jill and Terry had a huge mongrel dog called Abimelech after Terry's Armenian great-grandfather. She called me one day and asked me if I would accompany her to the Blessing of the Animals, which has taken place every year since 1930 on April 7 on Olvera Street, in downtown L.A., in the Mexican sector. We went with Abimelech and joined the mile-long line. There were cats, dogs, cows, donkeys—in its early days there had been llamas and camels—birds in their cages, hamsters, opossums, snakes—every animal you could think of. The bishop started at noon with this prayer: "Almighty Father, bless these animals for all they have done in supplying our food, in carrying our burdens, providing us with clothing and companionship and tendering a service to the human race since the world began." When we got in front of the bishop, who stood on a little platform, Jill gazed up at him with tears of gratitude as he swung the aspergillum so that the drops of holy water reached the animal. I snapped a picture. While we were in line, a person who was looking with respect at this huge, hairy dog asked what breed it was. Jill answered with aplomb, "It's an Abimelech." "Ah, yes," said the lady knowingly, "I've heard about them."

We were also close friends with Natalie Wood and her second husband, Richard Gregson. They came regularly to our parties. Natalie was fun-loving and sweet, but you had to say that she was Hollywood wise, having been around since the age of five. She always knew the latest. Then, suddenly, the split happened between her and Richard, with no warning that anyone could have seen coming. One day, soon after the birth of their baby—Richard had let it be understood that she had shut the door of her bedroom since she'd found herself pregnant—she caught Richard in an intimate conversation with her secretary. That was it. She ordered him out of the house within the hour and started divorce proceedings immediately. A great pity for all their friends, as everyone loved them both equally. I invited her to lunch to try to talk her into taking time for reflection, but I got nowhere. Unfortunately, there was also a financial problem between them, since, in those days of British socialist tax rules, Richard, who was British, couldn't get his money out of England. Being the breadwinner for the time being made the infidelity all the more bitter for Natalie.

Sometime later she invited me to her house in Bel Air to meet her newborn baby, who looked just like her, with her fine bones, delicate features, and huge brown eyes. I remember nothing about the house itself, only her swimming pool, which was surrounded by an iron fence with a gate and a padlock, at a time when this sort of security wasn't built on private estates. I remarked on it, and she admitted that she was terrified of water.

I was on holiday in Italy when the news of her death reached me. An immense shock! The gutter press and Hollywood gossip suggested a sinister murder. I'm afraid I believe the version related by my good friend Gavin Lambert in his book *Natalie Wood.* After heavy drinking that night, and several days previously as well, she had gone down to her cabin, annoyed at the quarrel developing between R.J. (Robert John Wagner, known as R.J. in the profession), her first husband, whom she had remarried after her divorce from Richard Gregson, and her co-star in her current film, Christopher Walken, both of whom had drunk considerably, too. The captain was in no better shape than his passengers and was probably sleeping it off. She found herself unable to sleep, even though she'd taken sleeping pills, as was her habit. The ocean was quite agitated, and the dinghy was tapping against the hull, just at the head of her bunk. After putting on her quilted jacket, she staggered up the deck to the stern and leaned forward to catch the rope with the idea of securing it tight—the ring was down the hull a little. Unstable with the liquor and pills she had swallowed, she leaned forward, lost her balance, and hit her head in the fall. Her quilted coat quickly grew heavy with water and dragged her down. If she screamed, the men below were too lost in their own drama to hear her. It took the two of them a while before they decided they'd argued enough. When R.J. went down to the cabin and couldn't find Natalie, he and Chris Walken got into the dinghy and searched the dark sea for a while, with no result. They even went ashore, thinking she'd gone back to the hotel, where she had spent the previous night, again after a fight. Only when they finally had to admit defeat did they alert the Coast Guard, which had to follow the currents to find her body, quite a long way off. The suspicion of foul play is not plausible to anyone who knew R.J. and Natalie. True, she was by then unhappy with her career and drinking much too much; they had fights, as they'd had during their first marriage, but R.J. was profoundly in love with his wife and always had been.

When school holidays came, the children flew in and Michael took us to the Santa Fe Ranch Hotel. Wearing chaps, we went horseback riding on an all-day trek, leaving me crippled for two days. On another holiday it was a Mexican adventure, when Christopher caught the fish of the year, a swordfish taller than he was, which the other guest on the boat wanted to buy from him. On January 1, 1972, we were changing planes in Taxco when we learned the news that Maurice Chevalier had died. Quite a shock, as Maurice had been such a frontline, glamorous personality on the French scene ever since I was born. Twice my co-star, he had asked me for an exchange of signed photos after *Fanny,* telling me that I reminded him of his partner and early love, Mistinguett. At the time I thought, *What a quaint old-fashioned custom.* Now I'm glad I have the picture.

Next it was Acapulco, in the kind of hotel where there's a pool with every room. We never even dipped a foot in the ocean, as the tale of the last guest's being eaten by sharks was still fresh on everyone's lips. We watched, holding our breath, the young divers plunge from a height of a hundred feet into a crevice between two rocks, no bigger than a bathtub. Michael was unbeatable for great holidays.

Professionally, however, everything had begun to seem so very quiet that my career appeared to have faded away. I didn't have the strength or the experience to know that this wasn't necessarily permanent. I thought, *It's over, I had it coming, I've always known it.* The fact that I was pushing forty but wasn't ready for maturity didn't occur to me. I missed a good opportunity to take the leap into middle-aged parts when I refused a play written by my great friend James Bridges about a woman of forty who destroys herself with alcohol. I suspect he wrote the play to help me mature, but I didn't see it at the time. In fact, I was slightly shocked by the proposition. With years of reflection, I've come to believe that another reason for the profession's neglect was that the new crop of filmmakers considered me part of the grand old studio system and wanted new faces. What it felt like from inside was failure. A feeling of inner vacuum. Did people see that? Did they detect it? Not necessarily. My press agent suggested a trip to New York, where a photographer was willing to take pictures. He hoped he could also get me on a talk show while I was there. I thought this sounded desperate— beneath me; I refused. In 1970 a B-movie was offered, *Madron,* which I accepted—why not, with nothing else on the horizon? Everyone has to accept an old chestnut once in a while.

In cowboy-and-Indian times—the nineteenth century, I guess—a nun with a stoic, stubborn personality (Sister Mary, me) is traveling alone on a mule to reach her convent. She has to cross hostile Indian territory and finds an unlikely traveling companion in the person of a carpetbagger who fears neither God nor the devil (Richard Boone, playing Madron) but who can't help being impressed by her courage. The plot is a cliché in the adventure/drama category, with *The African Queen* the winner of that genre—only it had John Huston directing, with Katharine Hepburn, Humphrey Bogart, and two of the greatest producers in the world: Sam Spiegel and James Woolf. I should not have accepted *Madron,* but I hoped against hope and gave a brave, honest performance against all odds. I did my best for authenticity. I wore a real nun's habit in black wool with petticoats, bloomers, and black cotton stockings, even though it was 104 degrees in the shade. But we were like a ship without a rudder. You can't fight a drunken director bullied by a drunken leading man. After the screen kiss, I rinsed my mouth with a strong mouthwash.

We filmed *Madron* in Israel, the only interesting aspect of this adventure. Soldiers stopped by every morning on their way to sensitive zones by the border and on their way back to the barracks at nightfall. They leaned nonchalantly on their guns while watching us for a few minutes. In Israel you're never more than half an hour away from the combat zone. Above our heads, during one scene in which we were both riding our mounts, the sound of airplanes swelled until the whole crew were craning their necks to watch three planes swooping and swirling in a dogfight, two of them trying to get in the right position to shoot the third one down. The director didn't stop the camera, so we had to go on, respectful of the rule that an actor never stops a take. Finally Jerry Hopper said "cut," and we could look up and watch the two Israelis hit the Arab plane farther out in the desert. In another scene I had to be buried with just a piece of straw to breathe with. While digging my grave, the grips found a scorpion. They dropped gasoline in a circle around the creature and lit it; the scorpion stung itself to death.

The production company that rented the material had none of the modern facilities you expect on a movie set; I remember they didn't have a wind machine, so one had to be concocted with some farm implement.

Nowhere could we find an old-fashioned nineteenth-century comb, so a prop boy carved one from a piece of wood (I still have it). The assistants and prop men were full of vitality, initiative, and goodwill and were certainly the most cheerful people I had ever met, perhaps because life didn't have the same certainty it had for young people in a developed country—these boys went into the reserve a certain number of weeks every year, with all the dangers involved. The first thing you were shown when entering any hotel was a chart of the different booby traps you could encounter on a walk; the manager at the front desk pointed his finger to it and told you to make sure you studied it.

Back in Hollywood I occupied my time with my house. I covered the walls with cloth—what the French call *tapisser*—and gave it back its original Spanish style. I also became interested in vintage cars; I restored and drove a beautiful 1948 Ford convertible painted cream (I called her "Mae West"). It was fun, and it attracted a lot of attention—a bus driver stopped in the middle of an intersection to chat about the car. I also learned about organic culture and grew my own vegetable garden. Talking of gardens, I must recount how very early one morning, while I was upstairs writing, I heard rustling in the bushes. We had about an acre of wild growth going downhill (into which I had never ventured), while Anthony Quinn had the grounds going uphill, facing us, also covered with wild undergrowth. Alerted by the sound, I tiptoed to the ground floor and nearly fainted with fright: There, barely five feet away from me, stood the most majestic, full-grown stag, with five- to six-foot-long antlers. A stag, in Bel Air! We looked at each other, and the same thought crossed both our minds: *I won't harm you if you'll leave me alone.* We each went our way, the stag down the hill while I reentered the house. I saw him again above our little road, Cuesta Way, around six in the morning, quite unperturbed, obviously the real proprietor of these wild gardens.

Those were years when I became better known in the film community for my hostessing than for my acting. I appeared in *House & Garden* rather than in *Variety*. On party days I would start preparing the dinner early in the morning. The chocolate ice cream took the longest, a recipe that I came to call "Oh-my-God!" I would start by blanching and grilling the almonds, then add the dark chocolate to the half-cream/half-milk and all the other delicious ingredients, a few drops of orange juice, a spoonful of coffee. While talking, the guests would take a spoonful of ice cream, followed by a pause—"Oh, my God!" they invariably exclaimed with appropriate fervor.

I came to think that you immerse yourself in decorating your house and give marvelous dinner parties and your reputation as an actress takes a dive in inverse proportion to the quality of your cooking. No, I'm not being honest. All those fringe preoccupations were just temporary remedies to hide the real problem: I didn't believe in myself anymore.

The only flailing of the arms that kept me afloat was an American tour of the Feydeau farce *13 Rue de l'Amour*. It was good, solid professional experience and very enjoyable for those two hours when the public was howling with laughter. Instinct led me right; that was my way of surviving. The children came on holiday and saw me play in Chicago and Fort Lauderdale. Great days when they were there.

Michael made two films with me that were never really released: *Chandler,* written and directed by Paul Magwood (who incidentally was never my husband or even a boyfriend, as IMDb claims—we never even had a meal together), with Warren Oates as my leading man—an independent soul, he was. MGM financed the film. At that time James T. Aubrey (former president of CBS Television until he got fired) had been named president of the studios by Kirk Kerkorian, the Las Vegas businessman who had taken over MGM. Nicknamed "The Smiling Cobra" by producer John Houseman, Aubrey alienated several filmmakers during his four-year tenure, due to his brutal handling of production. Blake Edwards and Bruce Geller were among his victims. At the end of our film, Jim Aubrey, without any warning, simply locked the cutting-room door to both Michael and Paul Magwood. The two filmmakers took a full-page ad bordered in black in the trade papers: "Regarding what was our film *Chandler,* let's give credit where credit is due. We sadly acknowledge that all editing, post-production as well as additional scenes were executed by James T. Aubrey Jr. We are sorry." *Chandler* is sometimes seen on airplanes or one of those film channels at night. Michael had a meeting with MGM's lawyer, who told him in colorful terms, "Don't worry about Jim Aubrey. The slide is greased." Effectively, Jim Aubrey was soon transferred to manage the MGM Grand Hotel in Las Vegas, where he belonged.

The second film was *Nicole,* also called *Purple Nights.* Two charming Hungarians were involved in that one, István Ventilla and Louis Horvath. The cans of this unfinished work were later found in someone's garage and thrown away. A sad affair. I had to admit that Michael and my professional collaboration was a fiasco, as, increasingly, was our personal one. In 1975 I parted from him following his hesitation waltz between London, Hollywood, and Paris. After I'd sold my house in Montpelier Square under his instructions, in order to settle in Hollywood, and again after his insistence on selling the newly furnished Bel Air house in order to move back to Paris—"the next center of world business," as he put it—he decided after only two weeks there, "I don't think Paris is for me. Let's go back to Los Angeles." I firmly said, "Sorry, I'm staying right here." This excess of mobility was the major cause of our discord. Michael was a nomad, happiest floating in the first-class cabin of an ocean liner or sipping Coca-Cola in the bar of the Orient Express. I'm the opposite. I am earthbound. I need my two feet firmly planted in my own home. An atavistic resurgence of the Carons' obsession with houses? Very possibly. Oddly enough, Michael was forewarned by a fortune-teller whom we consulted before going to Paris. "She needs her house," said the lady with insistence. "Don't make her sell it." Michael made me sell it. He eventually went back to L.A. alone, where he settled in a hotel for several years.

Without too much conviction, I acquired an agent in Paris, but I could feel a reserve toward me, and this rejection has remained for forty years. To the French film community, I was neither fish nor fowl—not really American nor believably French; how could I be French, since my name, Leslie, was American and since I had made a successful career in Hollywood? I am very much appreciated by the French only so long as I appear in American films—preferably musicals—but my star is tarnished immediately if I try to join the French scene. *Nul n'est prophète en son pays.*

Docile, my head hung low, I accepted that my film career was dead and buried. A great lassitude overtook me when I thought of looking at myself on the screen with signs of age creeping up. I thought gamely, *I must learn a new profession,* and looked forward to learning to write, which interested me. While still in Los Angeles, every day before daybreak with Michael still asleep, I had started to write a comedy about

Hollywood, *Ritchie vs. Ritchie.* Michael offered it to Tatum O'Neal, whose father (Ryan O'Neal) became very angry. It seems that by co-incidence my description of Tatum as a little racketeer hit too close to home. I went on to write two more scripts, and in 1982, encouraged by Doubleday, a book of short stories, *Vengeance.*

17

A New Passion

*H*ere is how I began writing. I received in my Paris flat a letter from the agent for the American publisher Doubleday, Beverly Gordey, who lived just one Métro stop away, asking for a meeting to discuss the possibility of my writing a book of short stories. This lady had seen the naïve portraits I had done of my children and wondered if I might want to write children's stories and illustrate them. I'm afraid I simply threw the letter in the wastepaper basket. Two weeks later the same letter reappeared in the post with this note: "Perhaps you did not receive my first letter." This second missive took the same route down into the trash can. When it appeared a third time, I couldn't continue my uncivil behavior. I called the sender, who insisted on meeting me.

I apologized for my rudeness but said as politely as I could that I wasn't interested in kittens, puppies, or duckies; she immediately proposed alternatives. Murders? Love stories? Anything that interests you. "Ah!" said I noncommittally. "I'll see." She concluded, "Write three stories, send them to me, I'll submit them to New York." She told me later that she never thought I would oblige. She was very surprised when she received three rather sinister stories—one about a child, all right, but not in the kind of plot she had expected: The little girl is murdered due to the negligence and immaturity of her parents. It took me over a year of hard work to put down on paper thirteen stories; at that time I didn't even type, so the 180 pages were written in longhand, and I wrote at least ten pages for one that was saved. English isn't my mother tongue, and I constantly had to dive into the dictionary or my *Roget's Thesaurus.* But I became passionate about writing and discovered that the exercise was enriching and therapeutic.

I was also learning to be a normal citizen. Out of Hollywood's hothouse atmosphere, I found real life to be at first a thrilling discovery—all those interesting faces in the Paris Métro. Then less pleasant little things started to happen. The police didn't recognize me when I'd asked what a demonstration was about. "Move on, lady," was the rough answer I got. I had to spell my name when I reserved a table at a restaurant where they ought to have known who I was. I'd be invited to the Césars (the French equivalent of the Oscars), and a photographer would ask me to step aside so he could photograph the new face. Or worse, I would simply be knocked aside without even an "Excuse me." Let's face it, the princess had lost her tiara.

I had to wait until 1976—nearly ten years since *Il Padre di Famiglia*—for a film offer of quality to come along. Ken Russell, who used to be a dancer—believe it or not—and ages earlier had done barre exercises behind me when we both worked out at London's Royal Ballet School, asked me to play the silent-screen actress Alla Nazimova in his eccentric and remarkable *Valentino,* with Rudolf Nureyev.

I plunged into a biography of Alla Nazimova (by Gavin Lambert) and discovered the most fascinating person. After a very difficult start in Europe, where she even had to resort to prostitution in order to eat, she went to Russia and managed to get hired by the Moscow Art Theatre. When the company came to New York in 1905, her realistic Stanislavski style of acting made her the toast of Broadway, to the point that MGM invited her to Hollywood at the phenomenal salary of thirteen thousand dollars a week. There again she had a huge success with her first film, *War Brides,* and started to amass a solid fortune. She was respected as a grande dame because she could speak five languages and eventually imposed herself as her own producer and scriptwriter. Among her claims to fame was the discovery of Rudolph Valentino, whom she made her co-star in *Camille.* The paradox is that, having revolutionized the theater with her naturalistic acting, she then became the most melodramatic actress of the silent-film era. To complete her life's trajectory with true Russian contrast, she lost her considerable fortune—stolen by a lesbian partner of hers—and had to rent one of the small bungalows in the vast estate she had built on Sunset Boulevard. I stayed there when it became a chic hotel, the Garden of Alla. The estate was finally torn down in the eighties to be replaced by a bank.

I rather enjoyed working with Ken Russell. He would draw lines on the floor and tell me, "You're in frame from here to there, so go ahead, do your stuff." I loved this permissiveness and also his excesses. He sometimes pushed us to act with operatic exuberance, but in a way it suited the subject of silent-film days. The film community and the public, too, I guess, were going through the opposite tendency—realism— so the film wasn't a success. Sad for Nureyev, who would have loved a film career. One of the most heavenly pas de deux in this film, or in any since the beginning of cinema, is the tango lesson danced by Nureyev (Valentino) with Anthony Dowell (Nijinsky), who then proceeds to give him a little demonstration in classical virtuosity. I always watch this moment of magic holding my breath.

I learned to love Rudolf dearly, the most vulnerable person I've known, hiding his tenderness under caprices and the foulest of language. I'm not afraid to use the word "genius" when I talk about him. He had exceptional intelligence, powers of seduction, humor, an open mind, and curiosity about everything. The world was too small for his appetite; he wanted to experience all that the universe had to offer, way beyond ballet. He was avidly interested in poetry, in the theater, in films, in opera—and furthermore he could sing all the great soprano arias in a falsetto voice.

We became close friends in the beautiful city of Bath, where we were filming the Valentino mansion. We were on our own every night for dinner, and immediately, as if we'd known each other for a long time, we began to exchange intimate information. Nureyev knew how to be a close friend. He wanted to know about my life, my childhood, and he asked questions in a soft voice—almost like a child. He was bluntly truthful about his own, though never vulgar. "I was born in the armpit of the world! There!" He would point to Tartar country on the map. His use of obscenities, said with a pronounced Russian accent, made him very amusing. He didn't get along with Michelle Phillips, who was playing his wife, Natasha Rambova; her star attitude didn't work with him. His reaction was as straightforward as a punch in the nose: "Just because you play c— in film doesn't mean you have to be c— in life!" He was quite nervous about his lack of social savoir faire and asked me to accompany him to the Iranian embassy when the ambassador gave a dinner for him in London. He wasn't sure he would pick the "right" fork. We sat, about twelve guests, around the largest round table in blond varnished wood. Two butlers came in with soup tureens full of the best gray caviar, offered with silver ladles—not spoons, ladles. No garnish, no lemon, just pure Iranian caviar with toast. I served myself a generous portion, which I ate with extreme pleasure. Just when I thought I couldn't eat another thing, the butlers came in again with the tureens replenished to the brim. I had to refuse, aware that I would later regret it.

Rudolf liked to be admired. During the film he kept up his training and would ask me if I wanted to watch him do the barre. Yes, of course I did. There was always a local theater with a barre in the wings, lit by one glaring bulb—he would sit on a chair and undress without the least embarrassment. He knew he was beautiful. But above his flawless technique and the rare proportions of his body he had a quality of tenderness and grace that gave meaning to the ballet steps. Despite the formality of classical ballet, his dancing wasn't mechanical; it spoke with lyrical poetry. Onstage he kept an intimate dialogue with his partner, enraptured by her, the two of them alone in front of a thousand pairs of eyes. One night at curtain call, amid the thunder of clapping hands and the cries of adulation, someone booed him. I can't think who would boo Nureyev; still, he may have had enemies. Holding his partner with his right hand, he took his bows with a humble tilt forward, but the middle finger of his left hand was definitely up in the air! An old Russian lady followed every one of his performances and always came backstage to congratulate him. Although a crowd surrounded him as soon as he left the stage, he would reach for her and stand respectfully before her—suddenly the little Russian boy in front of his babushka. In Paris, sitting in the restaurant after a performance of *Giselle* at the Palais des Congrès, a group of close friends surrounding him, he first drank one or two glasses of white wine (laced with water—oh, what a crime!), then sat back with a puckish smile and said, "Now, compliments."

A frivolous image forces its way back to my memory. During the filming of *Valentino* in London, Rudolf tells me, "Margot [Fonteyn] and I are going to see the first documentary to come out of China. Come with us." I accepted and found myself in a short line with a lot of politically involved people, to view a film about Mao Zedong's postrevolution China. In comical contrast with the dedicated Communist viewers, Margot was wearing a priceless black sable coat, Rudolf a black mink with matching toque, and myself a full-length silver fox. I was afraid they wouldn't let us in.

The film showed Chinese men and women with bland expressions, dressed in perfectly identical blue working clothes, riding identical bicycles to work in thick formation, like a flock of swallows. We were also shown an example of the "Great Proletarian Cultural Revolution," in which a few members of the intellectual class "confessed" in public. These scenes sent shivers down your spine.

In 1975–76 Federico Fellini was preparing his film *Casanova*. I was asked to go meet him in Rome at the famous Cinecittà studios—I was sent an airplane ticket, a room was reserved in the Grand Hotel, everything was elegantly organized for the meeting. I was thrilled at the idea that I might be working with the great Fellini, but also a little apprehensive. At the studio gate, the officer directed me toward his bungalow, and I walked along the straight studio street. At the end of the alley, nearly a hundred yards away, I saw a man who had stepped outside his door and was looking in my direction. After a while I recognized the famous silhouette, scrutinizing me with the concentration of a painter staring at his model before attacking his canvas. When I came close to him, he switched to a warm welcome, invited me into his office, and asked me genially about my trip—the kind of banal chitchat that goes on when you're meeting someone new. But I could tell that all the while, he was observing me and calculating in his mind whether his first impression was right. He asked about Renoir, whose friendship we had in common, and talked a little about his plan to shoot this film on Casanova.

When the lapse of time dictated by courtesy seemed right, he came to the point in a cheerful way. "You know I am very bad at keeping up with actors. I never go to the movies. That's really very bad of me. I saw you in *Lili*." He made several appreciative nods of the head, and I calculated mentally that roughly twenty-five years had passed since he'd seen me on the screen. I was hardly the young girl he expected to meet. We both burst out laughing, since it was now quite clear that the outcome of this meeting was going to be negative. Then, to soften the blow, he added with self-deprecation, "Last time I asked to meet an actor I hadn't seen for a while, when he came to my office I was really surprised by the change. He had become a woman!"

* * *

In the summer of 1977, I was approached to do an American tour of the famous, delightful stage musical *Can-Can.* We rehearsed in New York, the most stimulating town, my favorite for any artistic adventures. (On Fifth Avenue I saw for the first time black kids dancing on their heads. I stood there in amazement, and later learned it had a name—break dancing. I thought Fred Astaire would have loved this insane new technique.) Our show had good actors, good dancers, and only one flaw: It required me to sing. Singing is not my forte; I have true pitch, but since my failure in *Gigi* I had not exercised my vocal cords, and they were weak. I was given a full chorus to back me up in "I Love Paris," but I still feel I should apologize to the audience that paid good money and had to suffer me in that classic melody. Nevertheless, the performance was a joyous cavalcade—hoofers are a nice bunch, and we kept our morale up by smoking pot, all together, after final curtain. This musical was very energetic, and if you wanted to come down from the adrenaline high and fall asleep before six in the morning—and we often had to pack up and leave early for the next town—it was either pot or wine or pills. I chose pot as the least evil. You sleep fine and suffer no hangover the next morning. My son, who had just finished school and had a hiatus before university, came over and followed the show for a month. He tried the stuff with us all but showed more enthusiasm for a good-looking dancer nearly my age. Yes, I was surprised! Oh, well, my son was growing up. At one point on the road, the management warned us that we would have to cross into Canada to play Toronto the following week and that the border police didn't have a sense of humor about grass. It had to disappear from our luggage; the management couldn't help us if we got caught. At the border the baskets of costumes were indeed searched, as were we, but nothing was found. The dressers had sewn the stuff into the hems of the understudies' dresses, which were sent ahead because they were so seldom used. And thus we continued our nightly medication. When the show was over, Christopher and I stopped smoking—there was no reason to anymore. Years later I found a little pipe in my stage toiletries with some very dry grass. I threw it away.

While I was on tour in the summer of 1977, François Truffaut contacted me to offer a part in his next film, *L'Homme Qui Aimait les Femmes,* or

The Man Who Loved Women. The film is the autobiographical confession of a writer who adored women and collected them the way some people collect stamps. I was one of about twenty women involved. Here I must proclaim my admiration for the great filmmaker. His *Jules et Jim* was and is one of my favorites, and its charm, originality, and poignancy establish it among the masterpieces of cinema. Truffaut and I had become good friends since meeting at the Renoirs' in Beverly Hills. Knowing that I was alone in Paris, he used to call me every two to three weeks to take me out to dinner. I was then trying to become a writer and working studiously on scripts and short stories. He was my mentor, gave me advice and discussed my work (not if I wrote in English, which he refused to read—like Napoleon, he was incapable of grasping the foreign language, no matter how many lessons he kept taking). From time to time, we used to see films together that we then discussed during dinner—or, rather, he would give me a dissertation on the film. He was incredibly knowledgeable and enthusiastic but became mute if you mentioned anything outside films and literature. A leaden silence would then settle, only to be broken by my eager return to his themes of choice. His oft-repeated motto in case of fire was "Children and films first!" One day in a Hollywood restaurant, he said, "There's a film of yours on TV at three-thirty tomorrow morning. Are you going to see it?" I said, "No, of course not. I'll be sleeping." He added, casually, "I plan to put my alarm clock on to view it."

We were out for dinner on the night that writer/director Pier Paolo Pasolini was brutally murdered. François, upon hearing the news, exclaimed, "Oh . . . but he's finished his film!" as if to say, "It's all right, now that his film is completed." His opinions about most filmmakers had gone through a long analytical process: at first passionate youthful fervor, then the rejection of the disenchanted adolescent, to be followed by a slow maturation and eventual return to respect for the technical or artistic accomplishments of the director, which sometimes ended in a mellow clouding of the brain, close to sentimental mush. How else could this pronouncement, which he made to me—sober and in good health— be justified? *"A Countess from Hong Kong* is Charlie Chaplin's best film!" But no matter how irrational or provocative some of his critiques may have been, this simple pronouncement is the redeeming quote: "The only films that are of any value are films made with passion."

His partisan intolerance might have been tiresome if it hadn't been tempered by the most irresistible sense of humor. With insolent schoolboy quips, he would point to the comic aspect of human behavior even in dramatic or serious situations. We went together to the very first night of the Paris Film Festival. Photographers were crowded in front of a decorative pool to snap close-ups of us. François remarked with quick wit that it was lucky they didn't need full-length shots. (One step back and they would have fallen into the pool.)

He could sense the distress in inconsolable orphans and gave advice, paternal help, and friendship to those who had known the same indifferent or absent mother as he had. At his funeral I discovered a virtual orphanage, gathered from all over the world, in dire need of his assistance for life support. Twenty years after his death, the Antoine Doinels of this world (the leading character in *The 400 Blows* and of several subsequent films—a quite autobiographical figure) still leave flowers on his tomb daily, in memory of his compassionate understanding of adolescence. He was seriously involved in a program to help autistic children.

He died a good deal too early. A short time before a brain tumor took him away, he told me that he was now finished with all aspects of his adolescence and that he was ready to start working on the subject of love in maturity.

Although he was secretive till the end of his life, he confided to me, one evening at dinner, the circumstances of his birth. The secret was so heavy that I kept it locked in my heart until after his death, when his ex-wife, Madeleine Morgenstern, and his children admitted publicly their knowledge of it. His biological father was a Jewish dentist named Lévy whom his mother's family had refused to allow into its midst. After discovering the truth of his birth—just as in *Stolen Kisses* (more Antoine Doinel adventures), François had his real father traced by a detective. Of course, he couldn't resist the impulse to discover what his progenitor looked like. Recounting this emotional episode by way of an incidental detail, he described to me how, to his annoyance, his real father wore his scarf with the same particular twist as he did. There is no adequate word in English to translate the French word *pudeur*. Dictionaries suggest "sense of decency," "prudishness," "modesty," "chasteness"—none of which express the sort of distinction of sentiments and of behavior with which François was gifted. Just as he abhorred gratuitous nudity or any display of sex on the screen, he was "chaste" when it came to emotions. I think also that some emotions were too painful for him to address. For instance, he couldn't stand to gaze at the vast luminous or clouded heavens—the countryside made him uncomfortable, as he may have felt that landscape distracted one from human relationships. He wrote to me that while making *The Story of Adele H.,* which concerned Victor Hugo's daughter, his emotions were profoundly involved because of his attraction to Isabelle Adjani, who played the lead; for some reason he refused to ever photograph landscape, and even though the film has several scenes of traveling across Europe, he preferred to concentrate the camera on the wheels of the carriage rather than ever tip it up toward the hills, the sky, or the trees.

The Man Who Loved Women was filmed in Montpellier, the perfect-size town, with monuments in sand-colored stone, enriched with a first-rate university—sunny, orderly, and steeped in history with values of transmitted traditions. François loved filming on location, with the cast and crew gathered together to concentrate on the sole preoccupation of making a film, without any family interference to distract them. He loved the holiday-camp atmosphere—eating in groups and sleeping in proximity to work. I understood that; I felt the same warm conviviality when touring with the ballet company.

François had a great admiration for Ingmar Bergman, who made his films in six long beautiful scenes (or so he said), rich in emotions but economical in structure. He, on the other hand, always wrote short, sharp scenes—with an average length of a page and a half each. He used to say that if his structures were set far in advance, he had to write the dialogues during the weekends—as a result of which his actors didn't have time to learn long scenes. I have my doubts about this rationale; I simply think that the rhythm of short scenes suited his personality and also that he wanted to avoid endless actors' arguments. For this film Truffaut asked Charles Denner to play the lead. Denner insisted that because of his bad memory he had to get the dialogue early enough to learn it. And for once, François wrote me a six-page scene—quite exceptional. I was flattered. As the theme seemed autobiographical, I tried to find out whom I was interpreting. Was I Madeleine, his wife, whom I hadn't met yet? Or Catherine Deneuve, with whom he'd had a long love affair, or Jeanne Moreau, one of his first companions . . . ? In keeping with his secretive nature, he would never reveal the inspiration for her. Left to myself, I built up the character with what details the script gave me, and my doubts as to the profound reasons for the breakup between Bertrand Morane (Charles Denner's character) and Véra (my character) added to the pathos. My character in the script didn't know why the breakup had happened, and I didn't either.

I refused to believe the alarmist rumors about his health, even though I had heard them from a doctor friend. One day François himself called me from the hospital where he was undergoing more exams and scans. I was shocked by the loss of tone in his voice, which had become wispy and thin, what in French we call *une voix blanche*—a ghostly voice, you could say. I realized with shock that the rumors were true: François Truffaut was dying. His last call was to encourage me. He said, "Leslie, every time I have to go to the hospital, I take your book of short stories and I read one." My heart bled when I saw him at his flat. We tried to talk cinema, but there were long pauses where I heard the unspoken words, *Can it really be true? . . . Am I dying? . . . Why me?* At the door he said, "I feel so alone. I am desperate. . . ." Soon after this he accepted his former wife's—Madeleine Morgenstern's—hospitality and moved into her apartment, where he stayed until the end.

My respect for François was infinite, but I had to admit he sometimes surprised me with statements of sheer Parisian nonsense. Once in Los Angeles—where he seemed to thrive, with his pack of cigarettes in the crease of his rolled-up shirt—exasperated by his worship of "Tinseltown," I asked him, "François, why do you love coming here so much?" He answered quick as a flash, "Because there's room to park my car." Everything François said was scripture to me. Still . . . !

Soon after his death, Madeleine invited me to her flat for a meal. I was thrilled and a little intimidated. As I came near the building, I became aware that there wasn't a parking place to be had in this very elegant neighborhood—not for love or money. Suddenly I said out loud, in a state of irritated panic, "Come on, François, find me a place, for God's sakes! I'm here to visit your wife!"

Immediately a car pulled out, directly in front of Madeleine's flat. I snatched it gratefully, if a little surprised at his influence on terrestrial traffic. "Thank you, François!" Since that day, whenever I find myself in a terrible no-parking situation, I say a prayer to François. "Just once more, François, I really, really need it!" Can you believe it? I always find a space and never get a ticket in François's spots, no matter how approximately legal or illegal they may be. No, of course I don't believe in it, but still, I never forget to say, "Thank you, François!"

The year 1978 offered me one of the richest encounters in my professional life: the chance to work with Polish director Krzysztof Zanussi. That year we were both members of the jury at the San Sebastián Film Festival, together with Luigi Comencini, the brilliant Chilean director Miguel Littin, and sculptor Néstor Basterrechea, a bona fide Basque artist. Every day, just as the lights dimmed in the auditorium, a bomb threat forced the festival organizers to evacuate the cinema of paying patrons. Convinced that our Basque representative was our security badge, we never left the theater, although we did become a little cynical about our jury duties. The auditorium being empty, we would leave shortly after the credits, as soon as we knew that the film was a dud—and one can indeed tell after the very first frames. One of us would stay behind, to give the others a report, while the rest of us went off for a meal or a pleasant sightseeing trip. These forays near the Spanish-French border caused Zanussi untold anxieties. He had to be extremely careful to keep enough clear pages in his passport in order to be able to continue traveling to the West. Having his passport renewed by USSR censorship authorities, in those days, was for him a very uncertain operation. A wrong turn on the road and we might find ourselves inadvertently in France, where the police would ask for papers and certainly keep this citizen from the Communist Bloc for questioning, in the best of cases using one more page to stamp his document, thus endangering future travel.

One film in competition certainly got our attention: Bob Altman's *A Wedding.* I loved Altman's films—it is a regret of mine that the great man never asked me to work with him. Zanussi and I got into a quarrel about this particular entry. He argued that it was technically sloppy, while I maintained that this apparent carelessness was a precious quality in slick Hollywood. I'm glad to say that I did manage ultimately to get Altman the "Best Actress" prize for Carol Burnett.

Two years later Krzysztof sent me *The Contract,* his version of the same subject—a wedding. In his film, the conflict was the confrontation between the morally depleted bourgeois Polish apparatchiks and the integrity of the dissidents. I played the capricious rich capitalist from the West whose moral flaw is revealed through her kleptomania. Fascinating part. I accepted very happily and took off for Warsaw with a couture wardrobe. At the airport every actor and technician on the film was there to greet me. The customs officer was staring with disapproval at the great white cardboard boxes labeled "Nina Ricci." We had to open each one and give a detailed description of every garment. I remember particularly a coat made entirely of feathers of an indefinable color. Was it aubergine? Bordeaux? Or perhaps just purple? The group turned into a panel of advisers, making the guard very touchy. Then, for his written report, he had to determine what bird the feathers came from. The poor customs officer, who had never seen anything so frivolous, was about to refuse entry to the feathered coat, when I imperiously proclaimed that they were cock feathers from a French chicken farm. That was something he could relate to, so the coat was given a bill of entry.

Filming with Zanussi in Soviet Warsaw was quite an experience. Surprisingly, the most precious commodity was film. We had only enough negative for one take of every scene. To ensure that no film stock was wasted for technical reasons, the camera rested on the shoulders of Slawomir Idziak. There was no need to hit your mark, as Idziak had you in his lens. The Soviet authorities, who considered, with good reason, Zanussi to be a dissident, made it very difficult to film in the opera house, where my character insisted on going, having been a ballet dancer in her youth. All made up and in costume, we had to wait until one or two in the morning before being grudgingly granted permission to film.

Zanussi told me, "Film critics in the West discuss endlessly the whys and wherefores of black-and-white sequences in color films—they see artistic or political motivations. The reason is that we always film the important scenes first with our quota of color negative, but we sometimes run out of the stuff. If the authorities refuse to give us any more color, we have to finish the film with more-or-less stolen black-and-white negative. That's all there is to it."

I really became aware of the fear that motivated every public servant in a totalitarian regime when I bought at the local Saturday-morning flea market a modest little landscape on which a child had glued tiny airplanes, cut out from a boys' magazine. The frame had to go through

the "censorship bureau," where it was labeled "work of art—national
treasure," and I was informed that I could never take it out of Poland.

To say that Zanussi was brilliant is an understatement. He spoke fluent English, French, German, Italian, and Spanish, and of course Polish
and Russian. He could no doubt find his way in one or two other languages. Truffaut said of him, *"Ah, oui, le fort en thème!"* (Something like
"the school nerd!") Zanussi had studied physics despite (but combined
with) a strong religious and spiritual upbringing. However, his deeper
instincts were epicurean. The way he constantly cracked his knuckles
bore witness to his inner struggle. I think that what he taught me was
to recognize the complexity in human nature. I tended otherwise to
be quite simplistic in my judgments. When with artless logic I would
say, "She can't say this or do that, it's in contradiction to her nature,"
he would answer, "Ha, that's just it—people are full of contradictions."
Paradox was his element. He was a very good storyteller, and was also
generous and liberal. He never gave marching orders, and would ask
me to write my own dialogue, which was, I think, a little too trusting.
The set was crowded with too many crew members, as if labor were
the cheapest line of goods. I loved the sound of all those melodious
voices, going up and down the musical scale—to me a revelatory sign of
vitality. There was a happy anarchy on the set, even though things and
people usually fell into place. (Usually, not always.) He sometimes for-
got that I couldn't speak Polish and wouldn't know what to do or where
to go after he'd said "Action!" (in Polish) unless he had first explained
it in English. He also had a way of forgetting to say "Cut!" at the end of
a scene, which forced us to keep going, improvising as long as we could.
Finally I used to shout in distress, "Krzysztof! I don't know what to say
anymore! Why do you do that!" He would laugh and reply, "But it was
so interesting, I wanted to know more!" Apart from the gentle chaos
on the set, what I noticed was the warmth—we could have been in a
Mediterranean country, there was so much emotion flying around. The
remarkable Maja Komorowska, his muse, who appeared in several of
his films, had to go through heated arguments with Zanussi before her
luminous soul could express itself. I like to remember that the smallest
part in our film was performed by a young actor so accomplished that
he could have played Hamlet. Humor served an important function in
the survival of these oppressed people. My favorite Polish joke was the

official rhetorical speech: "Comrades, we used to be on the edge of the abyss. Since then we have taken a great step forward." And also how when the censorship bureau wanted Zanussi to cut the close-up of a dissident actress, he offered to replace it with an "American" shot (a medium shot), to the horror of the authorities. "No, no! Not an American shot! Leave it as it is."

As we never stopped for lunch, the food that was part of the wedding set kept disappearing slowly. When I made a polite inquiry about the lunch break, there was an embarrassed silence, followed by hushed whispers. I was then taken by an assistant to a restaurant, where I ate the worst goulash of my life. Yes, I felt guilty about this preferential treatment.

When we went to the Venice Film Festival, I complimented Zanussi on the remarkable music composed by Wojciech Kilar, whom I had met in Warsaw—a tall, intellectual-looking man with gaunt cheeks and prematurely gray hair. Zanussi thanked me and then added, "But I worry about his health. With his coupons he buys meat for his cat instead of for himself." The last shot of the film, underscored with a strident crescendo of strings, reveals the profile of a grand old stag standing in a clearing (about thirty years before the same shot in *The Queen*). The message of nobility is illuminating. There was a stunned silence in the festival theater before the thunder of applause.

I ultimately made three films with Zanussi: *The Contract* in 1980 and *Imperative* and *The Unapproachable* in 1982. We gave a stage version of the last one at the Little Odéon Theatre in Paris, the Piccolo Teatro in Milan, and at Spoleto for the festival.

While filming *The Unapproachable* in Berlin, I had the opportunity to witness again the paranoia triggered by the Soviet regime on its citizens. Krzysztof lived in fear that a malevolent taxi driver—or a practical joker, or even an amateur driver—would take him near the border with East Berlin, where the guards would be only too happy to grab him and force him across the border to the east for keeps. He had nightmares about being captured by mistake and refused to be steered anywhere near that neighborhood. He told me how he and his mother were arrested by Russian soldiers in the streets of Warsaw in August 1944. His mother, being a very tall woman, thought that if anyone got shot in the group, by mistake or as an example, she would be the one.

Afraid that her five-year-old orphan son would then not know who he was, she wrote his name and birth date in the palm of his little hand. A while later a guard who was marching them toward a camp made a discreet sign while passing a farmhouse and then turned his head away. She understood the signal and flattened herself and Krzysztof against the corner of the house, waiting for the group to pass. They were saved and later reunited with his father.

While in Berlin I had a letter of recommendation to a couple of German editors who were caught on the eastern side. Having a French passport, I could take the subway to the east (for a hefty border fee). When you stepped out of the subway, the decay and poverty of this neighborhood stood in shocking contrast to the affluent Berlin you had just left. My two hosts told the story of how, early on the Sunday morning of August 13, 1961, while they were out for a stroll, they noticed a few Russian soldiers starting to build what seemed like a wall, with cement blocks. Suspicious, the husband said to his wife, "I don't like this. Let's keep walking straight on." His wife told him, "I'm afraid, not right now. Let's see what this is, maybe nothing at all." By the evening, guards with machine guns were in place, stopping anyone from walking through. Their chance had passed, and so they remained on the wrong side of the wall for the next twenty-eight years. The surprising thing is that when they questioned me about news outside their eastern section, they were not so much interested in what was going on in London or on Broadway, or what was shown in museums in Paris, or what such-and-such a writer was publishing in the West—no, what concerned them passionately was, "What's it like at the end of our street, on the other side of the wall?"

While we were preparing the theatrical version of *The Unapproachable*, at the Little Odéon, Giorgio Strehler was rehearsing his *Illusion Comique* (by Pierre Corneille, 1636) on the large stage, and I would slip away every chance I could to see the great master direct. I admired his consummate creation of theatrical magic. First of all, he always rehearsed onstage with full performance lighting and with whatever costume was ready. This inflamed the actors' emotions to the right pitch. One detail to illustrate his mastery: A father in despair comes onstage to express his pain at losing his son. Most directors would have the actor enter from left of the stage going right, or from right going left, or from one of the back wings toward the front. Not Strehler. First we heard a pitiful moan ending in a howl of pain, so that our hair stood on end. Then emerged from the dark right side of the proscenium arch this old man reeling in despair, his back to the public, lurching slowly toward the rear of the stage in a diagonal, as if trying to flee from an odious scene—his voice gaining in intensity every time his eyes and his pointed finger returned toward the proscenium arch from which he had appeared. The drama was expressed by his body as well as by the fluctuations of his voice; an oblique shaft of light added to the dramatic effect. This was powerful theater.

I can't resist the pleasure of describing my favorite moment in a Giorgio Strehler production. In act 2 of *The Cherry Orchard,* Madame Ranyevskaya and all the gracious members of her family and entourage, out on a promenade, have stopped to rest here and there on a little hillock. Their voices grow quiet when we seem to hear the distant sound of a steam train. The sound intensifies, and presently a little toy steam train on miniature railway tracks appears at the foot of the hillock, with smoke blowing from its chimney, to trace its way across the whole stage and finally disappear in the wings. The play's message is clear: The industrial age has arrived in Russia! The aristocracy has lost its ascendancy over the workingman! Inevitably, the audience broke into applause.

In 1980 I was invited to be a member of the jury at the Cannes Film Festival, when Kirk Douglas was president. If he was popular with the photographers, he wasn't with the jury. Having been invited with several members of his family to stay at the five-star Eden Roc Hotel at the expense of the French taxpayer, he cared more for his tennis game than for discussions of the films in competition. For my part I lobbied forcefully and successfully for Zanussi to receive the director's prize for *The Constant Factor.* The award meant not only prestigious worldwide recognition but a precious *laissez-passer*—an important security badge for an intellectual in the Eastern Bloc. Thanks to this and other prizes, Zanussi was also able to protect his colleague Krzysztof Kieślowski, whose films he produced under his film company TOR. Similarly, during the Montréal World Film Festival in 1986, I was able to influence the jury to give the director's prize to the Czech director Jiří Menzel for his delightful *My Sweet Little Village.* The Czech delegation came to thank me with tears in their eyes, saying that this prize was sure to keep Václav Havel out of prison. I was extremely surprised to understand that although Menzel's film was quite removed from obvious political confrontation, the fact that "the West" had honored a Czech film meant that the world was keeping tabs. Western opinion might not accept another incarceration of the political opponent Havel . . . The support of the Western world, even in a film festival, had a way of making Soviet authorities very nervous.

In that same Festival des Films du Monde, another memorable incident took place. After a week of work, we had seen all the films except for one that had not yet arrived—a film by Peter Greenaway. The jury was eager to respect the voting deadline and have done with it. I insisted that we postpone our voting for twenty-four hours, hoping that Greenaway's film would arrive, and the jury grudgingly accepted. *The Belly of an Architect* arrived the next day. Naturally, it won Best Film hands down. I want to believe that this prize helped the film find a better release.

In the summer of 1980, a very nice offer came to play once again (in Australia and in English) the Feydeau farce *13 Rue de l'Amour,* this time with Louis Jourdan and a good director, the distinguished Basil Langton. The translation was superlative, as was the cast, with very accomplished Australian actors enriching the bill. Basil knew what was required to make a piece like this work. First rule: Express with total honesty the excessive naïveté of the characters. There are no straight parts in Feydeau; every character has flaws—physical flaws and personality flaws. Everyone is deceitful, acrobatically so. Second rule: Feydeau situations must be played with the hopeless, reckless despair of life-and-death consequences. Third rule: The whole cast must be very disciplined, and the tempo must never be allowed to flag. The ball must be kept in the air at all times. If played right, Feydeau is the most euphoric author to perform. There should be a laugh, like Swiss clockwork, every thirty seconds of the piece.

Louis Jourdan is an ideal Feydeau lover—he drew from his southern roots a kind of foppish self-conceit that was extremely comical. His own chronic dissatisfaction with life, however, had grown worse. Rehearsals became painful when Louis took it upon himself to reprimand every

actor if the slightest variation from text occurred. One fine day, unable
to take the torture he was inflicting on his colleagues anymore, I blew
up and denounced his rigidity, his pomposity, and his petty mind and
altogether took revenge for all the flak I had suffered since *Gigi*. Rehearsing became more harmonious after that, and we had a fine run. We
played in fifteen-hundred-seat theaters in Sydney and Melbourne, and
we were always full. Louis and I still did have our difficult moments,
but I was able to have it out with him when, for instance, he would cut
right into the end of my line so that I didn't get a laugh—I immediately
did the same to him, and he got the message. He also had a very unpleasant, even painful, trick of always looking at my hairline instead of
into my eyes. But why should I be so intolerant? Get on with your part
and don't expect from your co-stars a generous reciprocity.

In his hotel suite after opening night, Louis cooked a fine spaghetti
dinner for the cast and crew, and all the charm and generosity of his real
nature came forth. He was forgiven.

The 1985 summer tour of a French comedy, *One for the Tango,*
wasn't unpleasant. In the story one windy, dark night a woman past her
prime but far from her dotage hears a suspicious noise coming from her
living room. She tiptoes down to discover a young thief, who immediately tries to threaten her—but instead of being frightened, she bursts
out laughing and tells the young man that he is a pathetic amateur and
needs to take lessons. We learn at the same time as he does that she was
a cat burglar, the top in her profession. She takes him in to train him,
and the lessons go well until her son—an insurance broker—drops in
with his new fiancée, who unfortunaely recognizes too many objects in
the house. Mommy is caught with her hand in the cookie jar.

We were touring the states of New Hampshire, Maine, and Con-
necticut, three states with tradition and culture. My mouth salivates
when I think of the lobsters we ate in Maine. We used to go to a fish
shop before the show, where we each picked our lobster and indicated
the precise hour when the curtain would go down. Without even taking
our makeup off, we would pile into a cab and zoom to the fish shop. I
think we ate them on the spot, our chins shining with melted butter.

18

Black Days–the Eighties

What does it feel like to reach fifty when you've been known for your juvenile charm? Age crawls behind you and sneaks under your skin like an impostor. I felt guilty at the discovery of every little sag, every shadow, every wrinkle. Everyone knows that actresses have a duty to remain young; worse, I still didn't really think of myself as an actress. Now and again there were moments when I believed I had done a good job in a particular role, but I still regarded myself as a dancer who had given up dancing too early and hoped to convince herself and others that she could become an actress, given the right chance. Do all actresses think perfection is just around the corner, but somehow unreachable? I am relieved when I hear the same self-doubts expressed by other thespians. I hear them quite often, as a matter of fact. There was a face lift or two—because I felt I needed more time—a constant change of hairdos, a new companion, and with each new change I would think, *There, now, I've repaired the damage—I can get away with it still.* Delusion, of course. The years kept advancing inexorably, evident to everyone else.

I felt painfully starved for sex and wished I could attain some stability in my private life, while at the same time I kept hoping for the day when I could become independent and shake off the domination of men. I wasn't there yet. I had met a writer—black hair, black beard, part Corsican, part Greek, an explosive personality—Jean-Pierre Petrolacci, simply called Petro, the most promising scriptwriter in France. I always thought he should have written for Buñuel, as he had that kind of sinister, mischievous imagination. People died in his plots as they seemed to do around him in real life; his brother, a noted photographer, had committed suicide, and that inspired a kind of respect toward him, creating an aura of drama. When he was sober, he was humane, gentle, tender, amusing, extremely well read, and a remarkable writer. But he was sober only from two or three in the afternoon, when he woke up in a vulnerable condition, until around 8:00 P.M., when his first whiskey would start him on his revenge-on-life kick. When drunk, he turned into the devil and would hit anything that moved. I wrote one of my short stories about him: "The Boogeyman."

I firmly believe that Colette instinctively chose a writer for her first husband (Henri Gauthier-Villars, called Willy), no matter how inappropriate he was on every other level, so that he could teach her the discipline of writing. Without comparing myself to her in any other respect, I think I made that same calculation. There must be easier ways to educate oneself. . . .

If Petro taught me a lot about literature, he also taught me how to drink at night in order to become unconscious before the fight even started. I would knock myself into a deep slumber with whatever was available, and a sleeping pill if I had one. Our relationship quickly fell into the best Dashiell Hammett–Lillian Hellman pattern. First act, a drunken fight in his apartment; second act, flight to a hotel room, where the repentant lover came rushing in, full of contrition; third act, a flare-up of the argument; and the epilogue was a search into the bleak hours of the morning for a last bottle of whiskey and its inseparable pack of cigarettes. Of course there were vows never to fight again. Never again, sworn sincerely—until the next time. It wasn't that dramatic all the time, there were respites—wonderful evenings in the best restaurants, offered by Petro's generous friend Rodolph Ankaoua, the most romantic accountant ever. Petro and I parted, split up, and started life again at least once a month, and this lasted for six years, until the night of the great rampage when Petro, in a paroxysm of drunken rage, destroyed my apartment and rushed toward me with his arm raised to kill. I was rescued by a neighbor who rang the doorbell after hearing my screams, and Petro left my flat. Peering over the balcony to see his departure, I observed a dignified Petrolacci in his beige vicuña coat, hugging his vacuum cleaner—the last gift to our conjugal life. He hailed a taxi before disappearing from my life for good.

Through thick and thin, I kept on working—not only with writing (my book of short stories was published by Doubleday in 1982) but also as a performer. I also kept to the discipline of my morning ballet barre, no matter how shaky I felt. I didn't do any glorious work, except for a grand gala at the Met with the two superstars Nureyev and Baryshnikov. Yes, I can boast about being the only dancer in the world who has danced for seven minutes with both great performers simultaneously. The Paris Opéra Ballet Company, headed by Nureyev, was invited to tour the United States, but there wasn't enough money to fund the trip. Jane Herman, the Met's director, had the bright idea of hosting a benefit gala at the Met in order to raise a million or two. The bill presented the stars of both the Paris Opéra Company and the American Ballet Theatre. For a little dessert frolic, Jane had in mind a re-creation of my number with Gene Kelly, "Our Love Is Here to Stay," from *An American in Paris,* with the two Russian boys in tailcoats portraying the likes of Gene Kelly and Fred Astaire. Gene wasn't keen on the idea of our using his choreography, so a medley of tunes from my other musicals, (*Lili, Daddy Long Legs,* and *The Glass Slipper*) was arranged. At the time I was in Paris doing Zanussi's *Inaccessible* so John Richardson, a choreographer from the New York City Ballet, was sent to teach me the jazz number. Wherever I went with the play, a rehearsal hall was arranged so I could rehearse with or without my trainer. In Spoleto a disused chapel was put at my disposal, where I insisted on having a large, full-length mirror placed in front of the altar. The huge crucifix overlooked my swinging kicks. Pardon me, Jesus!

Two nights before the show in New York, a car came for me at Spoleto, after the play; we drove to the Milan airport, where I flew to Paris and slept in my flat that night. The next morning a car was at my door to take me to Charles de Gaulle, where I boarded the Concorde, arrived in New York three hours before my departure (that's the way the time difference worked). A limousine dropped me directly at the Met, where I found my costume sent from Las Vegas (Juliet Prowse's), rehearsed for the first time with the two boys, took a shower, ate a sandwich, and did the show.

The Met was packed—I can only describe the experience as an explosion of joy on my part and on the public's, too. The choreography by John Richardson was in the Jerome Robbins musical-comedy style—not difficult, but still, seven minutes of vigorous dancing. Rudolf never learned his part—he was far too nervous with his responsibility to the

Paris Opéra Ballet and Sylvie Guillem's introduction to the American public—so that Misha had to coach him until the very second when the curtain rose. The two boys looked superb in their tailcoats, white bow ties, and patent-leather shoes. Somehow, after four minutes of kicking and twirling, we had to leave stage right, and I had to run backstage and reappear alone on stage left to continue the number. To say that the wings were crowded is an understatement; every dancer from both companies was in the wings trying to catch a glimpse of the performance. Misha took me by the hand—this was his theater; he knew his way around backstage—and ran with me to my place of reentry, where he literally threw me on, totally out of breath, but with a smile from ear to ear. At the end the clapping went on and on until finally Misha said, "That's enough," and pulled me and Rudolf off. Nancy Reagan came backstage, and all the "society people" from Philadelphia and New York and stars from Hollywood and Broadway were at the supper party in the foyer—with Elizabeth Taylor on her most scintillating form.

The next morning a limo took me to Kennedy Airport, and the Concorde flew me to Paris, where I boarded the first flight back to Milan. That night I was on the stage in Spoleto—a little dizzy, I'll admit—to play my part in front of a much smaller audience (the theater held only 150 seats), which that night included Gian Carlo Menotti. My trip to New York had taken barely more than twenty-four hours.

I accepted all the acting jobs that came along, no matter how modest, and that same year, 1986, saw my daughter, Jennifer Hall, and me doing a *Love Boat* television series episode together. Jenny, after leaving Cambridge, had first decided to be an actress and had gone through the training required by the British theatrical union in order to get a professional card—forty weeks in the provinces (she actually did sixty)—before joining the National Theatre in London under the direction of her father, Sir Peter Hall. She was remarkably talented and was offered, after being heard singing in *A Midsummer Night's Dream,* a seven-record contract by Warners. Quite the hot girl of the day, Jenny was teamed with me for the first time, as we played a couple of crooks, the daughter seducing the good-looking young millionaire while the mother fleeced him at cards. I rather enjoyed playing the villain. Jenny was beautiful and sang and danced with the grace of a mermaid. We had a different costume every ten seconds; I've never had so many fittings for any film.

And why shouldn't I mention a turn with trained dogs I did in Munich, at the German international gala for the old actors' home? Those galas, based on circus shows—acrobatic acts, dangerous animal acts, and all—take place once a year in most countries of Europe; a lot of money is collected, and everyone in the profession gives his time generously. I did a good job wearing a white Dior evening dress. The professional trainers told me that the dogs loved working with me, and would I like to do a few shows with them on the road? *Is this my future?* I asked myself.

Lenin: The Train by Damiano Damiani, filmed in Austria in 1987, was a distinguished television film about the so-called sealed train that brought Lenin and his close collaborators back from Zurich to the Finland Station in Petrograd (St. Petersburg) to take over leadership of the revolution. I played Lenin's wife, Nadezhda Krupskaya, with Ben Kingsley as the Marxist leader. A charismatic actor, Kingsley was capable of a remarkable transformation of his personality to assume a particular role. We all took the project to heart and did a lot of research. We watched endless footage of Lenin and his close collaborators, listened to his radio speeches, and copied, from photographs, the clothing and looks of the group. Dear Ben Kinsgley was embodying, with scarcely any transition, one giant historical figure after another and found it difficult to keep his feet on the ground, especially when the press crowded him asking him to solve the world's problems. He had differences with Damiani and walked off the set at least once. In accordance with my role in the script, I served as the mediator and convinced him to come back to work. For some actors it is sometimes difficult to separate fiction from reality when the involvement is so intense. I liked my part, that of a very shy, modest, committed human being. A young man made his debut in our cast—Jason Connery, Sean Connery's very young son. I also met, during that film, Dominique Sanda, who became a dear friend. In *Lenin: The Train* she played Lenin's mistress, Inessa Armand; in our next film, *Guerriers et Captives,* by Edgardo Cozarinsky, filmed in Argentina, our roles were reversed, with her playing the wife and I the madam. We had something else in common, our love for cats. Hers had a Vuitton bag for traveling, of which I became quite envious. As soon as I returned to Paris, after Vienna, I bled my bank account and invested in a Vuitton for my cat, Misha.

Perhaps the last and least glorious of my jobs during this somber period of my life was a new version of *Heidi, Courage Mountain,* produced in 1989 by two of Kirk Douglas's sons, Joel (his eldest) and Michael, both rivals in cynicism. I didn't like them any more than I had liked the father. The director, whose name I couldn't remember (but Google did—Christopher Leitch) had a predilection for smoky photography. The cheapest way to obtain this effect is to burn tires, except that the fumes are very toxic, and we were working with five little girls.

In this film, in which I was playing a teacher, the script had me saying the most appalling nonsense about World War I—the wrong country declaring the war (Austria on Italy, whereas history has it the other way around). I was also expected to illustrate my point with the help of a map of Europe dating from 1960! Objections and complaints on my part were met with, "It doesn't matter, they won't know the difference!" What do you do when you are faced with such contempt for the public's intelligence? I played the history lesson standing firmly in front of the map so that neither the pupils nor the camera could see the faulty frontiers. Although the modest contracts with technicians and actors alike claimed that this was a television film, Michael Douglas had every intention to sell it as a feature. I felt vindicated when I was told later that the film was a financial disaster in the cinemas. It would have been too depressing if such a cynical project had fooled the public. However, it certainly harmed the actors involved.

A nice detail, though: We did the exteriors in Schladming, Austria, renowned for being the birthplace of Arnold Schwarzenegger. A rather modest village, where, suddenly, in the middle of the afternoon all the shopkeepers rolled down their iron shutters while a funeral cortege passed by. The shops still sold eighteenth-century silk and wool—traditional clothes—my Christmas shopping for the whole family.

Later, hoping to get a foot in the French film industry, I accepted a Swiss miniseries, *Erika Werner,* filmed in the glum city of Geneva, where I made a few nice friends and ate some very good meals. Back in 1980 I also did a little French film by Michel Lang, *Tous Vedettes,* which wasn't half bad but didn't get the support it deserved. I do not have much to say about an English television murder mystery, *Tales of the Unexpected,* from a story by Roald Dahl (who, having read my short stories, encouraged me to continue writing when I met him on a TV talk show), nor about a modest part in the French film *Dangerous Moves,* which won the Oscar for Best Foreign Film in 1985, and for which dear Liv Ullmann was also hired just to illuminate the credits. Among a number of indifferent projects, few memories survive: the narration for a documentary on Anna Pavlova pleased me—I felt I knew and loved everything about her. There was, I think, a guest performance in the American series *Falcon Crest,* where Jane Wyman acted on the set with the condescending charm of a First Lady. (She was, after all, Ronald Reagan's first wife.) As a matter of fact, I have just viewed my episodes, where I did my most extravagant acting. I thought the plot was so outrageous I could never remember if my character's request was for $4 million or $40 million. It all seemed ludicrous. (I smile as I write this, now that we are into thousands of billions!) I now think I was wrong; you should always try to humanize every character you play. I walked through these jobs, with a feeling of duty, without the joy and relish I used to feel in my first years of acting. Such work kept me from writing a novel—there wasn't time or strength for everything. Besides, I really wasn't ready for the long days of solitude and introspection that writing a book requires. After *Vengeance* was published in France, well translated into French by a friend of mine, my publisher told me ominously, "This is good, but I don't think you'll be able to write a novel." Did she mean that I didn't have the staying power? The time? Or the talent? I don't know, but she proved right. I knew, however, that the day would come when I'd be able to tackle the work on a full-length book.

Turning back a few years, in 1983 I missed an opportunity to make my debut on the London stage, and I'm still upset about that. The very good play by Jean Anouilh, *The Rehearsal* (written in 1950), was ready for a revival, and I was offered the lead with a six-week tour prior to the London run. The plot involves a rich, middle-aged couple busy rehearsing a play with their household guests, for one of their elegant house parties. The play within the play concerns a young girl of poor background whom the rich host lusts after. His wife takes her revenge and gets rid of the young girl. Peter Hall had taught me, ages ago, that actors shouldn't learn their text before rehearsals started, lest they become set in their ways. I wasn't all that experienced, so I made the mistake of arriving on the first day with a clean-slate memory. This being a very talkative part with only three weeks of rehearsals, I was more than uneven on opening night. A vengeful actor, Dinsdale Landen, who had it in for movie actors, made my life so miserable that I buckled under. The inexperienced director, Gillian Lynne (choreographer of the musical *Cats*—who had the worst characteristic of that species), didn't help. Since that experience I've read Laurence Olivier's autobiography and also Arletty's, and both made a point of being word perfect on the first day of rehearsal.

Although I was assured that the critics wouldn't come to the provincial town where we opened, they naturally made a point of turning up to see if the "Hollywood star" could make it on a British stage, and the unanimous response was "No!" The troupe blamed me for the bad notices after opening night—and they were partly right. They "sent me to Coventry," as the expression goes. This means that backstage your fellow actors don't see you—they look past you as if you were not there; they don't ever say hello, avoiding you as if you had the plague. The experience is extremely painful. However, I didn't give up but continued to work doggedly with an assistant to drum the text into me, and with a teacher to improve my voice projection. On the sixth and last week of the run, I had glorious reviews—really great reviews, but too late for the producer to book London. I still regret that failure.

In 1984, when I was fifty-three, an offer came that tickled my vanity: a U. S. national tour of *On Your Toes* by Rodgers and Hart, with choreography by George Balanchine and the ever loyal and supportive Donald Sadler. My first reaction was to refuse. Though I had kept supple and did the barre every morning, I had given away my toe shoes when I was twenty-three, some thirty years previously. The muscular training you need to get on pointe takes years to build up. A child will require four to five years of muscle building before she can stand on her toes, and another one or two before she can do her first pirouette. During my dancing days, I wondered every Monday morning if I still had the strength and the skill to rise on pointe after the Sunday off. For the moment my immediate concern was an arthritic pain in my hips. I told the producers that I first had to see if an acupuncturist could make the pain disappear before I would consider the offer. A Chinese acupuncturist was recommended, who said he thought three sessions would suffice, and they did. I now had three or four months of crammed muscle building to go through.

I arrived in New York, where Natalia Makarova was then playing my role, Vera Baronova, on Broadway. She was nine years younger than me and had never stopped dancing. My assessment was that her dancing was great, better than mine could now be, but her voice and her acting were not equal to mine. The character of Baronova was fun, a hot-tempered *primadonna assoluta*. I threw in the text a few Russian swear words, and Nureyev, who was in town, taught me some choice expressions (involving a mother, of course, as they always do) that only he and I could understand. Now that the frontiers are open, I wouldn't dare attempt this today, but there were few Russians around then. We were directed by the original director, George Abbott, born in '87—1887, that is—he who had cowritten and directed the show in 1936 and done a first revival in 1954 and was by now ninety-seven years of age. He had just remarried the previous year and was amazingly lucid. I remember a very tall man, with a slightly stiff walk, someone quite blunt who didn't waste time on knickknackery. He always spoke his mind with straightforward logic.

During the second week of rehearsal, I suffered a broken rib when my partner threw me over his shoulder a little roughly—I heard the snap. My rehearsals were interrupted, but I recovered in ten fast days, thanks to very painful sessions in a hot Jacuzzi. I kept up my muscle building by going to Pilates to exercise all the muscles not involved with the rib cage. The strange thing is that nature develops a little gelatinous egg over the broken rib, which disappears when the bones are sufficiently welded. Pain remains, however. The show went on the road, and I could do all the dancing, including my favorite number, the fabulous "Slaughter on Tenth Avenue," but couldn't yet do the little Scheherazade on toes. Makarova was asked to take half the performances for about two weeks, and my understudy did the ballet part when I began to perform. Finally the day came when I could do a complete performance. I don't ever remember being so scared in all my life. For at least twenty-four hours, during every waking moment, I thought only of the number in which I would have to do my two pirouettes. A musical-comedy show on the road is like a marching army, with a front line and a backup staff. For every actor, dancer, or singer performing in front of the public, there is a shadow cast in the wings—in full makeup and costume—going through all the numbers with the principals, ready to jump onstage if someone gets injured. On the night when I had to perform my toe number, the full cast, principals and stand-ins, had gathered in the wings to watch me. They applauded wildly when I succeeded with my pirouettes. I don't know if the audience heard the clapping, but they certainly saw my explosive smile of victory. After that success, with the superstition common to theatrical people, I thought, *That's it. I've gone through my accident. I'm safe now.* Not a bit; I was too optimistic, for a second one was in the cards.

But on that night my sky was cloudless. Row nine—the whole of row nine, all fifteen seats—was occupied by Plácido Domingo and his tribe— his wife, his manager, his press agent, dresser, and a few assistants and friends. He was going to perform *Otello* the following week and came backstage with an assistant who handed out some fifty small posters. The great singer was gracious enough to sign them for everyone in the cast.

My daughter, Jenny, was getting married the next day, in a sweet country church in Gloucestershire while I was tied up in Houston, Texas, on this six-month tour. By now I had become anorexic and was down to about a hundred pounds. The stress and guilt for not being with her on that important day were such that my stomach and bowels reacted in a fury, resulting in dehydration, with no doctor available on the weekend. A soft linoleum floor hiding malevolent holes caused me to twist my toe and fall. I heard and then felt the tissue in my hip tear—exactly like when you tear a piece of cloth at the shopping counter. Rushed to the hospital and stretched out on a gurney, I was slipping away fast from dehydration before a nurse noticed that I wasn't responding anymore. Next morning, after the proper X-rays, the surgeon diagnosed a torn hip ligament. He said, "The tour is over for you, young lady!" At the age of fifty-three, after six months' valiant effort, I had succeeded in getting back on my toes—which ought to qualify me for the *Guinness Book of Records,* but for what? The question is, why did I undertake such herculean tasks?

You pick yourself up and continue bravely. Playing the great Coco Chanel in the television film *The Man Who Lived at the Ritz* in 1988 was a nice treat. During the war Chanel lived at the Ritz, the only French tenant among German officers. I prepared well and went through a lot of research. I read Chanel's imaginative autobiography, where truth was the least of her concerns but her pugnacity offers a lesson. I read Paul Morand's bio of her and Edmonde Charles-Roux's, who were both friends of hers. I also met and talked extensively with the witty and elegant dancer Jacques Chazot, who was one of her friends and her escort in the last years of her life. I based my costumes on photographs of her taken during the war. The fittings were fun, though I tormented the poor seamstress, who had no idea how Chanel clothes were made and couldn't believe my uncompromising insistence on details. We nearly came to blows—we certainly came to words—and her acid comments about my visible collarbone would have pleased the great mademoiselle. I stood firm, and the clothes were remade, properly this time. The film was a bit of historical nonsense, but I did enjoy an improbable tennis game at the Touring Club de France between Coco Chanel and Hermann Göring (played by the excellent British actor Joss Ackland).

In 1991, just when an earthshaking event—the fall of the Berlin Wall—took place, I was asked to play Elizaveta Grushinskaya in a musical stage production of *Grand Hotel,* which had been the Hollywood Academy Award winner in 1932. (I seemed predestined to play Russian ladies—in fact, I'm quite good with the accent, given my childhood education with Russian ballet mistresses.) I received letters, faxes, and phone calls from the producers offering me the choice of (1) taking over the New York production where Liliane Montevecchi was finishing her contract, followed by the U.S. tour; (2) opening the new London production; or (3) taking on the new production planned for Berlin, in German, of course. I decided on the Berlin production, for several reasons.

The first was a question of integrity. The show is based on a German novel written by bestselling writer Vicki Baum in 1929, *Menschen im Hotel.* It made a lot of sense to play in the country where the intrigue takes place. The plot denounces the excesses of an overindulgent high society and presages the arrival of a police state—very interesting just now when the Russian occupation of East Germany had recently been overthrown. The second reason was that the German production was bound to be the most challenging—I don't speak German, and I would have to learn the language, and God knows I love a good challenge. The third reason is that for the last forty years or so, whenever I had a nightmare, it was about a brutal German soldier. Dislike for anything German was still in my heart long after the war; above all I hated the language. When meeting any German of the right age, I used to think, *And what did you do during the war?* I was determined to rid myself of this negative emotion. In the course of working on the show, I came to know and appreciate a few Berliners, actors and dancers. My hatred melted like fog in the sunshine. Since then I haven't had any nightmare involving a German soldier.

I started to work five hours a week with a German teacher. Barbarous sounds! Following my new pattern, I went over my text for several more hours at home, with a Dictaphone. I also started my ballet training again. Punishing schedule—I was in my element.

I arrived in Berlin word perfect but warned every member of the company—most were of American origin and could speak English— never to vary in their text when acting with me, because I had absolutely no alternative dialogue. I understood what I said but could not make up a word. My most serious problem was with the singing. Again, I used my dancer's voice, holding my stomach in, when a singer should breathe *with* her stomach. So in Berlin I started to take daily lessons with a remarkable soprano, Vicky Hall. Her voice was like a delicious spring that flowed out effortlessly. Just listening to her run through the warming-up exercises was lovely.

Apart from the five minutes that my song lasted, I was really happy on the stage—or, to be honest, almost happy. But stage fright can nearly ruin your day; the theatrical insurance paid for seven months of a nervous stomach and a tendency to anorexia. Each night two hours before curtain call, I went through every line of my text, rehearsed my song, then went through my barre warm-up. But I knew I was part of a beautiful show. The staging, by Tommy Tune, who won two Tony Awards for it, was dramatic and imaginative. The metallic sets and harsh blue lighting were in perfect correspondence with the text and music. The public was attuned. They participated because they remembered—they knew the subject matter. During the musical numbers, I found out what it is like to stand next to a tenor who sings out full throttle: The noise is so great you could go deaf! (As a matter of fact, many singers and conductors *are* partly deaf.)

Winter came, with the added burden of keeping clear of colds. The rules were to stay out of public places because of microbes; smoke-filled cafés were especially forbidden, as the vocal cords are fragile. I was witness to the surprising vitality of the Berliners, still going great at one in the morning, as no law enforced the closure of restaurants and cafés. Sundays, our days off, were spent on long walks with my co-star, Jürgen Wagner, on the frozen lakes around Berlin. Friends and family came to see me from London and Paris and stayed a day or two. We went to the Brandenburg Gate, newly opened, where on improvised stands East Berliners sold military paraphernalia left by their Russian oppressors. Naturally, we bought a piece of the wall, already a precious icon. We walked along the corridor where the wall had stood, witness to such very recent tragedies. Days were simple and regulated with the precision of military life. Every waking hour revolved around the show, for those two hours when emotions pumped your heartbeat to increased vibrations. Every evening was a major event; unfortunately, each one ended in solitude with my cat, Misha.

My dear friend the great Margot Fonteyn died on February 21, 1991, while I was in Berlin. My mind went back to the time in London when she had looked at my grandfather's automaton. . . . That evening the whole company held hands in a circle—as we used to do every night before the show. With tears in our eyes, we dedicated the performance to her memory. The best obituary I can come up with is one of her own quotes: "Genius is another word for magic, and the whole point of magic is that it is inexplicable."

Spring came with visits to Potsdam and the Sans-Souci Palace (where grumpy Russian-trained watchdogs made you take off your shoes and wear those filthy felt booties). I tried to take my cat to the park of the royal palace, but he didn't appreciate the collar and leash. The Pergamon Museum was awe-inspiring. The particular blue of the Ishtar Gate thrilled me. I'm a real tourist and visit everything there is to see.

The play's leading male role was taken over by an East Berliner when our theater director and leading actor Helmut Baumann found it all too heavy. I was impressed by the dedication and professionalism of these eastern actors. However, after the first wave of sympathy for the suffering of East Berliners, an undertone of anger appeared. The easterners brought pollution to Berlin—they warmed themselves with coal fires, and their poorly made cars were excessively polluting. Little groups furtively carrying television sets and mounds of consumer goods loaded on baby buggies could be seen walking back from the newly opened west, inspiring shame and embarrassment in their richer cousins of the west. The taxes started to rise. The great wave of patriotic jubilation slowly deflated itself to give way to a certain bitterness, marking the onset of a conflicting situation that lasted many years.

19

Changing Track

Years earlier, while we were on holiday in New Mexico, Michael Laughlin, the children, and I went on a trek up and around wooded areas, which involved riding our horses down a very steep hill. My horse, sensing an amateur rider, took it upon itself to stop and graze rather than chance toppling over and breaking its neck. In other words, it decided to avoid a potential catastrophe and do something more pleasant. In my fifties, while living in France, since no effort on my part could convince the French to employ me, I found myself in a similar situation; fearing that I was toppling over, I felt the urge to move in a totally different direction for a while. Was I right? Was I wrong? I still don't know. Here's what happened:

I was driving with my son, Christopher, by now a film and TV producer, over the bridge of the little town of Villeneuve-sur-Yonne, in Burgundy—an hour and a half from Paris, near the seventeenth-century millhouse I owned for weekends, when suddenly I saw on the left of the bridge a For Sale sign posted on one of four abandoned stone warehouses that lined the river. These near ruins looked so forlorn that my heart bled at the sight of them. This part of town, the slums of Villeneuve-sur-Yonne, had no streetlights, was deserted at night, and served as a cemetery for defunct cars. The street cleaners never ventured here, and the area was obviously doomed to be razed to become the town's parking lot. I looked at my son, who shares my love for old buildings, and asked, "Did you see the sign?" "Yes, I did." "Shall we?" "Why not?" We drove straight to the *notaire* (the public notary who deals with buying and selling real estate in France), who received us instantly. The price being asked for the little building was so minimal that we chuckled and agreed to buy it—just for a lark—but asked the *notaire* if he could obtain the other three boarded-up shacks that were part of the clump. Maître Lendais said he would try to convince the owners but didn't hide the fact that it might be a slow and difficult endeavor—quarreling families being involved. Some eight months later, my son and I owned the four houses on the river plus another on the back street—which came with the garage, a small shack in line with the front ones.

My imagination started to elaborate exciting plans. Why not develop a weekend colony for a group of writer friends? Something like D. H. Lawrence's Kiowa Ranch, near Taos, New Mexico? I started contacting architects and builders until I realized that if the barns themselves had cost next to nothing, their renovation would be a serious financial undertaking—and none of my friends was ready to invest that kind of money just for weekends by the river. Christopher, filming in London and about to be married, was far too busy to come up with answers. So the project was interrupted, and the houses were left to stand in forlorn neglect.

It was at that point that *Grand Hotel* was offered, which took nearly a year out of my life. I talked so extensively about the dear little stone warehouses by the river, showing photographic proof of their charm, and was so persuasive that I fired up the imagination of my singing coach and friend Vicky Hall. Our daydreams gave birth to the grand scheme of a festival. The opening of the festivities was to be announced by trumpet calls from the battlements of the gate tower facing west (Sens), answered by those of the gate tower facing east (Joigny). In the majestic Gothic church dedicated to Notre-Dame, a high Mozartian Mass, sung by my dear Vicky and her best pupils, would raise Sunday Mass music to a level of unsurpassed spiritual and musical beauty. And why not a small opera, sung for three performances only in the minuscule eighteenth-century theater, that would establish the town as musical center of the Yonne? Art exhibits were planned to promote my favorite painter friends—the Spanish-American Miguel Condé and the Belgian Caterina. A play done on a barge—*The Cherry Orchard*—using the thirteenth-century St. Nicolas Bridge for the arrival of Madame Ranyevskaya and her family in their carriage was sure to draw crowds. Our little buildings would house the offices, cafeteria, a room or two, to launch this grand project. My energy knew no bounds; I threw myself into action with the enthusiasm of Mickey Rooney and Judy Garland in one of their Andy Hardy films. For about six months, I prepared a detailed dossier, sure that the town would be thrilled by my project.

Of course we needed subsidies. In France you turn to the state to finance this sort of endeavor. The mayor of Villeneuve-sur-Yonne received me and with an elaborate gesture offered an armchair. He listened with a stone face, then said firmly, "I can't help you, the town has no money. You'll have to ask the president of the region if you want to do something like that." After a pause he added, "It's too big to do all at once anyway. Why don't you start by restoring the houses? I can see you are someone with taste and plenty of energy. What this town needs first is a hotel and a restaurant. Tell you what. I'll make a gift of some land in the front for a terrace."

My response was categorical: "Impossible! I know nothing about that business. Very complex, I'm told. You get robbed by the cooks. . . . No, absolutely not." I decided to ask for help at a higher level.

The president of the region of Burgundy was also a senator with an office in the beautiful Parisian Senate house, in the Palais du Luxembourg (built by Regent Queen Marie de Médicis in 1615). He asked me politely if I had launched a festival before. I had to answer no, I hadn't. He made some reference to Hollywood, and I could hear his thoughts as clearly as if he'd spoken them. He eased me out quickly and advised me to go see the cultural secretary of the region.

I took the train to Dijon, the seat of the rich dukes of Burgundy with their magnificent palace and houses that date back to the twelfth century—a beautiful town to visit, but I was on a mission. The gentleman in charge of cultural events was openly hostile. He clearly thought I was after his position. He said unequivocally that the region financed only projects that were proposed by him and his office. I was getting nowhere fast. I realized that, in Burgundy, when you say "culture" you usually mean corn.

By now the financial burdens—land tax, notary, and so on—were getting more significant, so I asked my son to find a third partner. A Cambridge friend who was in merchant banking and loved to invest in old buildings, Peter Sykes, agreed to join us as co-proprietor of the houses, which by then we decided to turn into apartments for rent or for sale.

In the meantime one of the roofs caved in. When the roof goes, the building deteriorates quickly. We had to make a decision: Should we forget about our investment or go ahead and restore? We agreed that we were all game to continue, and since I lived in France and had no acting work for the time being, I offered, in a moment of aberration, to supervise the work. For no fee, of course. I was a Patron of the Arts, in the mood to sponsor the revival of this perishing town, where nothing had been built for a hundred years except a retirement home with its attached hospital wing.

It must be said at this point that there wasn't a more untrained, inexperienced, inept businesswoman than I. I had no idea that there was such a thing as insurance if you embark on building. I had to find out what a "limited" company was all about, how to take out a bank loan, and that most French workmen want to have an official paycheck, which eventually gives them the right to retirement benefits. The first time I called the local social security office to legalize my workmen and was given the list of deductions and additions that must be included in their paychecks—some twelve of them for the worker and many more for the entrepreneur—I burst out laughing and asked the lady if this was a joke. "No, madame, not a joke at all," she said, surprised that someone should be so ignorant of what every French contractor knows. You calculate 22 percent of 65 percent of the salary, then 4.5 percent of 75 percent and so on for two columns. Suffice it to say that it is easier to learn Chinese. My *notaire* urged me to sell now before I lost more money. The civil servant who sold me the building permit said, "Madame, you are really making a big mistake!" The French are no entrepreneurs and certainly don't encourage you to be one; the taxes and work laws are not favorable to that kind of initiative. But I believed in my project and pressed forward.

My first task was to find a contractor. Locals were not in the habit of bidding for jobs, and several turned me down when they learned I had contacted others, as they would not waste their time with estimates. After several weeks the consenting contractor presented page after page of five- or six-figure numbers. I told him truthfully that we couldn't afford these sums and asked him to go back to his calculator and make an effort. The alternative, I warned, was to find foreign workers, now that the European market was open. The comical thing is that the builder came back with a new estimate—the same price per meter, but he had recalculated a larger surface. I decided there was only one solution: I was going to be the builder, and I would hire the craftsmen, the machinery, and all the material myself. Except for watching my grandparents building mansions throughout my childhood, I had of course no more experience as a builder than as a businesswoman.

Our English partner suggested a pair of British workers—one was a mason, his brother a carpenter—the Bramble brothers. A contract was drawn, the two brothers agreeing to come and work for three months, staying at my millhouse, where I would cook and care for them. The mayor kindly agreed to sell me (by now it wasn't "gratis" anymore) enough land to make a large terrace, and we started to restore the roofs and, soon after, to attack the heavy masonry. The mayor was very pleased.

My first concern was to raise the ground above water level. The bridge has marks indicating the last great water disasters—I aligned our level above the worst flood within the last hundred years. No wonder the inside of the buildings smelled as moldy as a cemetery—the ground, after repeated inundations, was nothing but damp, packed earth. On the top floor, in what is now our star apartment, "The Loft," reposed ten inches of dirt and pigeon droppings, witness to more than a century of solitude.

I bought a secondhand cement mixer and spent eighteen months in jeans and a pair of wooden clogs. Along with the British boys I hired other skilled workmen and supervised the work. Every once in a while—still in clogs and jeans—I zoomed up to Paris to my bank, which wouldn't release more funds without bills and paychecks. To find the right craftsmen I posted handwritten ads in local bakeries and butcher shops. In search of old tiles, I took ads in the village paper and drove far away to farms with my poor old Peugeot. I wound up buying some eleven thousand of them, quite a few of which were carried in my car trunk. They were often sold by Gypsies who had salvaged them from dumps and counted them correctly to the piece. My Peugeot also served as a truck to carry any number of plaster bags, nails, and screws of every sort, as requested by my workmen. In every situation I listened to their experienced guidance and to my own common sense. I was grateful for some helpful suggestions made by my architect but realized that one must sieve an architect's ideas through fine mesh before applying them.

Appalling mistakes were sometimes avoided, sometimes not. I heard from the workmen that my reputation in the local cafés was somewhat controversial, not to say negative. "Who does she think she is? A movie star from Hollywood rebuilding those ruins! Crazy! She doesn't even have a contractor." One or two locals stopped to stare at the slow progress as they went to work in the morning and as they came back home at night, usually too shy to engage in a conversation. One woman, Linda Delemont, was openly supportive and gave me good advice. Just one friend can be enough to keep your spirits up.

Working with men and giving them orders was a problem only once. A drunken plasterboarder threatened me with his electric drill when I told him that his bathroom wall was not straight and that he must do it again. (You cannot glue bathroom tiles on a curved wall.) I eased slowly backward until I came within the hearing of my faithful leading workman, Zoric, who shouted my attacker down. In the meantime I called the police, who said they were coming straight over. The drunk pretended to leave, at which point I called the police back to cancel their intervention. Five minutes later the man, who had not left at all, reappeared and really scared me. I had to call out loud for help while grabbing a piece of metal in my hand. As I did so, I thought of Marlon Brando in *On the Waterfront*.

The most nerve-racking moment was during the few hours of the day when the little house that is now the entrance to the auberge with its two floors above, stood gutted, with a gaping hole where doors were meant to go, upheld on just five metal struts or props ("acrows," the boys called them) and my prayers. Two of the props developed bowlegs under the weight of the huge timber beam, like cowboys after a lifetime of riding. Before sundown the builders managed to stack the brick column that now keeps the whole house standing.

Getting a license to sell alcohol was another amusing hurdle. There were already nineteen cafés in this town of five thousand inhabitants, and the licensing authorities thought that was quite enough. I went to see the mayor and asked for his support. He made a few phone calls and told me to buy the license from an out-of-town café. A transaction was arranged, but a civil servant who lived in another village had to give me his official signature. I found this bureaucrat up on the roof of his house, which he was restoring. He grudgingly came down the ladder, wiped his hands, found his seal, and signed. I seem to be aping, for folkloric charm, Peter Mayle's bestseller *A Year in Provence,* but that is honestly the way it went.

While Tony Bramble, the carpenter, was there, I had to find a workshop with the proper machinery to make all the doors and windows. The old man who owned a suitable place had had it since his military-service days. He had never even been to Paris and was surprised to have a request to rent his workshop to a film actress who employed a British carpenter who couldn't speak French. The men communicated with loud enunciation, as if that made the meaning clearer—gestures did the rest. I was recommended a lumberyard several miles out, a beautiful place with a pungent smell of wood, where I ordered three-year-old oak. I saved about 60 percent doing it this way and feel so proud of the skillful finish. The only drawback: Because my carpenter was left-handed, he installed the bolts on the left panels instead of the right ones. I think of him every time I have to shut a window with my left hand at the auberge.

At one point we attacked the decayed rendering on the riverside façade. It had been raining, and the men were working on scaffolds behind a tarpaulin until the job was finished. When we removed the veil, so to speak, an amazing surprise nearly took my breath away: Flint stones, lined up in perfect symmetry, were revealed, like precious jewels. I raced to the phone and called my partners. "It looks like a f— château! Of course, it isn't that grand, but you should see the beautiful golden stones!" I couldn't get over the rustic charm, the elegance, revealed by clearing the peeling stucco. I snapped pictures endlessly from every vantage point.

To my surprise, in 1992, around the beginning of the building work, when I had all but forgotten my involvement in the film business, a minor miracle happened. One of the world's leading directors, Louis Malle, wanted me to play Juliette Binoche's mother in his film *Damage,* to be shot in one of the studios outside London. The male protagonist was the very seductive Jeremy Irons. I accepted with enthusiasm but warned Louis and his brother Vincent, who produced for him, that they must pay me on the dates set down in the contract, because I was building an auberge and had bills to honor. Louis asked, "Where is your auberge?"

"Oh, you wouldn't know the place, it's in a little town in Burgundy called Villeneuve-sur-Yonne."

"On the river?"

"Yes, on the river," I replied, surprised.

"Above or below the bridge?"

"What? You know Villeneuve-sur-Yonne?"

"Yes, as a child I spent many school holidays in the tower [the Château, we call it]. It belongs to members of my family." Small world!

Three or four times during that spring, I had to leave the building site, drive to Paris, wash the dust out of my hair, and clean my nails thoroughly—a half-hour scrub—before a chauffeur would come to my flat, carry my suitcase to a limousine, take me to the airport, and see me off to London, where another chauffeur was waiting with the reassuring little sign L. CARON. This one drove me to the Dorchester Hotel, where a suite awaited Cinderella and I changed from jeans and clogs to a glorious yellow suit by Dior and jewels from Van Cleef & Arpels. The contrast was amusing. I remember calling the Bramble brothers from my Dorchester suite to warn them that the brick pilaster they were stacking in the back of the kitchen was one brick too thick.

What bliss to work for Louis Malle! There wasn't a director more discreet, tactful, sensitive, or patient. His sense of humor—a precious quality, in my book—was so very reassuring. You knew he wasn't going to hurt your feelings no matter how off you might be. But behind his polished façade there was a very independent, individual person, in conflict with his bourgeois family. Here's a story he told me to illustrate:

When his elder brother told his mother that he had enlisted to go to war (World War II), she said without a blink, "Good, that'll put some lead into your brain!" Of course, "putting lead into your brain" is a French expression—still!

Louis covered the scenes from every angle, and there were many takes. He was extremely particular about the exact degree of emotion—not too much, not too little, like a doctor watching the temperature of a patient. He came to whisper in my ear after a scene, "Leslie, please don't sigh so much. I don't like actresses who sigh." So right—such an interesting comment. I've watched that ever since. He was alert and vigilant, standing or sitting next to or under the camera, with his unlit pipe between his teeth, and both arms locked above his head for fear of a careless hand flashing in front of the lens.

I understand that there were conflicts between him and Jeremy Irons; the gossip in the makeup rooms also whispered about difficulties between Juliette and Jeremy. I never saw any of this. I thought all the actors, including the amazing Miranda Richardson, worked in close unison. What I saw of Juliette impressed me. There was a girl who couldn't speak English when the film started and who was fluent by its end. She has a knack for accents and is very determined, but I can well believe that the intimate love scenes must have been difficult for her.

I admit that I simply played the worst aspects of my mother, a selfish woman who nevertheless had one admirable quality—speaking the truth. It was a painful role in a sense, because of course one wants to be lovely and loved. Every time I showed too much humanity, or even emotion, Louis brought me back to the straight and narrow. However, I knew I was part of a very fine film.

Suddenly one morning Louis didn't come to work—no precise reason was disclosed, just something to do with his heart. The next day Candice Bergen arrived in London to look after him. Without knowing Louis Malle intimately, I would say that his was a fragile temperament. The sensitive masterpieces he gave us almost predicted a shorter life for him.

Back to Villeneuve—back to building. Endlessly. When would it be finished? It was the monotony of small details, day after day, that got to me. I now know that exhaustion brings depression—for me, at least. More and more, as the working day ended, I wished I could close the shutters and sink into oblivion. A glass of red wine, a piece of bread and cheese led to another glass until the bottle was gone and I hoped the slumber that overtook me would last the night. It rarely did.

Main construction went on for over a year, with six additional months spent on the decoration, and, surprisingly enough, that was the most exhausting part. A local young upholsterer agreed to do the curtains, and I had to run to the fascinating quarter in Paris called Marché Saint-Pierre, a neighborhood of genuine souks where you can find expensive French and foreign materials, end-of-season designs, at considerably reduced prices. It's fun to shop there and, except for the gray skies, you could feel you were in Morocco, as the local men and women wear tunics, caftans, and jilbabs; most women wear the head scarf.

Two weeks before opening, I started getting worried: my upholsterer wasn't answering the phone. I went to his village and found his shutters closed, an eerie silence surrounding the place. I asked around in the village, but no one had seen him for days. Someone knew his brother's number. I called and went to see him. The brother responded with shocking indifference, as if his sibling's disappearance weren't the first one. I told him that I was going to call the police and ask them to break down the door, so he finally agreed to come with me. I feared the worst, but it appeared the boy was in there and wouldn't answer or come out. I was finally forced to contact the police. We talked a long time through the door until he eventually opened it. The poor boy was going through a nervous breakdown, hadn't eaten for a few days, and was trembling like a leaf in the wind. I drove him to the hospital. Several months later he came to the auberge for a visit. He had now become a musician and was much happier.

For me, too, the pressure was gathering momentum. The cutlery and the porcelain came from England, as did the double-glazed windowpanes. England was still in a depression then, and those items were much cheaper there than in France. Peter Sykes drove several times from England with a heavily loaded BMW. He returned with an equally heavy trunk weighed down with French wine.

Finding a name for the restaurant and hotel was solved by the *notaire*. As usual I was short of time when he came up with the answer. "One of the houses is named 'The Owl's Nest' on the town registry— why not keep that? You can't find a better name." And so it was. Now I had to find an owl to use for our logo. In a state of panic, I wondered where I would find an antique print of the bird. I imagined an endless search in the "bookinists" on the quays of the Seine but thought I'd better ask the nearest shop first. I entered the print shop on the boulevard Saint-Germain, two hundred yards from my Paris flat, and asked the question in the negative form: "I'm sure you don't have an eighteenth-century engraving of an owl?" The answer surprised me. "Yes, we do." And the proprieter pulled out "our owl," our sweet and wise owl. There we were. I raced to the printer, designed and ordered the menus and the stationery.

We were just about a week from the date of opening to the public and had yet no lighting fixtures in the dining hall. I had seen in a chic Parisian shop chandeliers made with raffia—just the thing for a barn-like restaurant, but the price was extravagant. I snapped pictures, came back, and asked the workmen if anyone knew how to work metal. One man stepped forward. "I was a metalworker till I injured my eye." Showing him the photographs, I asked, "Could you make four of these?" He said, "Sure. We need a plumber's workbench, a blowtorch, and a few cowls of copper." Off I went with my little Peugeot to buy eight cowls of copper. I designed the shape and size on the cement floor with a piece of chalk. Our plumber lent us the tools. In the end I calculated that we saved about 70 percent by making them ourselves.

The raffia story is also worth recounting. Where does one find raffia? In a gardening store or an arts-and-crafts shop. A friend found such a shop in Paris, where she ordered twenty braids, hoping they would arrive before the opening date—dangerously near—of June 19. When the order was delivered to the shop, she rushed in a taxi to the Gare de Lyon, where, weaving through the travelers, she asked aloud (only an Anglo-Saxon would dare to do this) if anyone was stopping at or passing by Villeneuve-sur-Yonne. A young soldier said that yes, he was, on his way to Migennes. She thrust the bag of raffia into his arms and said, out of breath, "Please, please take this, it's perfectly legitimate—no drugs or anything funny, trust me. A workman called Manu will be at Villeneuve train station to take delivery. He'll look for you. It's just raffia to make chandeliers! Thank you!" The trusting young soldier took the big bag and a twenty-franc note. At the Villeneuve-sur-Yonne station, he and Manu found each other, and the raffia arrived safely at the building site. With the help of the newly hired waitresses, we dressed the chandeliers in time for opening night. The staff was eating dinner in the large dining hall while, perched on a ladder, I was still clipping the raffia pom-poms, throwing little pieces all over the place.

Of course I had not intended to manage the place myself, as I was perfectly aware of the perils involved. I wanted to include in the partnership a professional manager who would also invest financially. A friend found a highly qualified person who said he was interested in investing and would find a suitable chef. This man, whom I will call Mr. G., was then the manager of a top Relais & Châteaux hotel—with this recommendation, I had to trust him. However, three months before the opening, he announced that due to the death of a member of his wife's family he had new financial responsibilities that forced him to withdraw from investing. But he was ready to find me a good chef, for a fee. My education in sharp practices had started.

Three weeks before the inn's opening, I raced to the Élysée Palace, where President Mitterrand pinned a medal on my lapel. Aimery had flown in from the Virgin Islands, my children had come from London, and many good friends surrounded me. We were all immensely impressed by the dazzling crystal chandeliers hanging in the gilded hall. President Mitterrand came in nearly half an hour late. He managed a stupefying feat of memory. There we were, about eight of us chosen to be decorated with the Légion d'Honneur. He spoke for ten minutes to each one of us, summarizing each of our backgrounds, schooling, and achievements—all without a single note. When he came to me, I was eager as a child to be congratulated for building an auberge, for having saved part of our "architectural heritage," for helping to revive a dying town, but this accomplishment was deemed commercial—the president mentioned only the films, plays, or musicals I had appeared in "and a book of short stories with a very dark title, *Vengeance.*"

"I didn't choose it, sir," was my retort, "my editors did." He nodded his approval in a paternal manner and moved on to the next honoree.

I sometimes wonder if Churchill would have liked to be praised for the brick wall he built when, after leading England to victory in World War II, he was kicked out of the government, or if Daniel Day-Lewis wants people to admire the shoes he makes between playing unforgettable performances. I built an auberge and feel proud to think that it serves the community.

We opened our doors to the public June 19, 1993. I suspected that none of the locals would come for at least a year, as mistrust and shyness run deep in Burgundy. They were going to wait and see. I was not local; I was a "newcomer."

The night after the opening, the chef had kidney failure and had to be transported by ambulance to the nearest hospital for dialysis. What the young man (and Mr. G.) had failed to tell me was that he'd had a kidney removed three months previously. In June, the days are already hot, and standing on your feet in front of a blazing stove is not recommended when you have only one kidney. The cook spent every night for at least a week being driven to the hospital in an ambulance. I stood by him and tried my best to encourage him and give him moral support.

The chef had another drawback—a foul temper. He soon exercised the full volume of his voice on his kitchen staff, then on the clients, and finally on me. But his worst flaw was a sad lack of culinary talent. I found out later that he was just a short-order cook, good for "bacon and eggs with mash," who had had no serious training. Once again I had been taken for a ride by Mr. G. My naïveté and ignorance also worked against me when I let the chef go for incompetence. The young man complained to the Prudhommes (the local court that settles differences between employer and employee; they always—no matter what the case may be—take the side of the employee), who found me guilty of cruelty because I employed a handicapped person. I was heavily fined. But I must conclude my "Perils of Pauline" by saying that bad deeds don't always go unpunished, contrary to the general belief. Eventually Mr. G. was sued for malpractice by his other employer, sent to trial, and lost his job.

After a few false starts—including my second chef, an enthusiastic champagne drinker, given to mistaking my cash register for his pocket, followed by a female chef who couldn't stand the pressure—the auberge has been run for the last eleven years by a remarkable Japanese chef, Daïsuke Inagaki. He was fifty-three when I hired him, mature enough to know that he'd hit on a good thing. I was happy to have found someone passionate about cooking, who worked by the same culinary principles as I did. Never short of new ideas, he is not one to "torture" food, as some modern chefs do. His inventions are full of subtle flavors, artistically presented on the plate, and you can always recognize what you're eating. His French wife is totally reliable with the accounts—a great relief.

Several thousand Americans, Britons, Australians, and other foreigners have spent the night in one of our four rooms and gone through the Burgundy experience, thrilled with the fine food, the walks along the river, visits to châteaux and vineyards and all the charm of our historical town. When I'm there—and I go about once a week—I thrust into my customers' hands a detailed map highlighting all the rich excursions that are available. I never tire of boasting about our illustrious neighbor, La Grande Mademoiselle, cousin of Louis XIV, who was banished by the king for heading a small insurrection (La Fronde), wearing a feathered helmet and gleaming breastplate—banished, indeed, to the most enormous pile of pink bricks called the château of Saint-Fargeau. I positively force my guests to drive to Saint-Sauveur-en-Puisaye, Colette's birthplace, where they can visit the château full of her memorabilia, now a museum celebrating her life and work. Also nearby is a medieval edifice with moat and pigeon tower, the Château de Ratilly, where the present owners make the most attractive earthenware. Robert De Niro came to the auberge for three days, swearing he didn't want to visit anything at all, but the driver had orders to drive past the châteaux I wanted him to see, and he was as charmed as everyone always is.

I'm particularly pleased when the busload of the American Women's Group in Paris (AWG) comes once a year, to hear me ramble on about Fred Astaire, Gene Kelly, and Cary Grant and all my other famous partners, while eating chef Inagaki's refined cuisine. And I do love to hear English accents in our dining room. Having made the trip from England in a Bentley, a Rover, or a BMW, they never fail to go visit Chablis, where they stock up for the year. Somehow Australians, who travel everywhere, found us on the map, and there is now the beginning of an Australian community. Fearlessly adventurous, they buy houses, convert them, and settle by our lovely river. Finally even the locals adopted La Lucarne aux Chouettes. Our restaurant is the place to celebrate in style the end of the harvest every July. We welcome engagements, wedding parties, and business lunches, and also welcome Parisians who want a breath of fresh air while watching the river flow by in majesty.

When a German businessman came for the weekend by private plane, we were quite impressed. Another gentleman in retirement took off from Germany on a barge with his whole family, enough bicycles for everyone, and a car that was either driven ahead or left behind the barge. In a slow progress across Europe, through rivers and canals, he was headed for the Mediterranean. Early one summer morning, the dew still shimering on the leaves while I was watering, I saw his barge glide by slowly. I waved at him, standing on his deck. He stopped the barge, said hello, and decided to stay for lunch. He found the food so good he moored for three days; we all became quite friendly during the several meals he took in our restaurant.

The most amusing event was when a Dutch couple on their twenty-fifth wedding anniversary was offered a surprise trip by their children with only a treasure map to lead them each step of the way. "What shall I pack in our suitcase?" asked the mother, totally mystified. "Are we going to a hot or cold country?" "Neither one nor the other, but pack something elegant, for a smart dinner," answered the daughter. The first riddle had to do with "the country where food is best in the world," and the driver taking them to the airport had plane tickets for Paris. At the airline counter, the hostess, in on the game, held an envelope with the name of their Paris hotel, where the concierge had a note suggesting that next morning they must drive a car put at their disposal down to the part of the country "that made their favorite wine." That spelled Burgundy to them. The third riddle was this: Seventy-five miles south of Paris, find a very old town called "Newtown on . . . a river" that spills into the Seine. They plunged into a map of Burgundy and found that the river Yonne is a tributary of the Seine. The next riddle proposed a hotel owned by a famous Hollywood dancer who had made a musical film with Maurice Chevalier after one with Gene Kelly and another with Fred Astaire. The phone book of Villeneuve-sur-Yonne mentioned "Auberge La Lucarne aux Chouettes," so they phoned to check on the identity of the owner. Two hours later they turned up with their riddle in hand, just as I was going through the lobby. Of course there were shrieks and welcome kisses and a bottle of champagne opened with a loud pop! I kept a copy of the mystery plan for many years; it must still be in my archives somewhere.

20

Breakdown

*B*ut nothing could relieve my anxieties and my exhaustion during the first few years of running the auberge. The struggle had been too hard, and there was no one with whom to share the burden. Pressed with staff difficulties—we were still in the red, thanks to the chef's knavery—one black morning in 1995 I woke up feeling, *I don't think I want to live through this day.* Loneliness and distress had bored a hole inside me; my will to live was quite deflated. I had no resistance left. Two mornings later when I woke up from a pill-and-wine-induced slumber, I called my son. Christopher's wife, Jane, came on the phone and said, "I know of a psychiatrist who has treated one of my friends for the same problem. Come on over to London and meet him."

The doctor sat me down in his office and put forth this simple request: "Tell me about yourself." The floodgates opened, my life seemed to me such a failure, such a list of mediocre work, a series of foolish mistakes, a road full of wrong turns, that the imperfection of it submerged me and tumbled me like a pebble in the waves. An hour later I was still crying uncontrollably. The doctor took me into the clinic that same afternoon and kept me for a month. I was made to repeat my life story to several doctors, one of them an alcohol specialist. Their conclusion was, "You are not an alcoholic"—frankly, it had not occurred to me that I might be—"you're having a nervous breakdown. We have the best pills. Don't worry, we'll put you on tranquilizers and antidepressants. We'll start today; they will take full effect in about a week. Right now you're going to take this sleeping pill and have a good night's sleep." That sounded heavenly. I could think of nothing more comforting than to be tended by ladies dressed in blue and white. I quickly felt better because

I wanted to. Being healthy is a matter of pride with me. The doctor said, "Stay a couple of weeks more. You're safe here."

That's when another great script dropped down from heaven, through Peter Chelsom and Peter Flannery: the zaniest comedy, *Funny Bones.* Chelsom—a Shakespearean actor–turned–director—had written the part for me, and another one for Jerry Lewis.

Here's the story: A family of vaudevillians on the skids tries to survive in Blackpool, England. I play the mother of autistic and brilliant young performer Jack Parker (Lee Evans). A rich American comedian, Tommy Fawkes (Oliver Platt), arrives to buy material for a show. His father is the very successful Las Vegas star George Fawkes (Jerry Lewis), who worked with the family years ago and left, stealing all the good gags but leaving something behind—a son. The collateral damage that was done to the family is far-reaching. We see the murder taking place while the unsuspecting crowds roar with laughter.

To convince me that he was a serious filmmaker, Peter Chelsom sent me a cassette of his first film, *Hear My Song,* which immediately took place among my top five for charm, wit, and originality. I pulled myself up by the bootstraps and went from the hospital to the first reading. I remember that I had to hold my cup of coffee with both hands because they were shaking so much.

Peter Chelsom described my part: "Katie Parker is the only sane person among a group of insane people. She is the center pole of this bizarre family, the only one who has a hold on reality." Ironic to be playing the only sane character when I had just been released from the psychiatric ward.

Funny Bones saw me through—playing Katie Parker saw me through. I suppose I'm a competent enough actress, because I am believable as "the only sane person" in that cast. A nice detail: Katie comes from Charlesvilles-Mézières, where Arthur Rimbaud was born—no coincidence. And what is the grandest gift a scriptwriter can offer an actress? The part of Cleopatra, of course—even if she is only a tinsel queen prancing about in a circus ring. Peter Chelsom gave me Cleopatra—the full kit, complete with her asp, making a majestic entrance on a dais with a profusion of ostrich feathers and carried by four Egyptian slaves.

What divine madness runs through this film! I love it like you love people who saw you through a desperate situation and kept you laughing. I appreciate the eccentricity of all the British variety artists who figure in it; I love it for the teddy-bear ingenuity of Oliver Platt and above all for the genius of Lee Evans, who plays the natural son of Jerry Lewis and of my character, Katie Parker. Jerry Lewis kept the whole town laughing for the five days it took us to film in the Blackpool circus. Simon Fields, the producer, had no difficulties in finding willing extras to fill in the circus benches.

The film done, I was a very good girl, taking all my pills regularly, but the problems weren't resolved, my troubles with the restaurant weren't over yet. It took me a while to get wise to the second chef's game. When I told him, "Someone is fixing the till," he looked at me with candid eyes and said, "Goodness, you must be very worried." The next day he came to me with an unexpected piece of news: "I've just been offered the greatest job in my life, in an exotic resort." He mentioned his daughter's school fees . . . his wife's alimony . . . the debt he still had to repay on his bankrupt restaurant . . . his old mother, et cetera . . . I let him go, unsuspecting. Two weeks later, checks paid to his account confirmed his culpability—a court case found him liable in absentia for damages, but he's still on the run. Panic seized me again. Where could I get another chef? Of course I had a relapse. Back to the hospital for another round. The doctor said, "That's disappointing. I guess what you need is a stronger dose of antidepressants."

With my eyes glued on the television set—so as not to think, I guess—the reassuring hospital routine kept me believing that I was improving, but for several years the relapses occurred with almost monotonous regularity. Every few months the black dog would grab me by the throat and wouldn't let go. Any news, good or bad, was enough to trigger a sudden crash, when breathing for the next minute, let alone the next day, took too much of an effort. I can only gauge the depth of my depression by this reaction: Every time I passed the freeway toll booth to go to Villeneuve, I seriously wondered how the lady in the little glass cabin could carry on that job without committing suicide. Going to the auberge caused me almost insurmountable pain. The lush landscape of Burgundy, under sunny or cloudy skies, caused me wrenching pangs. I could not read, or feed myself—local cafés for lunch and dinner were my only recourse. Listening to classical music seemed to touch a neuralgic spot and had to be avoided.

With every relapse I was carted off to London by ambulance or on my own steam, thinking naïvely—because the doctor said so, "You're getting nearer to being cured." Five years later the doctor finally admitted, "Well, after all, your mother committed suicide. There might be something in your genes. You really ought to get help in Paris." I was then exactly the age my mother was when she decided she'd had enough, sixty-seven.

21

Recovery

With the obstinacy of the ant who skirts a leaf and rises above sticks and pebbles to reach home, I worked at the reconstruction of every molecule in my body. I asked around, listened to advice, and found the right doctor to start serious analysis—my second one. From two to four hours a day, every day including Sunday, I worked at trying to heal myself. The human soul is resilient and can repair itself as long as blood courses its veins. I had to acknowledge that overwork, exhaustion, and depression had brought me to abuse alcohol to the point that I couldn't do without it, no matter how much I wanted to stop. I don't think I had an alcoholic predisposition—alcoholic tendencies usually declare themselves between the ages of eleven and fourteen, sometimes earlier, and I was into my sixties when I started to abuse. Nevertheless, I was drinking alcoholically and didn't want to take a chance, so I went to the right program to tackle the disease. I stick to it because it works for me, as it has for thousands.

My recovery took several years, but what does it matter when there are daily improvements, albeit almost imperceptible ones? The smallest achievement—clearing a cupboard, being able to call friends, feeding myself properly—took on the importance of Olympic gold.

An inner equilibrium, which I now manage on most days, is the most precious gift I have received in my recovery. After ten years of reconstruction, I have regained respect and affection for myself—I think my children trust me, respect me, and, now that they are more mature, recognize the obstacle course I went through.

I have come to appreciate all the lovely surprises life has in store for me. In the last few years, there have been acting offers that were small but fun. One of them was reciting *The Story of Babar* at the Windsor

Festival and *The Carnival of the Animals* at Wigmore Hall in London. In 1997, while still hospitalized, I forced myself to start learning the text of a piece for the Chichester Festival Theatre in England and, later, for the Melbourne Festival in Australia, based on George Sand's letters and memoirs, while, at the piano, the sensitive David Abramovitz played Chopin. It took me seven long months to commit the text to memory. At first, I hyperventilated so that I had to take a breath every three words; my power of recall was deficient, and I had no confidence left. Learning an hour and twenty minutes of text by heart was a grand achievement. George Sand lived inside me while I played her, giving me strength and wisdom.

In the year 2000, the lovely script of *Chocolat,* to be directed by Lasse Hallström, came as a blessing. I found it difficult, and still do, to play "and also . . ." parts, and though my ego was bruised, I have to admit those small roles were just the right size and length for me at the time. *Chocolat* is a fairy tale narrating the magical accomplishments of a mysterious woman (Juliette Binoche) who receives the GPS directions for her next destination from the North Wind. Chocolate is her only weapon to overcome prejudice, hidden violence, and bigotry in a backward little town. It was very nice to meet Johnny Depp, the Gypsy troubadour who wins Juliette's heart. Judi Dench lends her warmth and humanity to this film, which was nominated for five Oscars. We filmed in the medieval town of Flavigny-sur-Ozerain, where history started with Julius Caesar when he camped on the hilltop with his army in 52 B.C., to fight the Gallic chieftain Vercingetorix. Nothing new has been built there since an unfinished nunnery in the seventeenth century, and most of the town dates from the eleventh century. We lodged in Saulieu, at La Côte d'Or, the four-star restaurant of Bernard Loiseau (who was still very much alive). Eating dinner there was an event I repeated only twice. Food at Bernard Loiseau could be too good to eat—besides, we really did gobble down a lot of chocolate on the set.

In the year 2001, an irresistible little film called *The Last of the Blonde Bombshells,* an HBO production written by Alan Plater, made in London with Judi Dench (who won the Golden Globe again and the BAFTA miniseries as well), Ian Holm (nominated for an Emmy), Olympia Dukakis, Cleo Laine, Billie Whitelaw, June Whitfield, and other great girls, put me back on track. The story was charming: Judi Dench reassembles, for her granddaughter's school dance, the all-girl swing band she led during World War II. I was carting around an enormous double bass, which I played with enthusiasm wearing a flaming red wig, convinced that you have to be an eccentric to still play the double bass at the age of seventy.

Even the unremarkable TV version of *Murder on the Orient Express,* in which I had fun playing a South American dictator's wife with a Spanish accent, did me good, and it was nice to work again with Alfred Molina, "Inspector Hercule Poirot," whom I had met on *Chocolat.*

Then suddenly, in 2002, a dream fulfilled: working with Merchant and Ivory on *Le Divorce,* based on the novel by Diane Johnson (part of the trilogy *Le Divorce, Le Mariage,* and *L'Affaire*). The book was a brilliant comedy of manners that spares neither the French nor the Americans and where frivolity hides nasty foibles in both cultures. A young American woman, Roxeanne (Naomi Watts) is married to a fickle Frenchman (Melvil Poupaud) who wants out of the marriage just as his young wife becomes pregnant again. Anticipating a possible divorce, the French family, led by grande dame Suzanne de Persand (me), immediately plots for the repartition of the couple's assets, especially an old painting in the style of La Tour. Experts are invited from London and New York (Stephen Fry and Bebe Neuwirth), who declare that the painting is a real La Tour, worth a fortune. The American family (Sam Waterston and Stockard Channing) arrives to defend the interests of their daughter. The suicide attempt of Roxeanne is considered tasteless exhibitionism by the French grande dame, but the murder of her son, the guilty husband, is a more serious matter. Roxeanne's American sister (Kate Hudson) takes advantage of this trip to Paris to have an affair with Roxeanne's uncle by marriage (Thierry Lhermitte). She will stay in Paris, for a while at least. Glenn Close, playing a well-known American author in Paris, has survived the end of her affair with him. The Kelly bag from Hermès, a gift he gives to all his mistresses, binds the two women in competitive complicity. The considerable sum resulting from the sale of the La Tour painting assuages a lot of ill feelings, and everyone takes off for new adventures.

I had met the two filmmakers, Ismail Merchant and James Ivory, years, years earlier in London—in 1965, to be precise. We had a mutual friend, the naïve painter E. Box—Edna, who called herself Eden, an infinitely more evocative name. Merchant-Ivory's *Shakespeare Wallah* had just come out in London, creating a stir, but even though Eden encouraged me to see the film, I had yet to do so. I had no idea that I was having dinner with two of the most enchanting, sophisticated filmmakers, all at once unique and independent, rated very high among film lovers around the world. Personally, I cannot see *The Remains of the Day* or *Howards End* often enough. The magic of their films reflects their rich and diverse personalities.

Jim Ivory is so well read and refined that everyone thinks he's British—in fact he's an American raised in Oregon. He was educated not at Eton, the Guards, Oxford, Cambridge, or Harvard—but at Oregon University. Which goes to show. With Jim directing, every part is of Academy Award quality—it is quite clear, given the brilliant cast list of *Le Divorce*, that it is the way actors feel. No one ever refuses a role, no matter how small or how modest the salary. Jim directs in an offhand, almost nonchalant way—you don't feel you're being directed. As a matter of fact, he starts the day by asking you politely, "How do you see this scene?" And that is really clever. At that point the actor, liberated from any constraint, gives free rein to his imagination. Jim intervenes only if you're going off the rails. Balance and economy rule his style, with immense hidden reserves of emotion. He is a master of the "iceberg style," not because the effect is cold—on the contrary, his films are full of emotions—but because you see only the tip of the drama, while the rest is concealed behind civilized attitudes and is all the more poignant because of its subtlety. Jim Ivory is also one of the most thoughtful individuals I've met. I was witness to several examples of his discreet kindness. He will ask you to sit alone in the back of his car while he remains in front, in the passenger seat, because he doesn't want his driver to feel that he's "serving." He takes photographs of crew members with one of the leading actors and never forgets to distribute these pictures to the crew first. The "star" will have to wait her turn for "her" stills. On several occasions I heard him speak in public after Ismail's death, insisting, with touching modesty, that the greatness of his films was entirely due to Ismail's talent.

On the other hand, Ismail—the fund-raiser—was the bombastic one, genial energizer and mobilizer, the one who could convince a countess to lend her château for free and furthermore get her to cook every meal for the film crew. He turned out to be the one who suffered from an ulcer and died suddenly of it. His technique for producing magnificent productions on wishful money was remarkable. Added to his financial conjuring abilities, he was the most delightful company. With him you were sure to meet interesting people. A maharani organized the evening where celebrated writers and politicians came to rub shoulders with the cast. Old friends welcomed new ones, who became groupies by the end of the evening. When Ismail and Jim were in town, you wanted to bask in the sunshine of their presence. As promotion for the last or the next project, exotic, colorful buffets were whipped up during the course of the day—the collaboration of Indian genius assisted by worshipping admirers.

What charms me as much as the subtleties of their films is the flair with which they found the right sets. They were both passionate about houses and decors. Their Paris apartment was the famous interior decorator Madeleine Castaing's own Paris dwelling. In an eighteenth-century mansion, right in the heart of the Latin Quarter, the noble floor that was hers and now theirs has an interesting L-shaped floor plan. The corridor, almost spacious enough to be called a gallery, runs overlooking a vast inner courtyard, where a horse carriage can turn around. The ceilings and windows are as tall as in a royal residence, and each room has the right proportions.

All the sets for *Le Divorce* are the kind you long to live in when you visit Paris. For years I'd been spying across my street into a lovely eighteenth-century private mansion with garden that faces my apartment. I knew that it had belonged to the Count Daru, cousin of Stendhal, and that the great author had lived there when he'd arrived from his native town of Grenoble. One evening I was given the call sheet for the next day and thought the assistant had made a mistake. I pointed it out. "No, no, no mistake. Your character, Madame de Persand, lives at number five." The next morning, in slippers and curlers, I crossed the street and could finally satisfy my intense curiosity. I was quite moved to step onto the same floor on which Stendhal had walked and rest my eyes on the same mellow wood paneling. I think this feeling of historical transmission helped to give authority to my character. The country house in the film was in Senlis—royal residence before Compiègne, Fontainebleau, Le Louvre, and Versailles.

A year later, in 2003, with the film cut and mounted, we were invited to the Venice Film Festival. In my memory the sixteenth/seventeenth-century Palazzo Mocenigo, on the Grand Canal, glows now and forever in a shade of golden blue morning haze. We became guests of the doge's family for three glorious days, while presenting *Le Divorce* at La Mostra! As the senior member of the cast, I was given the grand lady's faded bedroom "with a view" onto the rarest of back gardens—en suite with a 1920s bathroom, so chic in those days when the swan-shaped chrome taps shone.

We arrived by vaporetto, and the canal entrance doors were opened for us. The hall, suffering from the ravages of humidity, led us to the steep staircase and up to the reception floor. Four salons, with marbleized or silk-lined walls, en suite with one or two small bedrooms and one immense one, filled me with wonder. An inner staircase led to one or two more modest bedrooms. We invaded the rooms like a flock of swallows at sunset, then went to spend the evening at a more rustic-looking restaurant. The next morning a discreet knock on my door woke me at six-thirty for makeup and hair before the presentation to the press. Walking through the succession of rooms and drawing rooms, where all the doors were left open to allow the night breeze to cool the air, I could see the bodies of my colleagues abandoned, half naked, to their sleep. Just like in a boarding school, I thought. A table and chair were set right in front of the large bay window, and while the makeup lady painted my face, I sat down for one hour of a rare spectacle: Venice waking up! No tourists, just a few empty *traghetti*. This was the workingman's hour when small barges (*burci*) bring the building materials (bags of plaster, cement, sand, and wood), foodstuffs, meat, fish, vegetables, fruits and flowers, wine, beer, soft drinks, water, and everything needed for a city's running day. Busy traffic. The surprising difference lay in the fact that it all came floating on water instead of rolling on wheels. A policeman, standing up in a smaller boat, was posted at the corner of the Grand Canal and a smaller one, directing traffic.

At eight o'clock breakfast was served on the house monogrammed linen—scrambled eggs and bacon, all sorts of cereals, toast and jams, tea or coffee—and we all sat in the palatial dining room lined with green silk in our dressing gowns and slippers—and I thought we were . . . ? What could I compare us to? Certainly not the legitimate owners of this grand decor—we were what we were, thespians playing at being princes at home in our palazzo. I've had supper in the lavish Salon de Mars at Versailles, with the queen of Morocco and President Chirac's wife attending, but having breakfast in the Palazzo Mocenigo in my dressing gown, slippers, and curlers was something else entirely. . . .

We had our evening of glory at our presentation in the Lido. The girls, Naomi Watts and Kate Hudson, were very much admired by the press—Kate Hudson, pregnant out to here, was the target of all the cameras—while Jim Ivory made a nice introduction speech and was applauded at great length for all his past, present, and future work. But the ball! The next day's ball given by Ismail was, once again, a fabulous event. People from all the other films in the festival came in boatloads and crowded the four magnificent salons. There was music with an American jazz singer, and the windows on the Grand Canal were wide open to let in the evening breeze and for the guests to live through that magic moment when you stood on the balcony, memorizing for the rest of your life the splendor of Venice, in its night's glitter. It was the party not to be missed.

Even though I think I had now come to behave as a reasonable citizen, no member of my family cared to have anything to do with me for my seventieth birthday. I had already gone through three years of reform—so to speak—but they were understandably bored with my histrionics. (I will whisper here that it took longer to convince my family of my good behavior than anyone else around.) But I was determined to celebrate, so I decided to organize the event on my own. A week before the date, I hired a bus and invited fifty of my Parisian friends to the auberge for a splendid dinner. A really joyous evening took place. At the French revelers' table sat the intellectuals, headed by the writers Bernard Minoret, Jacques Fieschi, Claude Arnaud, James Lord (who qualifies as a French writer after having lived in France since World War II), and Ivan and his wife, Claude, Nabokov, whose Paris flat floats on a river of books overlooking the magnificent department store La Samaritaine. An art dealer and a princess or two filled the large table. At the American table were all the gallant journalists from *Time* and *People* magazines, the *New York Times* and *European Travel & Life*—all in love with Paris, ready to suffer the hazards of the dollar exchange to live in the city of grand avenues, palaces, parks, gardens, and great food. At my table was Jean Babilée, seventy-nine then, and his young wife, Zapo, each having driven on his or her own motorcycle, with helmets and leather jackets designed in the style of Sonia Delaunay. Everyone whom I invited came, and I feel an immense gratitude for their joyous participation in my celebration.

But on my proper birth date, the first of July, even the last of my friends canceled their plans to come and join me on holiday. Remembering Renoir, my mentor, I thought, *Only thing left is to get a dog.* Two days before my birthday, I went to the Quai de la Mégisserie and bought myself a three-month-old black-and-white Jack Russell, whom I named Toto. I don't need to explain his name; filmgoers who love Judy Garland will understand. A mischievous little rogue he was, who devoured more shoes, silk pillows, elegant bags, and fur-coat edges than any colony of rodents. I loved him dearly, and he loved me with passionate, exclusive devotion. I tried to have him trained so he would adopt good manners. Yes, he went to dog school—several times—and then to reform school. Toto was perfectly obedient for the first hour after he came back from training school, but I soon realized that he was fundamentally a misogynist, capable of behaving responsibly only with a strong man, preferably tall, with a stern voice. I, a female, could never be leader of the pack. Toto made me fall in the staircase of my building; then, when a friend tried to take him for a walk, he pulled on his lead so hard that he nearly dislocated her shoulder; later, in the park, I tried to stop him from biting the ear of a harmless little bichon, and he snapped around and bit my thumb with the speed of lightning. I had to have an operation in which half my nail was removed, and it took two years before I could button a shirt. On the sidewalk Toto fought garbage trucks the way Don Quixote fought windmills. He loathed roller skaters and would have bitten a few if I hadn't been alert, but when they sneaked up on me from the back, I was powerless to stop the carnage. Toto was also a passionate surfer—walking along the banks of the river, he pretended not to notice that a barge was coming up, but as soon as the boat had gone past, he would pull his lead till I let go and throw himself into the water with a swallow dive to ride the waves endlessly. There was nothing for me to do but to sit on a bench and wait until he'd had enough. He also used to jump in the river Yonne, in front of the auberge, to try to catch the swans and would swim back only when he understood that he couldn't beat the strong current. He tried every forbidden pond in the Tuileries gardens in the hopes of catching a duck. Fat chance! In the meantime the guards would blow their whistle, and strollers would frown and point to the sign stating DOGS ARE FORBIDDEN. If I took him for a walk in the forest near the auberge, he did the vanishing act until his sixth sense told him I was ready to abandon him for the night. He would then graciously agree to climb back into the car.

I tried to give him away, but his reputation had preceded him. No one wanted him. Our parting took place on an autumn day when a neighbor who had a raucous voice that Toto particularly disliked—or feared—stepped out of her doorway. Toto jumped across the road to attack her and made me fall on my kneecaps. The pain was hideous, I couldn't get up. The friendly sandwich-bar owner, Virgilio, tied Toto to a post, picked me up from the gutter, and carried me to my apartment, where I called an ambulance, convinced that both kneecaps were cracked; before being carted off to the emergency ward of the hospital, I had time to call the trainer who had unsuccessfully tried to civilize this little hood and asked him to take him away for good. I had finally understood that it was either him or me.

It was three months before Toto found a new master in a man who stayed at home and lived near a park—a writer, perhaps. I understand that he was smitten by Toto's incredible intelligence. I didn't ask too many questions. I hope that age has finally mellowed Toto. Regardless of all his crimes and misdemeanors, I loved him dearly and missed him more than I could say.

A few months later, the trainer's girlfriend called me, pleading with me to take on an old lady's Maltese bichon. The lady, who had Alzheimer's disease, was being taken away to a home, and her dog needed immediate adopting. Prunelle (French for "apple of the eye") was in a sorry state—deaf, blind in one eye, and trembling with shock. After a long visit to the vet's, proper grooming, and lots of love, she stopped trembling and started to enjoy life. She wasn't eight, as I had been told, but something closer to twelve. She never learned to play, but she became frisky enough. She lived for three years in perfect harmony with me. She told me when she'd had enough by refusing to eat or walk anymore. She went away peacefully in my arms with a last little lick of her chops as a good-bye kiss. Dogs face death with such great dignity that they can really break your heart.

After Prunelle was gone, I was in mourning again. All dog lovers will understand what it means to lose a beloved companion. My heart was heavy. My friends said, "Quick, get yourself another dog!" I thought, *No, I don't want to go through training a pup again. Too many training hours—too many shoes and pillows eaten.* I tried the SPA (Société Protectrice des Animaux) with the idea of getting an adult dog. In France the SPA is state-subsidized and receives many donations. You get the civil-servant attitude—snooty indifference—and most times I couldn't even get a human being on the phone. And then I found a Web site that actually showed pictures of the orphans and gave you a phone number where a human voice answered. Yes, they had a small dog looking for a home—a shih tzu. They said he was eight and a male, not too sure about the weight. I got in my car and drove to meet him—in fact, quite far away. He was called Whiz and hardly looked the name; in truth he looked like a bum who'd slept in the rough for quite a while. He had a little slit above his left eye, as if a cat had scratched him. Fearing he might get hurt again, I said I would take him, even though I really wanted a female. I rebaptized him Tchi-Tchi and took him to the vet, who said, "He's not eight at all, I would say he's between one and three." Tchi-Tchi got an expensive grooming job and now looks like a little Tibetan prince. His tail is curled up like a feathered hat, and he has a proud chest-forward stance. When he walks, he picks up his four paws as if on parade. He's friendly, untraumatized, and very bright. He learned his new name in a couple of days. He loves to play but loves equally to stay home with me while I write. He's willing to accompany me to dinners (if the evening doesn't drag on) and loves meeting other dogs. He has another striking quality—his unblinking stare. His eyes focus on mine while he tries hard to translate the strange sounds we call words; in a touching endeavor, he tries to imitate those sounds much more often than his own dog's language—the bark. He seems to understand my meaning in any language.

Every morning, from seven-thirty to nine, a group of dog lovers go walking up and down the Tuileries gardens' long alley and over forbidden grass patches, watching their pets with the pride of nannies walking their prams in London's Hyde Park. The masters and mistresses are from all walks of life. There is a therapist, two painters, a lawyer, a female jockey, an American stockbroker's wife, a retired art professor, a yoga teacher, and a film actress. We know one another, enjoy meeting in the mornings, talking about last night's show on TV or the elections and mostly about our dogs, who love to play together. From time to time, an unknown dog comes along, led by an apprehensive or suspicious owner—beware of muzzled dogs when yours is free. We call our dogs in and veer to the far side of the alley, nodding politely, thinking, *Poor dog, why don't they take him off his leash?*

22

Latest Adventures

*I*n 2006, I was invited to New York to play a dramatic part in an episode of *Law & Order: Special Victim Unit,* titled "Recall." The producer, Neal Baer, thought of me on the plane from New York to Los Angeles when *Gigi* was offered on the entertainment menu. He convinced his young son that he might enjoy the film. After the boy's favorable reaction, Neal decided to write a part for me in his series.

The difficulty was in getting a quick work permit after the September 11 horror. Senator Ted Kennedy's office helped by recommending me as a harmless, nonterrorist French citizen, well known to the American public. Still, I had to enter the States through Canada—easier for some reason. Since then I have taken my American citizenship. All it required was for Aimery to get a copy of the 1900 census report for Topeka, Kansas, where my mother—Margaret Petit, three months old—is listed as number 83. My grandmother, Cora Petit, is number 82, and my grandfather, Harry Petit, whom I never met, is number 81. All rather moving. The lady at the American embassy in Paris looked at the photocopy, smiled at me, and said, "You're American! Please stand up and raise your right hand." I was just in time to vote for the election of Barack Obama. An immense satisfaction.

I adored staying at the Lowell Hotel in New York and receiving the star treatment again. My room was "The Hollywood Suite," with pictures of the great stars of the thirties and forties—Betty Bacall, Rosalind Russell, Judy Garland, Ida Lupino, Ava Gardner. (They asked me for my photo—I don't know if I have the honor of hanging on the wall yet.) Two bathrooms, a kitchen, and a proper dining room, all on the eighteenth floor overlooking water towers and roof gardens. The view was spectacular, and I felt a nostalgic thrill every time one of those sirens that characterize New York wailed past.

We filmed the interiors in an abandoned cookie factory in New Jersey. All the sets are interconnecting after the production's front offices. In rapid succession you walk through the jail cells, the district attorney's offices, the spacious courtroom and judge's chambers, and the lawyers' offices.

Working in television is tremendously hard. No matter what, you must finish the episode by the end of the week. On the day of my biggest scene, sixteen hours passed from the moment the car came in the morning to the moment I could take off my shoes in my suite at night. You need tremendous stamina, which is probably why the company feeds you constantly. A meal was served every two hours. Breakfast is followed by a mid-morning snack (what the English call elevenses), then lunch comes along—a minute later it's four o'clock tea, and as you usually go overtime, dinner is also served promptly. Supper is available past 10:00 P.M. Everyone, except for the actors, is overweight.

Every time you work in the streets, company food trucks open their side flap on the sidewalk to feed the whole crew and also the homeless who converge when the aroma of coffee reaches their nostrils. I've seen businessmen in smart black overcoats (with the collar turned up to protect their shirt from the New York soot) stop and order a bacon sandwich and then reach into their pocket for a few bills, not realizing that the food is prepared for the movie crew. The cooks serve everyone generously.

There are several ways of delivering the line "You raped me!" to the villain who assailed you. I chose to boom it out, with forceful outrage to a courtroom full of actors who were visibly shaken. Seriously, I was particularly pleased with the part because, at long last, I was asked to play a vulnerable woman who had gone through real trauma and who finally expresses her pain. After having portrayed innocent victims for many years, and then without transition nothing but cynical bitches concealing a selfish heart under couture clothes, finally here was the part of an ordinary woman willing to reveal her frailty. I welcomed the change. I always longed to show to Zanussi, Louis Malle, and others that I could also play human beings. Chris Meloni (who plays chief detective) is as deeply involved with his part as he seems on the screen—a real pal. I didn't get to act with Mariska Hargitay, beloved by public and crew alike—she was having a baby. And Juan Campanella, the director, made all the difference; thanks to his sensitive guidance I could rely on him. I found that I had new technical and emotional capacities and that my pleasure in acting had come back. I wasn't anxious about my looks anymore; what the public expects to encounter in an actress past seventy is the sum of her experience, not her beauty.

Winning the Emmy for this guest performance is one of the very good moments in my career. I realize it is out of proportion with the success of such films as *Gigi, An American in Paris,* or even *Lili,* but at last I felt I deserved the accolade. It took me some sixty years in film to realize that I am indeed an actress and that I do belong in the professional league. Oh, my mother's indifference! Such echoes of doubt reverberated throughout my life! My only regret remains the closed door the French have maintained to my willing collaboration. From time to time, a rash television producer says, "Goodness, why don't you play in French films?" I answer modestly, "It may happen yet." And he says, "Let me do a special on your life and career. It will swing things into action." But the decades fly by, and the French phone line remains stubbornly silent. By now the die is cast; I am firmly ensconced in the French collective mind as a Hollywood product, unreachable, untouchable, part of the great celluloid myth. So be it. I am at peace but still willing to try to convince French producers that I exist.

The best part of my life is over. Now is the time to reflect. What do I think of my journey? It has certainly meandered through many side roads. A journalist made this scattered dispersion the subject of her article without coming to the obvious conclusion: Every step of the way, obstacles made me change the course of my life, and at this point I recall what Jean Renoir and his father, Pierre-Auguste, before him said: "Just bob along life like a cork on the river." With opportunistic clarity, it became evident that once I was launched in films there was no question of my returning to ballet on the stage. Hollywood welcomed me as "the little French girl," and I should have considered myself fortunate. My particular difficulty was and is to accept the fact that although I adore London, New York, and Hollywood, I will never really be at home anywhere. I remain unmistakably a foreigner where my children live and where I am professionally welcome.

When the need to love was too powerful to deny, I had to listen to my heart, and I think it steered me right, since I have great memories of this love and am blessed with two wonderful children and now a batch of remarkable grandchildren. But the part of the road on which I accompanied Peter Hall couldn't last if I wanted to fulfill my own destiny. Later, when the lull in my career seemed to announce a definitive full stop, in my forties, I started to write. Learning a new craft was my answer, and if the result didn't make the news, I had the feeling of going forward.

Building and running an auberge was again a departure from the straight line. My theory is that talents mustn't lie dormant. I used the gift I had and served the French community in a way my fellow citizens found acceptable. Good for me. I am secretly proud to have imposed myself as an innkeeper when I was refused entry as an actress. It will have to do me.

The question remains: Have I been happy? The answer is, Yes, I have often been happy—even very happy. Not consistently, but in spurts, and, strange as it may seem, I believe that happiness grows with age. Of course, having children gave me the greatest joys, after which must be counted successes in my professional life. Happiness with men, I will admit, comes in third—not last, but third.

The fruits I picked along the way were rich—the bad experiences just as enriching as the successes. I have learned that it is important to try to overcome the failures and turn them into productive lessons. I think I am especially grateful for the incredible individuals I have encountered. I didn't go to school and university, but I met extraordinary teachers.

Life compels me, just as it does with everyone else, to face the decline that advancing age imposes, at the risk of turning bitter, and I see bitterness as a cancer of the soul. But although I now accept the wrinkles that line my face, I'm not at all pleased with the loss of energy that urges me to slow down. I still resent that part of aging as I would resent defeat. The lesson clearly is to become an onlooker rather than a doer, but I emphatically refuse to surrender my boxing gloves.

e there other adventures in store for me? Theatrical adventures hrill me to bits. Oh, I do hope it is written in heaven.